GO
Google

20 Ways to Reach More Customers and Build Revenue with Google Business Tools

Greg Holden

AMACOM

American Management Association

New York • Atlanta • Brussels • Chicago • Mexico City • San Francisco
Shanghai • Tokyo • Toronto • Washington, D.C.

This publication is designed to provide accurate and authoritative information in regard to the subject matter covered. It is sold with the understanding that the publisher is not engaged in rendering legal, accounting, or other professional service. If legal advice or other expert assistance is required, the services of a competent professional person should be sought.

Library of Congress Cataloging-in-Publication Data

Holden, Greg.
    Go Google : 20 ways to reach more customers and build revenue with Google business tools / Greg Holden.
        p.   cm.
    Includes bibliographical references and index.
    ISBN-13: 978-0-8144-8059-5
    ISBN-10: 0-8144-8059-4
    1. Google. 2. Business—Computer network resources. 3. Internet marketing. 4. Internet advertising. I. Title.
    HD30.37.H648 2008
    658.8'72—dc22

                                                    2007043440

Printing number
10   9   8   7   6   5   4   3   2   1

Contents

GO
Google

PART I

Getting Ready to Go Google

CHAPTER **1**

Learning from Google:
A 21st-Century Model for
Success

You know what Google is. At least, you *think* you know Google. Chances are you associate Google with being among the most successful high-tech businesses in the world, as well as being the most popular search service on the World Wide Web. And you have probably heard "google" used as a verb, meaning "to search for or find something online," as in: "I Googled my professor and found his home page . . . I Gmailed him my report." (Gmail is Google's email service; you'll hear quite a bit about it in the pages that follow.) If that's all you think of when you hear the word "Google," you're missing the latest Internet revolution. What you can learn from this book will improve your life immeasurably, especially if your goals are to work more efficiently and to do a better job of marketing yourself or your company.

What's So Great About Google?

Back in 1996, two graduate students started their own Web-based search service, which they called BackRub. By 1998, the project had gained a lot of attention, secured some investors, and turned into a corporation called Google—a Web site that made specific Web pages, discussion groups, or even individual words and phrases easy to locate. In recent years, Google has expanded its services for businesses in a dramatic way. Its Gmail and AdWords services are now in widespread use. For example, Google offers scheduling, word processing, spreadsheet, email, and other applications both separately and as part of an umbrella package called Google Apps. These days, Google is also an increasingly popular solution for small businesses that need to increase their visibility and build their brand. Google is fast becoming the most affordable and effective marketing venue for businesses.

Through its expansion into the business services space, Google itself provides you with a role model that you can follow as you develop your own business online. It all starts when you create a service that gives you a solid foundation. After a steady stream of customers are knocking at your virtual door, you can expand into new areas. Google can help you make that exciting move.

This book will give you comprehensive descriptions of the site's search engine, advertising, marketing, workflow, and communications features. Not only that, but you'll be provided with tips on how they can best meet your needs. Google's search tool and other services can help businesses get organized and on the same page, often for little or no cost. The new Google Apps will let businesses take their online communications and data sharing to a new level. This book will examine ways in which businesses like yours can communicate messages and make Web sites more visible to prospective customers; it will go a step beyond what has previously been said about Google to describe how clients and coworkers can use it to communicate with one another more effectively.

These days, Google is much more than a directory of the Web's contents. It's on the verge of becoming an integral part of many small business operations. Google is itself a model for a 21st-century business. You can learn a great deal about how a successful company operates by reading the sections that follow.

Googling Google: Researching an Internet Success Story

Plenty of books have written about Google and how it started. In a nutshell, the business was founded by two men, Larry Page and Sergey Brin, who first met in late 1995 when they were graduate students at the University of Michigan. They spent a lot of time and programming effort to come up with a complex algorithm for finding content on the Web with amazing accuracy.

It should come as no surprise that the best way to find out about Google is to Google the company history yourself. If you enter the search terms Google History on the home page (http://www.google.com), you will see that the first returned result is a link to Google Corporate Information: Google Milestones (http://www.google.com/corporate/history.html). This will reveal a comprehensive and up-to-date timeline detailing the company's achievements. Here you will find personal anecdotes from and biographies of Larry and Sergey (who are shown below), as well as a detailed history of their company's humble beginnings and remarkable growth. Don't be afraid of being bored. You won't be. It's all told with the straightforward and laid-back style that have become synonymous with the name Google.

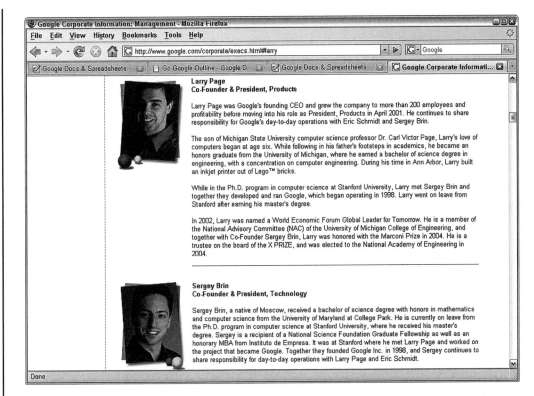

For more information, you can also scroll down to the bottom of any page on the Google website and click on the link labeled About Google (http://www.google.com/about.html). This will take you to a map of all of the products, services, and support features that Google offers, as well as provide links to more corporate information.

The "take away" point here is that Google succeeds by providing a service that everyone wants and needs: access to information and links to virtually any kind of online content.

Information Sells

What's the first lesson you learn from Google's story? Having identified a need that is shared by each one of the millions of individuals who go online every day, Brin and Page stuck to their core business and kept improving it. They spent many years building their company, slowly focusing on the basic activity of searching for content on the Web. Only when that process became widely accepted did they begin to sell ads that would appear alongside search results pages. Only after several years did the company go public. Only recently have they begun to provide the business applications described in this book.

When you start up your own Web site, whether or not you use Google, you need to identify your mission and stick to it without trying to take on too much at once. Define the kinds of customers, clients, or visitors you want to reach. Determine how you're going to meet their needs by making your own products or services available online. Start with a few pages or business applications and build your presence gradually. Once you have a firm base—a Web site created with Google's Web Page Creator (see Chapter 11), a domain name obtained through Google Apps (Chapter 6), or a sales channel created with Google Base (Chapter 15)—you can expand your presence to build a wider audience.

On the Internet, the more prospective customers who can reach and the richer the level of content you provide, the more effective your business will be. As you'll learn in subsequent chapters, you improve your search engine rankings for both venues when you are able to make links from one Web site you own to another one you own. If your sites have three or four "levels" of content (in other words, if your visitors are able to click through from one page to another and keep finding new forms of information) your site will be "stickier." You'll be able to hold those visitors on your site for a longer period of time, which makes it that much more likely they'll perform the action you are hoping for—whether that action is making a purchase, filling out a form, or sending you an email inquiry.

Google gives you a virtual toolbox full of options for creating a Web presence that is expansive and extensive. It can help you in one of two ways:

- If you already have a Web site dedicated to your business or club (or to your own personal exploits), Google provides you with a set of tools that are sure-fire ways to help you meet your goals. (And you can use Google's Page Creator as described in Chapter 11 to create another Web site, too.)

- Google gives you a free and yet powerful way to establish a full-fledged Web presence if you don't have one already.

Keep It Simple

When you look at the Google home page shown in Figure 1-1, what do you see? Along with the search box and heading and links, your eyes will rest on lots of white space. While other Web sites (such as that of Google's competitor Yahoo!) are cluttered with links, words, images, and corporate logos, Google's remains remarkably

Figure 1-1. Google's home page points to a model of simplicity you should try to emulate.

uncluttered. No doubt Google could make millions by placing a single ad or two on its well-traveled home page. But the site's managers know the value of simplicity, and you should appreciate it too.

There's no doubt about it: You can go ahead and hire Web designers and computer programmers to create a complex and world-class Web site that will "Wow!" everyone who visits it. But chances are you have picked up this book because you want to avoid just this sort of expense and complication. You want to be in control and plan your online site in a way that reflects your personality and your interests. And you don't want to pay an arm and a leg—or, unless you sign up for the premium Google Apps service that is aimed at businesses, anything at all. You want to "Go Google," in other words.

Focus on Your Core Business

Even as it expands to the desktops of individual business users, Google hasn't lost sight of its core business: providing accurate search results. Google doesn't make money off the search results by themselves. However, its paid advertising programs such as AdWords, which place ads alongside search results, have proven to be highly lucrative. Google has found a way to preserve its original mission and maintain the quality of its product for the millions who search the Internet each day. At the same time, it enables customers to take advantage of that product by providing advertising in a targeted way. This system is based on making a decision on how much they will pay each time a visitor clicks on one of their ads.

The lesson for you is to focus on your own core business and establish a base of operations on the Web first. Then you can begin to think about branching out into trying to boost productivity as well as revenue. Suppose you are starting from square one: you have a Big Idea for an online business and you have identified the target audience you want to reach. But that's as far as you've gone so far. You have Internet access through your office, your school, or your home. But you need to set up your own business online. If you only wanted one service to get you started, the logical first choice would be to sign up for email with Google's Gmail service—email, after all, is central to all online communications. But if you want a complete solution, sign up for Google Apps and look around at other Google services.

Table 1-1 presents you with a road map for Google services that can help you take your first step online: establishing a Web site, email, and a domain. That's all you need to do to make you or your company visible online.

Once you have a Web presence, you can follow Google's example and start to branch out. Google can help your company's internal operations by improving collaboration and workflow among your employees. You can create shared business documents, set up user accounts, and schedule meetings. The Google offerings listed in Table 1-2 are relatively new and exciting in many ways. That's why they have the potential to take business away from Microsoft, to mention just one example of other companies that develop expensive business applications.

Table 1-1. Step One: Tools for Establishing an Online Presence

What You Need	How to Get It	Where to Find It
Gmail only	Sign up	http://mail.google.com
A Web domain, Gmail, Google Calendar, Web Page Creator, Google Talk, Docs & Spreadsheets	Sign up for Google Apps and buy a domain name for $10/year	http://www.google.com/a
Get out news and updates to your customers quickly and frequently	Create a blog with Blogger	http://www.blogger.com
Make your business's physical location easier to find	Add your business to Google Maps	
Make your Web site more content-rich and timely	Add Google Gadgets	

Table 1-2. Tools for Working More Efficiently

What You Need	How to Get It	Where to Find It
Save money on long distance phone calls by typing or conducting voice chat sessions	Sign up for Google Talk	
Creating group discussions	Start your own Google Group	http://groups.google.com
Set appointments, plan meetings, and share your upcoming schedule	Use Google Calendar	http://calendar.google.com (also part of Google Apps)
Set up a Google search engine on your own computer to search through your own files or other computers on the same network	Obtain Google Desktop	
Translating Web pages and text in a foreign language	Translate with Google Toolbar	
Get the latest business statistics and trends	Google Trends	
Organize your electronic image files	Use Google's Picasa service	

British company uses Google to Collaborate

Rock Kitchen Harris (http://www.rkh.co.uk) is an advertising, design, PR, and web agency based in Leicester, England. There are eighteen employees working in the same office but, as in any organization, staff people frequently need to work from home or go on the road. The solution that has worked best for this company is to use Gmail to keep in touch and Google Apps to share files.

"Google Apps has been particularly helpful in allowing some of us to work from home and all of us to check our email and schedules wherever we may be," says Paul Sculthorpe, Senior Web Developer for the company. Sculthorpe says that aside from giving everyone on staff the ability to schedule upcoming meetings with Calendar and share files, it's made his job easier, too. "It has taken a big load off our general IT administration staff. Now we can focus on our real work. The calendar and docs sharing is particularly good."

Email is the primary Google service used by the company. "All of our emails are stored at Google. We figure their systems are more resilient and secure than our own shoddy solution that failed a few months back. Those using desktop clients still down-load all of their emails too." A desktop client is a program like Outlook Express that is installed on your computer and that gathers information from a networked re-source—in this case, an e-mail server. Google's Gmail service provides an alternative for those who want to take advantage of it.

Although Google's Docs & Spreadsheets service, which enables a company to pre-pare, edit, and share word processing and spreadsheet files online, isn't as full-featured as, say, Microsoft Word or Excel, as Sculthorpe observes: "for simple day to day stuff that needs collaboration, it's ideal."

Google can also help a business market itself and sell products and services on-line. In this arena, Google is challenging e-commerce hosts like Microsoft and Yahoo! and even the popular marketplace eBay.

Twenty Google Tools for Boosting Your Productivity

Google has extended far beyond its core search business to provide a variety of new services, including free email, Web hosting, and business applications. It only makes sense to pay attention to what Google has to offer and take advantage of the services that can help you. Go Google does not attempt to be a comprehensive examination of all of Google's online services. For one problem, a book like that would be far too large to fit on your bookshelf. But more importantly, the book would become obso-lete between the time it is written and when it is delivered from the printer. That's because Google is constantly expanding its services and acquiring new technologies.

There is also the important matter of your time and energy. The truth is that if you look through all of the services and utilities made available by Google (a list that seems to grow all the time), you'll find many more than 20 tools. But in a manner of speaking, we've done a significant portion of your work for you. Rather than trying to cover everything comprehensively, this book has chosen 20 services to describe in detail. Learning to make the most of what these services have to offer can make a difference to anyone wanting to get a new online business off the ground or improve the reach and success level of an existing small- to medium-size company. Here is a list of 20 of the tools you're likely to find most useful and that are described in this book's subsequent chapters:

1. *Google's search service.* Google indexes and organizes the contents of the Web in a huge database; it's this database that you use to search the Web (see Chapter 2).

2. *AdWords.* This is a paid search placement program; you create ads and bid on how much you'll pay for each click the ad attracts. Each time someone clicks on your ad, you gain a potential customer or client (see Chapter 5).

3. *AdSense.* This program enables blog and Web site owners to run targeted ads alongside their content; the content of the ads is intended to complement what you've published yourself (see Chapter 12).

4. *Google Apps.* This service provides you with a domain name (for a one-time $10 fee) and enables you to use a suite of business applications, which multiple users can access (see Chapter 6).

5. *Google Docs & Spreadsheets.* This exciting and easy-to-use service gives you a word processor and a spreadsheet application that you can use and access for free (see Chapter 7).

6. *Google Calendar.* A default calendar is created for you when you sign up for Google Apps; you can also create custom calendars and even embed calendars in Web pages (see Chapter 8).

7. *Gmail.* Google's e-mail application comes with lots of storage space and an integrated chat client to boot (see Chapter 9).

8. *Google Talk.* Google's chat application lets you send instant messages and even conduct real-time voice conversations through your computer (see Chapter 10).

9. *Google Page Creator.* This Web page editing tool lets you create your own Web site to go along with your Google Apps domain name (see Chapter 11).

10. *Blogger.* Google's popular, and free, blogging services lets you create your own Web-based diary, complete with an index, an archive, and a comments feature (see Chapter 13).

11. *Checkout, Google Product Search, Catalogs.* I'm fudging a bit and lumping these three separate Google services into a single unit. Each one can help commercial businesses sell products online (see Chapter 16).

12. *Google Base.* A growing number of entrepreneurs are posting merchandise, property, services, jobs, and lots of other things for sale in this Web publishing area (see Chapter 15).

13. *Google Gadgets.* These easy-to-implement bits of Web content can make your Web site more valuable and attract more repeat visits (see Chapter 16).

14. *Analytics, Trends.* These two analytical tools provide you with information about visits to your own Web site and trends in Web searches, respectively (see Chapter 17).

15. *Desktop, Toolbar.* These two tools help you search more effectively, both through files on your own computer and your local network (Desktop) as well as the wider Internet (Toolbar). See Chapter 18 for more.

16. *Picasa.* This powerful photo viewing and editing tool automatically organizes all the files on your desktop and lets you edit them as well (see Chapter 19).

17. *News, Book Search.* These tools provide businesspeople with important up-to-the-minute data they need to keep on top of trends and events (see Chapter 19).

18. *Google Apps Premium.* This corporate version of Google Apps guarantees nearly 24/7 reliability and gives businesses the ability to write custom programs that interface with Google's services (see Chapter 20).

19. *Gmail Mobile and SMS.* These tools let busy professionals search Google and exchange messages when they're on the road (see Chapter 19).

20. *Google Pack.* This suite of applications will boost the functionality of virtually any workstation (see Chapter 20).

Go Google!

In this chapter, you hopefully expanded your vision of what Google has to offer. Rather than just a single page where you enter a search query and get back a page of results, Google is a business resource. Its shared applications, email, and other tools can help small businesses work more efficiently; their marketing and advertising tools can help companies that are strapped for advertising cash improve their visibility, too. In the chapters to come, you'll learn how to take full advantage of Google's cutting-edge tools for working online. It's not an exaggeration to say that Google's shared applications have the potential to change the way the world works. The end result is likely to take business away from well-established software vendors like Microsoft, as well as from prominent Web services providers like Yahoo!. It's all about options: you no longer need to spend hundreds or thousands of dollars on expensive productivity programs. You now have the option to Go Google—explore the resources described throughout this book, and you'll be glad you did!

Searching and Finding: Getting Started with Google

Everyone you ask about Google has the same response, "It's that Web page where you search for something." Google's search service is its core business. It's also the activity that allows many of its other services to work so well. The huge database of Web page contents compiled by Google and used to present its search results is also used to search your own page and present you with AdSense ads that are relevant to your particular content. AdWords ads work because they are placed next to Google search results. And specialty search services like Google Product Search make use of the same technology.

If you want to know how Google works, you need to understand the searching and indexing processes that are at its core. In this chapter, you'll get a brief overview of what makes Google search "tick." Lots of other books describe Google's search capabilities, so we'll spare you the details here. (It's not possible to reveal too much on this topic anyhow, because Google keeps its precise searching and ranking technologies a closely guarded secret.) What is of real interest to you at this point is learning how to take the first step in integrating Google's business services into your own operation: signing up for a Google Account.

Googling the Web: What Makes Google So Successful

As you can tell from the title of this section, Google, like Frisbee and Kleenex, has become a household name. Web surfers everywhere use the word "Google" to describe the act of searching for something, many times not even realizing (or caring) that there is a powerful company that shares the same name. That works both ways, too; businesses both large and small hope they will be "Googled" by those same consumers, who will go on to find out more about what they have to offer and eventually make a purchase.

The place to start with Google is to determine how it can help your site become more visible on the Web. And the way to understand that is to understand how the Google search works. Here's an overview to give you the gist of it.

1. Google's founders, Larry Page and Sergey Brin, came up with formulas for indexing the contents of Web pages, storing them in a huge database, and retrieving pages based on keyword searches.

2. Google uses automated programs to scour the contents of Web pages on a regular basis (just how frequently is one of those trade secrets I already mentioned). The programs record the contents of many pages and the URLs and store them in a database.

3. You, the end user, type a word or phrase like "Irish dancing" into Google's search box and click the search button. When you do this, a program is activated on Google's servers. The program searches the pages that have already been stored in the database. That's right: when you click the search button on Google's home page or in the Google Toolbar, you are searching Google's database of Web pages, not the "live" Web itself.

4. Google compiles a set of search results ranked in the order of highest relevance to your search. It's Google's system of page ranking—of determining which items are on the top on the first page of the results—that's as notable as anything in this system.

As an end user, you already know how the search system works: it helps you find Web pages that contain information you're looking for. But "Going Google" means you want to make use of the system from the standpoint of someone who wants to do better business. You can take advantage of the system of keyword searches and page rankings to achieve the business objectives outlined in the sections that follow.

Objective 1: Making Your Business Easier to Find

One way you can manipulate Google's search system is to make your online business more visible. For many businesses, the primary goal is to be ranked higher than the other entries in a search for a given set of keywords. For example, my brother Mike has gone to great pains to improve his search engine ranking for his Web site Lp2CD-Solutions, in which he restores old vinyl LP records and converts them to CD format. There are a number of competitors in this field, and a search for the phrase term "LP to CD restoration" finds his site (http://www.lp2cdsolutions.com) second from the top of the first page (see Figure 2-1). And as he will tell you, once you end up on the first page of a set of Google results you get far more visits. That results in more inquiries from interested parties and, ultimately, more sales.

Figure 2-1. You can leverage Google's database to improve your Web site's visibility.

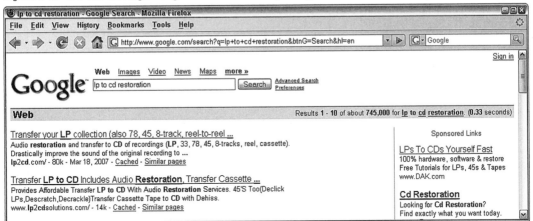

Objective 2: Working Smarter

Knowledge of up-to-the-minute business trends and news is important for anyone who needs to make business decisions. By searching Google's many specialty search sites, such as its News area, you can look up critical facts and figures and back up your business reports. Not only that, but by scouring Google Trends, which presents reports based on recent searches of Google's storehouse of information, you get an idea of what shoppers are interested in online.

Objective 3: Improving Your Web Presentation

You can create your own Web site with Google, and you'll find out how to use its Page Creator service in Chapter 11. The Warehouse Department of Paper Mart, a family-owned packaging store in Los Angeles, was able to create a simple Web page and link it to the company's main Web site. The page describes any job openings in the department—or, in the case of the page shown in Figure 2-2, the fact that there are no job openings.

The Web pages you create will get more attention if your site contains useful and timely content. The information sources mentioned in the preceding section can help you with the content in the main body of your Web page. You can enhance your page content by adding "gadgets" such as a display of the current date and time or a miniature search box to your site so your visitors can search Google, for example. You can add the current time and weather, as well as maps. You can even add a calendar showing upcoming events related to your company or your interests.

Objective 4: Advertising Your Business

When you understand how keywords and good writing can help your Web site gain better exposure on Google search results, you can use the same system to write ads

Figure 2-2. Page Creator helps you create a simple yet effective business Web site.

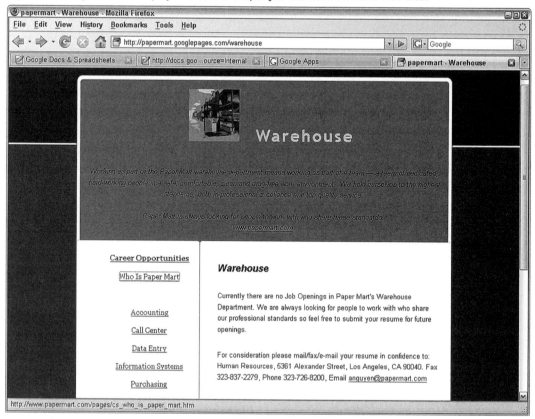

that gain more attention for your business on Google AdWords. AdWords is a successful program for delivering targeted cost-per-click ads alongside Google search results. By including critical keywords in your ads and placing bids on each one, you can increase the chances that your ad will appear in a prominent position—again, near the top of the first search results page. That is the best way to get visitors who are looking for what you have to sell to click on them and check out what you have to offer. Find out more about AdWords in Chapter 5.

Selling Your Products or Services

You probably don't realize it, but some of Google's online services provide you with channels where you can list tangible consumer goods or professional services you want to sell to the public. Google Base gives you a way to list items for sale in a classified ad format much like the popular Craigslist sites provide. You can also create a file of your catalog sales descriptions and submit them to Google's Product Search

search service for retail goods. You can even send electronic versions of your printed sales catalogs to Google Catalogs so that shoppers can "flip" through the pages using their Web browsers, clicking through to your Web site if they want to complete a purchase. You'll find out more about such services in Chapters 14 and 15.

Getting the Word Out

Every business wants to stand out from the crowd, and all those who offer a service want to share their expertise with interested readers. Google gives writers, publishers, and marketers alike a range of forums where they can get their expertise and their experience before the general public. By posting a blog on Google's Blogger service (http://www.blogger.com), you gain the ability to get your words online instantly and to update them on a regular basis. You can also post sales descriptions, recipes, instruction manuals, and reams of customer service information to Google Base (http://base.google.com). Not only do you get published, but also your words are indexed and included in Google's search databases so people can find them more easily. (See Chapter 13 for more details about Blogger, and Chapter 15 for Google Base.)

Google offers many more services to businesses; the ones mentioned in this part of the chapter are those that make use of Google's search methodology and its seemingly limitless database of Web pages. No matter which Google service you choose, you need to start the same way: signing up for an account with Google will enable you to use any of its services.

Obtaining a Google Account

Before you can sign up for any Google service, from Gmail to Google Apps, you need to obtain a Google Account: a username and password you'll use to log onto the site. If you only use Google as a consumer of information—for search, for finding news stories, for reading newsgroup messages—you don't need an account. But if you want to take advantage of any of the business services, you need to sign in.

Google Accounts start out simple, but things get more complicated as you sign up for more services and move onto the suite of applications called Google Apps. If you prepare accounts for your colleagues so they can share a calendar and other files with you—and that's the whole point of Google Apps—you've suddenly got a whole handful of e-mail addresses and passwords to maintain. There are a few general principles you need to keep in mind:

- If you sign up only for Gmail, your e-mail address is your account username. You have a single username and password.

- If you sign up for Google Apps, you have to obtain a domain name. You get an e-mail address that is part of that domain name: for instance, I have the domain literarymidwest.com, and the e-mail address is greg@literarymidwest .com. However, greg@literarymidwest.com is not the username for my Google Apps account: that is gregholden57@gmail.com. It's another example of the multiple e-mail addresses you might have to maintain when you start using multiple Google services.

- Beware of being logged into several services at once so that multiple windows are open. That can cause Google to get confused. If you're logged in with one username with one service and you try to sign in with another username to access another service with the same computer, you might be prevented from doing so. You need to sign out of one account before signing in to another.

 Note: You don't need to proliferate Google Accounts if you sign up for, say, Google Apps, Google Base, AdWords, AdSense, and so on. In theory, you can use the same username and password for all these services. But if you sign up at different times or if someone in your office signs up for one service and you sign up for another, it is possible to end up with two or more accounts for the same thing. This isn't a problem unless you mix up or forget your passwords, as I am prone to do occasionally.

Your username, in fact, will take the form of your e-mail address when you start using Gmail or another Google business service. So give some thought to the account name you'll choose: if you plan to use Google Apps for business purposes, you want your account name to look businesslike rather than "playful" or mischievous. Don't choose a username like Deedlebop, which might result in an inappropriate name like deedlebop@consolidated-industry.com. For personal use, deedlebop@gmail.com would be fine. But I recommend that you use your own first and last name if you set up a Google domain for your business. If your name is Lucy Evans, your username would be lucy.evans. This would give you the e-mail address like lucy.evans@consoli-dated-industry.com.

While you can set up your Google account using a pre-existing email address, and then set up a Gmail address later, you can also take a "shortcut" by setting up a Gmail account first. This will automatically create a Google account for you, and it allows you to sidestep the process of creating both separately. Since I personally feel that simply creating a Gmail account is the most logical course of action, assuming you ever plan on having one at any point in the future, I'll list the instructions for this option first.

Follow these steps to obtain a Google Account and sign up for Gmail:

1. Go to the Gmail home page (http://mail.google.com).
2. Click the *Sign up for Gmail* link, which appears in the blue box below the blank fields for entering Email and Password.
3. Type your first and last names in the Firstname and Lastname fields.
   Note that it doesn't need to be your real name on your ID card; Google isn't going to check it.
4. In the box next to Desired Login Name, type a simple, easy to remember word that will serve as the first part of your Google Mail (Gmail) address. This is the part of the address that will appear before gmail.com. If you use two words, you may want to follow the common convention of separating them by a dot (.) or the hyphen character. (Following this convention makes it clear to visitors exactly what your first and last names are.) Click the check availability button to see if the name you want is available; if not, try a different name or choose one of the options Google suggests. Remember that suggestive or funny names might give you a chuckle now but could be a problem later on if you use them to apply for a job, or to correspond with your college professor or supervisor, for instance.
5. Fill in the rest of the page, and click the *I accept. Create my account* button at the bottom of the page.

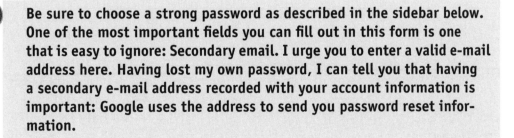

Be sure to choose a strong password as described in the sidebar below. One of the most important fields you can fill out in this form is one that is easy to ignore: Secondary email. I urge you to enter a valid e-mail address here. Having lost my own password, I can tell you that having a secondary e-mail address recorded with your account information is important: Google uses the address to send you password reset information.

6. An email verification page appears stating that a mail message has been sent to the e-mail address you entered at the top of the registration form. When the

message arrives, click the link included in the message to verify your account—if everything works correctly you should go to your new account.

Once your account is verified, you should now be able to sign into your account at the Google Home Page (http://www.google.com), or at the Gmail page, (http://mail.google.com).

Choosing Passwords that Pass the Test

Passwords are always important. But with a Web site such as Google that provides business applications, choosing a strong password is even more critical. You're trusting Google to keep your e-mail secure. If you store shared text or financial_files online through Google's Docs and & Spreadsheets application (see Chapter 7), you obviously need to protect those files. If they contain personal information, identity theft becomes a real concern for individuals who do business with you. Choose a password that:

- Is not a recognizable word in the dictionary
- Contains a mixture of characters, numerals, and possibly punctuation marks
- Mixes both capital and lowercase letters
- Does not contain a birthday, address, or other recognizable number—and especially not your social security number.
- Has six or more characters: Six to eight characters is good because it is easy to remember.
- Is something that will stick in your mind, such as an acronym. You can turn the phrase Google Is My Business Applications Host into gImbAh. If you then add a number, it becomes gImbAh29, for instance.

Google's security measures can be undone not only by a weak password but also by bad password management. Never write your password on a piece of paper that could be lost. What's even worse is keeping your password near your computer, especially taping it to your monitor. Never give your password out to someone who could misuse it. Do everything you can to guard your password so no one can gain access to your information without your knowledge or approval.

Once you have a Gmail e-mail address, you can use it to sign up for another service, such as Google Talk. Here's how to sign up for a Google Account using a pre-existing email address:

1. Go to the Google Home Page (http://www.google.com).

2. Click the *Sign in* link at the top right hand corner of the page.

3. When the page refreshes and the blue login box appears, click the *Create an account now* link. The Create an Account page appears.

4. Type your current e-mail address in the box required: this can be a Gmail address or another Google address, such as one you assign yourself if you have Google Apps.

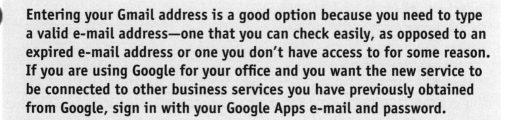

Entering your Gmail address is a good option because you need to type a valid e-mail address—one that you can check easily, as opposed to an expired e-mail address or one you don't have access to for some reason. If you are using Google for your office and you want the new service to be connected to other business services you have previously obtained from Google, sign in with your Google Apps e-mail and password.

5. Fill in the rest of the fields on the page, read the Terms of Service, and click the button at the bottom of the page.

6. In some cases you can start using your service when you gain access to its home page—the Google Apps home page, for instance. In other cases you'll need to check your e-mail for a message from Google welcoming you to the new service. The message contains a link you'll need to click in order to complete the signup process and start using the service. You can now log into your account at the Google home page or the home page of the service you want to set up.

In this chapter, you examined the core activity that makes most, if not all, of Google's other services possible—its system for searching and indexing contents of networked documents, and of ranking relevant pages in response to a keyword search. You learned how that system can help you take advantage of Google's business applications. You also took the first step in Going Google—signing up for Gmail and obtaining a Google Account. In the next chapter, you'll start to establish goals and objectives for running your business with Google so you can take advantage of the features mentioned in this chapter.

CHAPTER 3

Goals for Google-izing Your Business

If you're a small business owner or manager, you're used to setting goals and drawing up plans to achieve them. It makes sense to do the same with Google. How do you decide which Google services to choose? People considering this question usually begin by going to the More Google Products page (http://www.google.com/intl/en/options) and scanning the long list of available services. That way, you can pick the ones that seem useful to you on an a la carte basis. You don't necessarily give a lot of thought to your business objectives for doing so. The fact is that a little advance planning can make your effort to incorporate Google into your business activities much more effective and goal-oriented.

One direction small businesses should consider taking is to sign up for a suite of applications called Google Apps. It's hard to overestimate the potential impact of this suite of productivity applications. For years, businesses have had to throw around terms like *intranets, extranets, application servers,* and *hosted applications*, all of which cost thousands of dollars to install, configure, and maintain. Google Apps makes all of these functions available for free. Even if you sign up for the Premium version of Google Apps (described in Chapter 18), the $50 per-user annual fee is far less than you'd have to pay to install a comparable program, Microsoft Exchange, for instance.

But Google Apps won't do it all. And Google definitely contains many more services that will help you work more efficiently. Now I'm saying it's more effective. But is it really? When you tell your boss or your staff (or even yourself!) that you want to keep your spreadsheets and word processing files on Google and publish your catalogs there, they might be surprised. But by touting some of the business objectives you can achieve with Google's many services that are described in this chapter, you'll be able to make a good business argument.

Improving Your Visibility

For most online businesses, simply being found is half the battle. Google is the newest and best known single online resource for businesses around. It's the equivalent of running a Super Bowl ad, renting a billboard along a major highway, or putting your corporate name on a baseball stadium. When consumers hear the name Google, they remember that it's a place to find information. When businesspeople with Web sites think of Google, at some point they inevitably ask themselves: How can I get better placement on Google? By that they mean that they want their site to appear higher up in search results. I go into this subject in more detail in Chapter 4.

Increasing Your Advertising Revenue

Some businesses go on the Web with the goal of generating extra income through advertising. By creating a Web site that gets a high number of "hits" (that's Web-speak for visits), they are able to attract advertisers who will pay them to display ads on their pages. But things get complicated when you—the busy Web site owner and businessperson—have to negotiate who will place the ads, where they will appear, what size and format will be used, and how you'll get paid. Google handles that for you through its AdSense program—and at the same time, ensures that the ads you display will complement your own content. You'll find out more in Chapter 12.

Collaborating More Effectively

In today's global economy, many companies have branch offices around the world or contractors who work from far-flung locations. Getting everyone in the same place for staff meetings can be costly when it comes to the time spent traveling and money spent on transportation costs. Establishing a business presence with Gmail, Google Apps, and Google Page Creator gives employees a way to keep in touch and share files, no matter where they are physically located. A Google Apps site gives colleagues a place to access word processing and spreadsheet documents.

Collaboration is also fostered not only by having a virtual workspace online, courtesy of Google, but by having a single way to access Google's e-mail, spreadsheet, word processing, and other business applications: a Web browser. Once you are able to do all of your work—including e-mail—with your browser, you can work from anywhere. It doesn't matter whether you are using a Macintosh or Windows computer, whether you have Microsoft Office installed, or if you have Office, whether you use

Office 2003 or 2007. Your Web browser lets you get the work done. Some of the benefits of the Google-ized collaboration model are described below.

Behind the Scenes: The Client-Server System

You'll get a better understanding of Google Apps—and all of Google's online services, in fact—if you think of the *client-server system*. Imagine that Google is the server, and you and your individual Web browser are the client, which connects to Google to get information or perform functions like sending and receiving e-mail or reading news headlines.

The whole Internet, in fact, is built around the client-server system. The networked information made available on the Web is on computers that are connected to the Net and that are designed to *serve* files or applications; neither you nor your office must be connected all the time to exchange messages and files. (It's great if your office has a high-speed connection called a T-1 or T-3 line; it's just not mandatory.)

For example, if you are working outside the office, both you and the company can communicate by sending e-mail messages or files to a central server that is always available, such as the mail server or Web server operated by your Internet provider or your service provider (in this case, Google). An e-mail message you send to someone in your office is stored on the server until that individual connects from a coffee shop or library and retrieves the message later. You can also upload a file to your Docs & Spreadsheets (D & S) space on Google's server. Someone in the office can connect to the same D & S site and download the file at their convenience.

The client-server system is always present on the Web. Normally when you are on the Internet you access a Web page stored on someone else's Web server with your client program, your browser. In the case of Google Apps, your client browser can now access your pages, files, spreadsheets, and other records that you have stored on Google's application servers.

Streamlining Communications

Using Google as a central communications point helps you connect more efficiently with coworkers and business colleagues. You can exchange e-mail, communicate in real time using chat or conferencing software, or post messages on company bulletin boards. Your Google Start Page (see Chapter 12) gives you and your coworkers a single point of access to both your company's business data and to fellow employees. So rather than having to e-mail files to one another or be physically present in the office so you can log into the company's file server, you can browse to Google and log in from your hotel room. You can then post your files online through Docs & Spreadsheets and even discuss them while you're viewing them by typing instant messages to one another. In the early days of the Web, there was much talk about intranets—internal networks that used Web technologies to share data within work-group members. Google's services point toward a new and more efficient way of communicating. Being able to store data not on your own servers but on Google's saves you the expense, maintenance, and need to upgrade the necessary machines in-house. It's also very helpful to be able to use Google's e-mail and chat clients to share information if you already have one of the applications open and want to send a file to the person with whom you're communicating; you don't have to connect to Google Apps and move the file to your shared space, but can send it immediately from within the application you're using.

Increasing Your Mobility

Connecting to the Internet in general, and to Google in particular, enlarges your world. That applies to the world of work, too. When your office is online, you don't have to physically be on the premises to exchange messages, share files, and compare schedules with your coworkers. With a computer and modem at home or on the road, you can communicate with the home office by e-mail, fax from your computer, FTP, chat, or a number of other alternatives. Google gives you an even greater level of freedom: you don't have to worry about whether you use a Mac or a PC, whether you use Fetch or Cute FTP for file transfers, or Thunderbird or Outlook Express for e-mail. By using Google, you get a uniform interface to information. And it's free: you don't have to pay a monthly fee to an Internet Service Provider for e-mail service. As long as you can get access to the Net at school, at work, in a public library, or other location, you can access your free Google e-mail and file sharing services.

But moving some of your business communications online with Google gives you a new set of options that go beyond simple e-mail messages. For example, one trend in the American workforce is the increased use of "contingent workers"—temps, part-timers, and freelancers. By collaborating through Google, it is possible to make as-signments to subcontractors and with employees who work out of their homes or other offices. Using Gmail, Talk, or other applications, you can exchange schedules, transfer files, and work on projects collaboratively. It's faster and cheaper than long-distance phone calls or courier services.

It's all about being open to adopting new business strategies. When employees have new ways to communicate, their entire way of doing business shifts. E-mail conversations that go on for days and that are spread out over one's crowded email inbox can be complicated and difficult to track. With Gmail, your conversations are grouped together so that the back-and-forth with a particular individual can be viewed in one place, for instance. If you are in a hurry and the correspondent is online, you can open a chat window and "talk" to that person immediately by typing messages, without incurring long-distance phone charges. Forums like Google Groups help foster a many-to-many community atmosphere, which has promoted customer loyalty, expanded the outreach of companies to new global markets, and increased productivity.

 Tip: Instead of working in isolation, employees should ideally share data and collaborate as colleagues. Your want to make sure the different parts of your company will talk to one another and work together. Resistance will cause your efforts to integrate the Internet into your daily business operations to fall short of expectations.

If you and your business colleagues who work in different locations need to share images in order to develop projects or do collaborative problem-solving, the Internet gives you a variety of options. You don't have to use expensive conferencing centers or set up leased lines in order to conduct virtual meetings. You can share your images with Picasa. When you use conferencing software such as Google Talk to literally talk with your own voice through a microphone and headphones connected to your computer, you no longer have to make expensive long-distance phone calls. All are options to consider if you need to cut back on travel and telecommunications expenses.

Achieving More Efficient Workflow

Reducing paperwork and increasing effective communication were essential business goals long before the Internet became a household word. An increased sense of being in a world community joined by network technology, however, has heightened competition and increased pressure on businesses to work efficiently. When workers in developing nations like India and China are competing for work on a level playing field, businesspeople in older industrialized nations need to do everything possible to improve speed and eliminate duplication of efforts. Whether you're a lone entrepreneur or a business manager, you need to be aware of new technologies that can increase not only profits but also the efficiency of day-to-day administration.

Free software like Google Docs & Spreadsheets has the potential to change the way work takes place in offices around the world. Everyone needs to type letters and reports on their computers, and most businesses need to keep track of financial records using spreadsheet applications. Since personal computers first gained widespread acceptance in the 1980s, their users have had to download and install software programs to perform these functions. As new versions of the software are released with better features, those same individuals need to purchase updates and install them as well. When new computers are purchased there is often a different operating system involved, so new versions of the software need to be obtained.

You're probably quite familiar with the process of making sure you have the disk space and processing power needed to run the programs you buy. And chances are you use some version of the most popular business application around, Microsoft Office. Instead of having to pay hundreds of dollars per user (depending on the version of Office you typically use) to install or update the program every few years, Google provides you with a new and exciting alternative: using common applications by connecting to them online. Google Apps is an example of an approach to delivering computer programs known either as "software as a service" or "hosted applications." Instead of installing a word processing spreadsheet, a calendar, and another application that will consume disk space on your computer, you use your Web browser as the interface to those applications. Google Apps has Google poised to take on Microsoft and directly challenge its dominance in the business productivity area. You'll find out more about Google Apps in Chapter 6, and about many of the components of this suite of applications in subsequent chapters.

Strengthening Your Marketing Pull

By going online with Google, you increase the number of potential customers you can reach. The Internet gives you access to new leads and markets worldwide. Access to the Internet is now a necessity, and businesses are performing ever more functions online. Internet communication technologies such as Web pages, e-mail, bulletin boards, videoconferencing, and chat can help you find new business partners.

Here's an example: the Cato Institute, a nonprofit public policy research foundation in Washington, D.C., hosts a variety of public events such as talks and discussions held by well-known figures. Go to the Institute's Events page (http://www.cato.org/events/calendar.html), and you can view a list of upcoming talks and other gatherings. Each of the descriptions shown in Figure 3-1 includes a Google Calendar button at the bottom (as well as buttons for other popular calendars by Microsoft and Yahoo!).

Figure 3-1. Your organization can use Google Calendar to help promote your upcoming events.

Click the Google Calendar button, and your browser jumps to your default calendar space on Google. You open a form that contains automatically entered information about the upcoming event and its schedule. Click Options, and you can tell Google to e-mail you a reminder. In Figure 3-2, I'm specifying that a reminder will be sent to me 30 minutes before the event takes place.

Does the Google Calendar button attract more attendees to the event? It might, especially if those attendees are sent automatic reminders so they don't forget. It's also a subtle nudge on the part of the savvy Web business that to attract increasingly busy professionals, you need to provide them with all the tools they need, and increasingly, that includes Google's business applications.

Research More Efficiently

Google won't come out and tell you what to say in your blog or on your Web page. The general topic is up to you. It might give you some ideas about what to say,

Figure 3-2. You can tell Google to e-mail you an automatic reminder about your newly scheduled event.

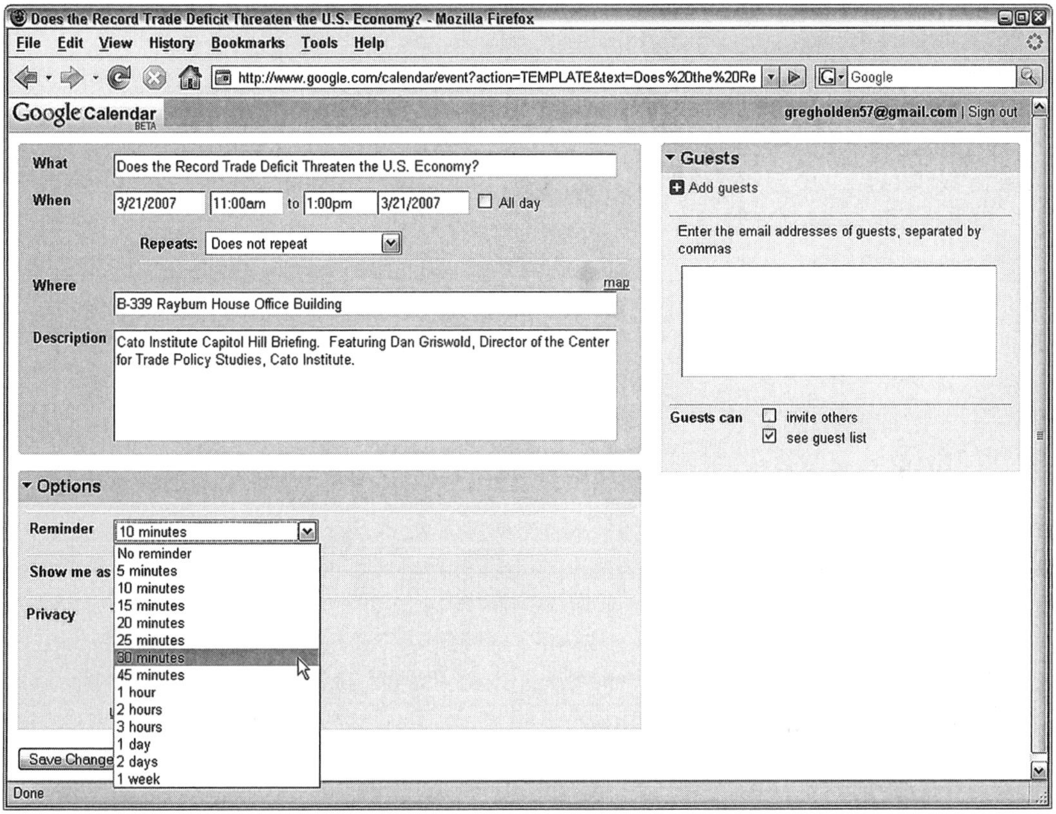

however, and it can also provide you with some add-ons that will make your site more worthy of repeat visits.

First, there's Google's News service (http://news.google.com, shown in Figure 3-3). At this writing, the site had just released a feature that enables anyone with a historical question to search news archives for stories going back several decades. For anyone wanting to answer a question or prepare a more accurate report, such archives are a gold mine of information.

A variety of other specialty services will save you the time that you would have spent trudging to the library or making phone calls to research centers:

- *Book Search*. This service (http://books.google.com) lets you search the full text of many books.

- *Blog Search*. If you are trying to gauge current opinions and the "zeitgeist," try this service. It searches the text of the many online Web logs, otherwise known as blogs (http://blogsearch.google.com/).

Figure 3-3. Google's news service can help back up your business research.

- *Finance.* This site (http://finance.google.com/finance) specializes in stock reports and business news.

- *Patent Search.* Search (http://www.google.com/patents) the text of patents to see who's in competition with you for that innovative product you're developing.

- *Specialty Searches.* If you're looking for information limited to a specific topic, you might find it here (http://www.google.com/options/specialsearches-.html). You can search through government Web sites as well as those of Apple or Microsoft.

Streamlining Administrative Functions

Many businesses handle essential administrative tasks such as payroll, training, and maintenance online. You can avoid expensive purchase orders and cut down on paperwork by ordering goods from suppliers through Gmail or through Google Apps. If you set up an account for a trusted supplier, that company's representative can send orders directly to your Google Apps workspace by logging in with a password you issue to them and uploading (a techie term for transferring) the file using Google Apps' user-friendly tools. Security is definitely a concern, however. First, Google protects you in two ways: it restricts access to shared Google Apps workspaces and you need to guard your passwords and account information closely if you plan to publish information online that you don't want the whole world to see. Even if you or your colleagues do upload information to Google Apps, you have a second level of protection: you have to specifically share each file with selected individuals; otherwise, they'll only be seen by the people who upload them.

Some larger companies convert their entire operations to make use of Internet technologies like e-mail, file sharing by means of intranets (internal networks that use Web browsers to give access to information). They order supplies from electronic catalogs, create vertical portals, set up employee intranets, and more. They spend millions of dollars installing proprietary software such as Microsoft Exchange, as well as setting up complex servers to manage information. Google is revolutionizing this by making the same technologies like shared workspaces, applications like calendars, spreadsheets, and word processors, available online for free, taking them out of the province of technical experts and organizations with "deep pockets" and making them available to everyone.

Using Google to Search and Be Found

CHAPTER 4

Improving Google Search Results

When I scan the message boards of services that host Web sites for small businesses, one of the most common topics is this: "How do I get my site to show up on Google?" By "showing up on Google," the site owners mean that they want their pages to appear near the top of a set of search results. Let's say that you have created a site focusing on bird cages, and your site turns up on page 56 of a set of 80 pages of results. Few, if any, dedicated bird lovers are going to dig that far into a set of pages. In my experience, you need to get on the first one or two pages to have any chance that someone will click through to your site and make a purchase. The Holy Grail for many online businesspeople is a ranking right at the top of the first page of Google's search results—or, barring that, to appear somewhere on the first page of search results.

The practice of optimizing your content to get the best placement in Google's search results is so common that it has been given its own name: search engine optimization (SEO). Google's exact formula for ranking pages in a set of search results is a closely guarded secret, but enough of it is known that you can follow some relatively simple, low-tech practices to improve your page's rank. The increased attention that comes from being on page one of a set of Google search results in the form of Web site visits is both effective and cost-effective. It's something you can do yourself for little or no money. But yet it's among the most important ways in which Google can help small businesses. Here's how it works.

A Mathematical Formula for Success

Google's exact formula for determining search result rankings is a complex algorithm. It's partly mathematical, and partly based on many factors that indicate how active and how popular a site is—in other words, how valuable it is as a resource. Google continually re-indexes the Web, and ignores sites that are considered "dead." A "dead" site is one that hasn't been updated for a long time and that doesn't receive many (or any) visits. To avoid ending up "dead" in Internet terms, you need to update your site regularly by changing some content.

For instance, if you publish a blog online using Google Blogger (see Chapter 13), you only have to make an entry every week (or better yet, every day) to keep your site fresh. Otherwise, make a commitment to change something—anything—on your site every week or so. This can be something as insignificant as the "last updated" date at the bottom of your Web page, or as significant as the page title. One Web site developer who is related to me explained that every week or two, he goes through his site page by page and rewrites headings and other text just so his site will be new when Google does its re-indexing. Just add a bit of information as often as you can to improve your search results. Of course keeping the cobwebs off your site is a good practice just to keep your visitors coming back to you on a regular basis.

Search Engine Rankings

The idea behind the desire for favorable search engine placement is probably borne out by your own experience. The whole point of doing a search on Google is to obtain a set of search results that you can scan. If you're like me, your tendency is to start clicking on links that are near the top of the first page because they are either most relevant to what you're looking for or they exactly match what you're seeking. Your job as a Web site owner or business marketer is to get your own site as close as possible to the top of the first page of results when someone does a search for products, services, or topics that match your own.

There are two simple and practical ways you can improve your search engine ranking: (1) submitting your site for inclusion in Google's directory and (2) exchanging links with other Web sites.

 Tip: There are online businesspeople whose particular goal is to increase their links to other sites. These networks are called Like Exchanges. If you want to participate, simply access the Google Directory: to GoGoogle's home page (www.google.com), click the link more, click the link even more in the popup menu that appears, and when the More Google Products page appears, click Directory. Then go to this category: Computers > Internet > Web Design and Development > Promotion > Link Popularity > Reciprocal Links. You'll

find a long list of Web sites that will match you up with "link partners." Make sure to approach sites that aren't direct competitors,
but that offer products and services that complement your own.

Playing the Keyword Game

A keyword is a word or phrase that someone enters in the search box provided by
Google or another search service. The user submits the keywords to the site, and a
sophisticated computer program scours a database that the service has compiled. The
database consists of some of the contents of every page on the Web that the search
service's automated computer program, called a spider, has been able to index. The
exact operations of the spiders, the databases, and the means by which individual
pages and contents are culled from the database are a closely-kept secret. But one
Google employee, Matt Cutts, wrote in 2003 (at http://www.mattcutts.com/blog) that
Google moved from a system in which the database was updated once a month to
once a *day*.

What does this all mean for you? When you design your Web pages, it's important
to keep them updated. It's just as important to sprinkle the keywords your customers
or clients are most likely to enter in prominent locations on your pages. Those locations include:

- *Each page's title bar.* This area at the very top of the browser window is believed to be indexed by Google: the search program doesn't scan an entire
  Web page but only indicators such as the title that describe its subject or
  contents.

- *Headings.* The headings at the top of your page are important because it's
  believed Google's automated indexing programs don't scour the entire contents of Web pages. The theory is that the ones that count are only the biggest
  headings (the ones labeled H1 or Heading 1 by the Web editing programs
  used to create those pages) and those near the top.

- *The first paragraph or two.* Most Web sites spell out their "mission" or provide
  a summary of their contents at the top of the home page, and this is regarded
  as an important location for keywords by those who study search engine optimization.

 Tip: Don't worry about terms like at, is, or, a, or the; these are
ignored by search engines. Focus on nouns and verbs that describe

your site's contents. If you need suggestions of keywords that are related to what you sell or promote on your Web site, do a free search at Wordtracker (http://www.wordtracker.com). This popular service (which includes a paid version with many more suggestions) provides you with a list of likely keywords based on your site's content. (See Chapter 5 for more about Wordtracker.)

The words "Google is believed to . . ." are used in the preceding list because, as I mentioned earlier, Google's exact formula for making searches relevant and accurate is secret. However, you get a glimpse into some elements of Google's method when you look at Google's patent application, which it filed with the U.S. Patent and Trademark Office (USPTO) in December 2003. The application contains a list of 63 criteria that will be used in evaluating search ranking. According to the document Google assigns each page is a numeric figure called a PageRank, which is determined by factors such as these:

- How frequently the page's contents are retrieved as a result of search queries.
- The number of new pages that are added to the site, or that are linked to the page being retrieved.
- The amount of text or photos that are changed on the site.
- The length of time the page has been online.
- The time that passes between changes to the page; the more frequently the page changes, the higher its PageRank number.

When you take the 63 factors (or at least the ones you can absorb most easily) into account, you will probably write and design your pages differently than you have been in order to improve your own page rankings. Make sure your titles aren't blank or that they contain a generic word such as Home or About Us. Make sure they have at least one or two keywords in the visible content of your Web page that describe who you are and what you do. Both the title and keywords can be controlled in virtually any Web page editing program. Microsoft's latest Web editor, Expression Web, uses the dialog box shown in Figure 4-1 to specify the page's title. In addition, you can also add keywords and a brief description to the HTML code for your page.

The keywords and description don't appear in the body of your Web page that is actually visible to anyone with a Web browser. It remains in the code, behind the

Figure 4-1. Take a moment to add keywords to your title in your Web editing software.

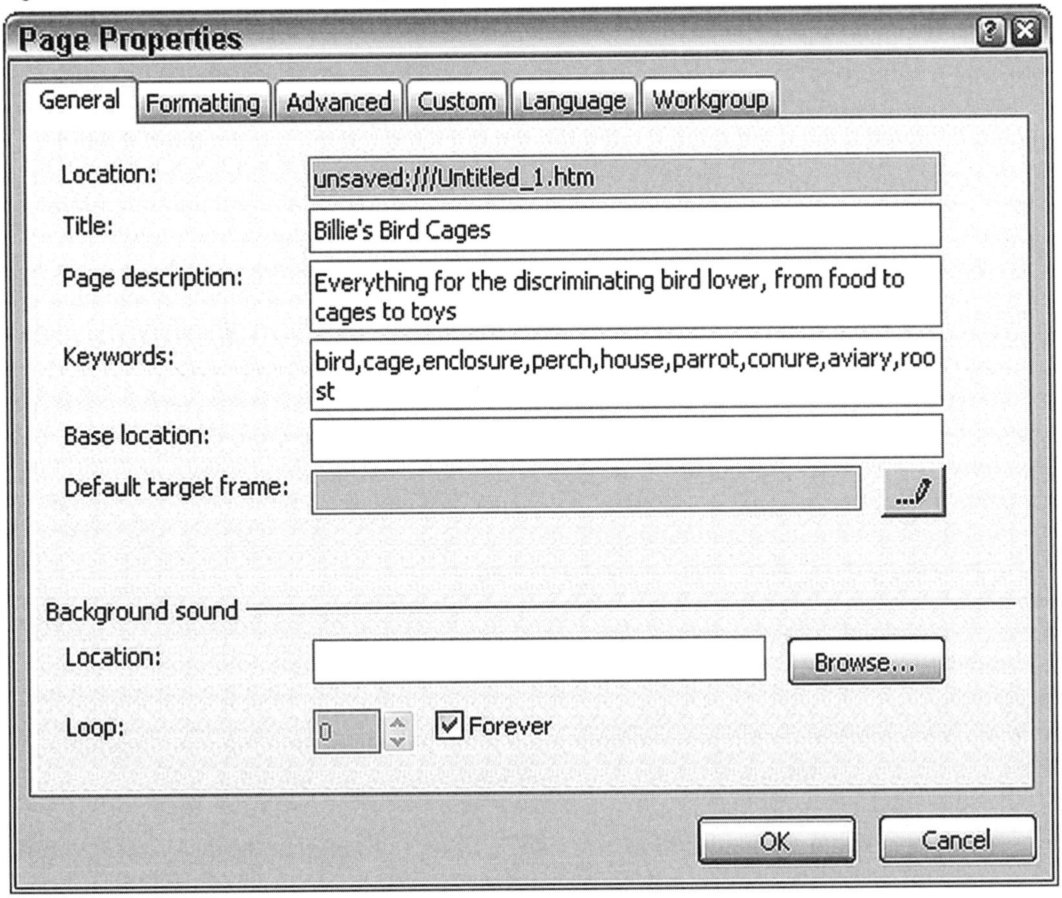

Page Properties

| General | Formatting | Advanced | Custom | Language | Workgroup |

Location: unsaved:///Untitled_1.htm

Title: Billie's Bird Cages

Page description: Everything for the discriminating bird lover, from food to cages to toys

Keywords: bird,cage,enclosure,perch,house,parrot,conure,aviary,roost

Base location:

Default target frame:

Background sound

Location: Browse...

Loop: 0 ☑ Forever

OK   Cancel

scenes, where it can be read by one of those automated "spider" programs that index your pages. The keywords (in theory) help make your site more visible; the description is incorporated into the brief description that appears when your site is added to a set of search results. In fact, many Web site owners who pursue SEO techniques to improve search rankings realize that adding keywords to the Web page code for a page doesn't affect rank much, if at all; the factors listed in Google's patent application and elsewhere in this chapter, such as links, updates, page history, and searches, carry more weight when it comes to page rank.

Besides creating page titles, try to build important keywords into critical areas of your site, as described elsewhere in this chapter. And make an effort to commit yourself to a schedule whereby you update your site regularly. Make sure the links you make to your pages and from your pages to other sites are valid (in other words, they don't lead to "dead" or nonexistent pages).

Tip: The Google PageRank patent application can be found by doing a search for its application number, 0050071741, USPTO's Web site (www.uspto.gov).

Adding Your Site to the Google Directory

Unlike the philosophy that if you pad your essays in creative writing class you'll get a better grade, length here is not your friend. If your descriptions are too long, they won't fit in the search results. You make sure that what will actually be seen is a message that you want to get across. Here, control is the name of the game. If you compose your own description for submission rather than waiting for Google's spiders to index your site, you can be the one to decide exactly what appears in the search results. One option is to compose your Web site description jut the way you want it, and to submit it to the Google Directory.

The Google Directory is a style index to the contents of the Internet. With a style that is similar to Yahoo!, it is arranged by category. Most people access Google's database of Web sites by using its well-known search page, which is also the site's home page. To find the Directory, you first need to access the site. Go to the home page, click More, and click Even More. When the More Google Products page appears, click Directory under the heading Search.

You can also take advantage of a simple and perhaps more practical approach to getting your Web site before the eyes of potential visitors: add your URL to the Google Directory. You do this by accessing Google's form for submitting a Web page URL to the directory (http://www.google.com/addurl). The form is shown in Figure 4-2.

You have two options for adding a description to Google's directory (or Yahoo!'s, or any other directory, for that matter). You can submit your description to Google as described in the preceding paragraph. You can also add a description to the HTML code for your Web pages What does it mean to add your description to the HTML code? Every Web page consists of a visible set of contents (text, colors, rules, and images) that appear in a Web browser window, and the underlying markup that tells a browser how to format a page's contents. The underlying markup is written in a language such as HTML (HyperText Markup Language). The HTML code for a page is a text file formatted with a file extension such as .htm or .html so a browser knows that it's a Web page file and that the contents need to be formatted accordingly.

An HTML file consists primarily of commands like this:

Figure 4-2. Fill out this form and submit it to Google's directory.

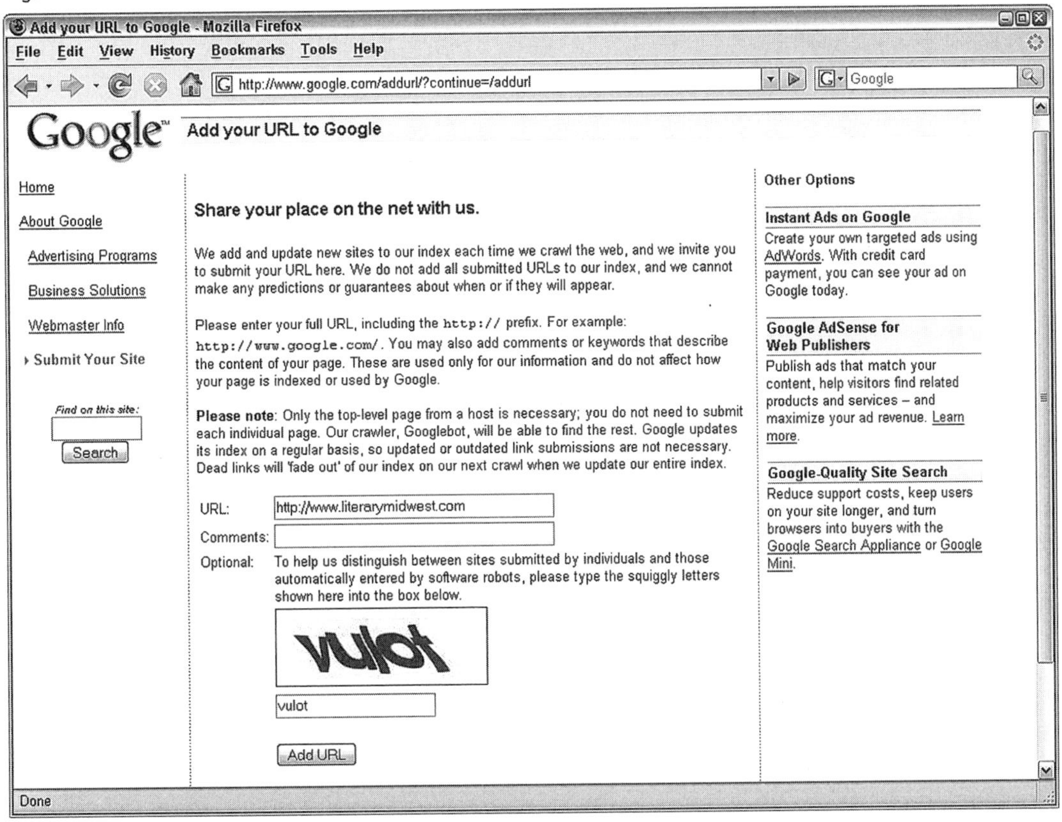

```
<b>Format this sentence in bold.</b>
```

The `<b>` and `</b>` commands describe to a browser what is supposed to be bold. In addition, a markup file can contain text that is not intended to be displayed in a browser window and that does not appear on a Web page. For instance, you might see comments left by the page's author, like this:

```
<!--This document was created by Martin Smith using Expression Web 1.0 -->
```

Another type of content is bit of META information. Such information is only meant to be interpreted by a browser or another program (such as an indexing program used by Google or another search engine). Some META commands can enclose keywords associated with your Web page, or a description that tells a search engine exactly how to describe it. For example:

```
<meta name="description" content="This is a web site devoted to the care
```

and feeding of parrots. Our fine feathered friends and their owners will find food and custom toys, and other parrot owners with whom they can discuss their favorite pets!"

Whether you embed your Web page in a META command in your page's HTML or whether you submit it to Google's directory, in either case you get a chance to characterize your site the way you want to present it. You can be businesslike, or you can be irreverent. Suppose you create a Web site devoted to parrots and parrot toys. You want your site to be distinguishable from Jimmy Buffet's Parrot Head fan club, or any other organizations that use the name Parrots, such as baseball teams. You can create a description of the site in a set of search results; the description that appears reads like this:

A Web site intended for parrot lovers. Includes custom-made parrot toys and houses.

The point is that if you take a proactive approach to search listings, you can control how your site is described in those results. That way, you'll get the visitors who are actually looking for what you have to offer and who are more likely to make a purchase, send in an inquiry, or perform another action.

It Pays to Be Popular

You've heard the saying that more leads to more, and here's another case in point. Google's engine is partial to sites that have frequent updates as well as those that get lots of hits. Just adding keywords and descriptions to your Web pages won't necessarily result in a good ranking. Being popular, however, has nothing to do with getting a date for Saturday night. From the search index program's point of view, popularity is defined as a lot of links being made to a page.

No Web site exists in a vacuum. Every site contains hypertext links that lead visitors from one location on a page to another or to another page, image, or file somewhere on the Web or even on your own computer network. Google gives a good page rank to a site that contains lots of valuable, valid links to other sites A *valid* link is one that is accurate: the link goes to an actual Web page rather than one that is "under construction" or that has moved because the Web address has changed. A valuable link is a link to a site that has many other sites pointing to it. It turns out that on the Web, as in other areas of life, being "well connected" matters. In this case, a page that has lots of connections to other pages is seen by Google as vital and worthy of a prominent place in search results.

One way to improve both the quantity and quality of the links on your Web pages is to contact other sites and ask them to link to you.

A useful approach is to look for sites that have products and services that complement yours. You should then approach the owners of those sites and ask to exchange links: "I'll publicize your site if you publicize mine."

Selecting Business Content for Google

Not all of the business content you publish online is for public consumption. You might not want search services like Google to index certain pages. You can block a search indexing program from including all of your Web pages or just selected ones.

- You include a simple text file named **robots.txt.**
- Identify the automated program you want to block, or the pages on your site that you don't want indexed.
- Post this text file on your Web site. Google itself provides instructions for people who want to block indexing programs at http://www.google.com/support/webmasters/bin/answer.py?answer = 40362.

Doing It Yourself: Linking to Your Own Web Sites

Many enterprising businesspeople increase the "linkage" associated with their Web site by connecting to themselves. They create lots of different Web sites and point them to one another, creating their own mini-network of interconnected pages. Publishing a variety of Web site increases the chances someone will find you simply because you have multiple "presences" online. Having the pages link to one another or at least point to a primary Web site lifts all of the sites in page rank.

Lars Hundley, who owns the site Clean Air Gardening (http://www.cleanairgardening) is a real online entrepreneur. One of his Web sites sells environmentally friendly tools such as manual push-type lawn mowers. But he also has a variety of other Web sites. As mentioned above, the number of sites that link to your own makes your site more "valuable" in Google's eyes, and improves its search placement. Google's indexing programs don't know whether you are linking to one of your own Web sites or someone else's. Enterprising businesspeople like Lars create multiple Web sites. By linking them to one another, each site appears to Google to be well-connected—in other words, with plenty of links to other sites. This improves the Google search placement for all sites. In addition, Hundley uses blogs and even the photo-sharing site Flickr to promote his business. His sites include:

- Practical Environmentalist (www.practicalenvironmentalist.com)
- Gardening Gift Guide (www.gardeninggiftguide.com), a blog for gardening products that frequently links to and promotes products for sale on Hundley's primary site, Clean Air Gardening.
- Compost Guide (http://compostguide.com/info).
- Flickr (http://www.flickr.com/photos/cleanairgardening). Hundley posts photos of satisfied customers happily pushing his lawn mowers or using other tools they have purchased from him on this site. The Flickr page contains a link back to Clean Air Gardening.

The best way to get a good ranking on Google, however, has nothing to do with links, keywords, and titles: it's simply to have a good Web site. The more valuable your site is and the more frequently you maintain it, the better its rank will be. That's the genius of Google's search system: it rewards good behavior with good attention.

Sure there are quite a few non-technical and low-cost strategies you can pursue to improve your search ranking on Google. But no single activity will function as a "cure all" to take your Web site from the 50th page of a set of search results to the coveted Page 1 position. You have to try all of these different activities, and keep at it on a regular basis. In the next chapter, you'll learn another way in which rolling up your sleeves and trying some new marketing strategies can pay off for you: by initiating some AdWords paid search campaigns that will gain more attention for your site in an efficient way.

CHAPTER **5**

Improving Your Visibility with AdWords

Google first became popular and eventually gained widespread acceptance for two reasons: its search service delivers what it promises, and it's free. But Google, like any business, couldn't give away its services for free indefinitely. Rather than charging a fixed fee for conducting searches, however, Google made a fortune by coming up with an innovative advertising system called AdWords.

AdWords takes advantage of Google's search technology for delivering context sensitive ads: ads that match the item that someone is searching for. AdWords enables Google to convert its search service to a revenue-generating system, while at the same time giving anyone the opportunity to *set their own fee* for displaying the ads. The cost-per-click payment system used by Google has largely supplanted the old-fashioned banner advertising system in which Web publishers displayed fixed ads on their pages and were paid based on the number of times those ads are viewed. This chapter provides you with a brief introduction to Google's main advertising tool and how you can get started with it to attract more attention for your business.

Understanding AdWords

AdWords (http://adwords.google.com) is the program that comes up with context-sensitive advertisements that appear just above and to the right of search results on Google. It gives everyone from lone individuals to big corporations the chance to compete in a level playing field for the same valuable advertising space. Because Google is the most popular search service around, and because millions of people conduct searches on Google every day, its search results pages are viewed by many. And if you can create an ad that will offer products or services that are similar to, if not identical to, what they're already searching for, it's worth paying for those ads.

An example is shown in Figure 5-1. I've conducted a search for a brand of shoes I frequently sell on eBay: Allen Edmonds. The natural search results—the results generated by Google through the mysterious formulas described in Chapter 4—are presented in the main area of the page on the bottom left. You'll notice that Allen Edmonds' own Web site appears right at the top of the list, followed by links to stores that sell this manufacturer's shoes. Some of the AdWords ads appear on the right; others appear at the top.

It's interesting to notice that none of the AdWords ads shown in Figure 5-1 direct the shopper to the Allen Edmonds Web site itself, although this manufacturer does sell its shoes online through its Web site. Instead, the AdWords ads you see on the first page lead shoppers to the e-commerce Web sites of various companies that sell shoes. The manufacturer could place an ad for its own products if it wanted to; on the other hand, since it appears right at the top of page one, it might not be necessary.

Who places the AdWords ads seen in Figure 5-1, if they aren't the manufacturer of the shoes? The AdWords advertisers fall into two general categories:

- *Online retailers.* Lots of stores sell shoes on the Web, and these store owners want to drive customers looking for shoes to their Web sites. When you're looking for shoes, for instance, you'll see plenty of AdWords ads for Zappos .com, an online shoe store.

Figure 5-1. AdWords ads appear alongside natural search results.

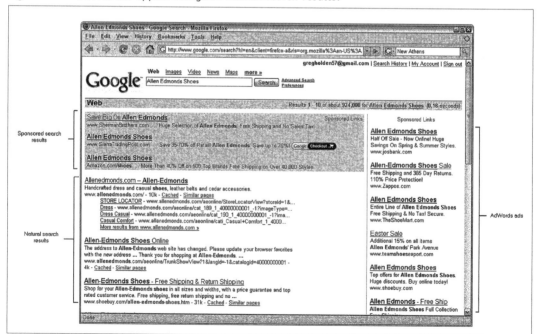

- *Affiliate advertisers.* An affiliate is someone who places an ad on behalf of an advertiser. The affiliate promotes the advertiser's products and services and steers potential customers to the advertiser's Web site; the affiliate pays a fee every time someone clicks on an AdWords ad. But the affiliate earns a far larger fee if one of the shoppers ends up making a purchase or performing a specific action, such as registering for the site or submitting information.

Affiliate advertising is a multifaceted subject that could easily require a book of its own. But it's something you can pursue through Google. Often, Internet-based companies like the job search site Monster.com and the bookstore Amazon.com run their own affiliate programs. You sign up with them, you place an ad on your Web site, and you earn a fee if someone registers, places an ad, or makes a purchase (the criteria depends on the advertiser). But the number of clickthroughs (clicks on your ad that take a visitor to the advertiser's Web site) your ad receives depends on the visibility of your Web page. The more visitors you receive, the more ad revenue you'll generate. If you place your affiliate ad on one of Google's search results pages, you'll probably receive a lot more attention than you would otherwise.

You can use AdWords, then, as either an affiliate or as an online merchant advertising your own business. Affiliate advertising is an activity that can be very lucrative, and one that has made a few enterprising individuals rich. I'm only going to discuss it briefly at the end of this chapter, however. For the bulk of this chapter, I'm going to assume you're a businessperson who wants to advertise your own Web site or online store by placing AdWords ads on your own behalf.

Does AdWords Make Sense for Your Business?

Suppose you've taken steps such as those described in Chapter 4 and optimized your Web site so it will receive prominent placement in Google's search results as well as services like Yahoo! and MSN Search. Should you take the next step and pay for ads that appear alongside the natural search results? It's not an either-or thing: competition is becoming so fierce among e-commerce Web sites that most businesspeople optimize their sites for search placement and take out AdWords ads as well. Of course, you could also consider one of the other tried-and-true advertising options like these:

- *Paying for directory placement.* Yahoo!, one of the most popular directories to the Internet, now charges commercial entities several hundred dollars to list themselves in the directory at http://www.yahoo.com. But simply being included in the directory can get you more attention. (Google, of course, has its own directory at dir.google.com. You don't have to pay to add your URL to Google's directory; see Chapter 4 for more.)

- *Banner ads.* A banner ad is an image, usually rectangular in shape, that is displayed on someone else's Web page. You are the advertiser, and you pay the publisher of the site a fee for showing your ad. The fee varies depending on the publisher: you might pay on a CPM (cost per 1000 impressions) basis. Or you might pay only when someone performs a desired action, such as clicking on the ad to go to your Web site, or making a purchase after clicking on the ad.

The problem with directory searches is that your site is listed alongside many others that offer similar items or services. The problem with banner ads is that they aren't always targeted: you can't always control what Web surfers are looking for when they come to a site. They may or may not be interested in the substance of your ad. And if you agree to a CPM payment structure, you are at the mercy of the publisher: if the publisher attracts many thousands of visitors due to a special promotion, it will hopefully end up with more visits for you, but whether you get visits or not, you still pay for that ad.

One of the big advantages of AdWords is that you are in control. You can begin or end ad campaigns at any time. Not only that, but you can determine how much you will pay every time someone clicks on your ads: you can bid as little as a penny a click or as much as $10. It's not a good idea to bid as little as a penny, however, because you are competing with anyone else who has already set a price-per-click level on the same keywords. If you bid a penny and someone else has bid .10, that person will get higher ad placement in a set of search results for your specified keywords. The challenge is to bid as low as possible while still ensuring placement near the top of the page; bid too high, and you'll spend too much on your ads. Bid too low, and few people will ever see your ad. And the success of your ad also depends in large measure on how you write it. You have an agonizingly small space in which to create your ad. Count the number of characters in one of the ads that appear on a set of Google search results, and you get the idea: the typical ad consists of only two lines of 30 to 35 characters each.

Another advantage is targeting: your AdWords ads only appear in search results when someone enters a keyword or phrase that matches a keyword that you associate with the ad. For instance, suppose I am advertising a line of golf gloves I have received in bulk from a wholesale supplier and want to sell quickly. I create the Ad-Words ad shown in Figure 5-2.

After creating the visible part of the ad (the part shown in the preceding figure), Google gives me the opportunity to choose keywords to associate with my ad. These are words or short phrases that consumers are likely to search for when they are looking for my gloves such as:

Figure 5-2. AdWords ads have keywords associated with them that you specify.

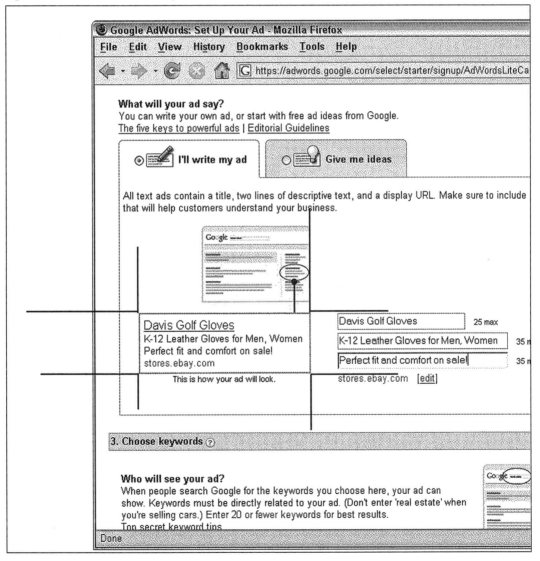

- Gloves
- Golf wear
- Golf accessories
- Men's golf gloves
- Women's golf gloves

Google will display my ad when someone's search terms match one of my keywords: But where the ad is displayed depends on how much I want to pay for each one of those keywords. I might bid, say, ten cents on the keyword "gloves." That means every time someone clicks my ad after searching for the keyword "gloves," I pay 10 cents. If someone else has bid 15 cents or 20 cents for the same keyword, their ad appears above mine in the search results pages. The important thing is that I determine how much I am willing to pay, and I only pay when I get results—when someone clicks on my ad. I can also adjust my ad copy and bid amounts based on performance; a keyword that gets a lot of results for me might be worthy of a higher bid amount, while one that doesn't attract any clicks can be reduced or deleted at any time.

Creating Your AdWords Campaign

If you have already signed up for another Google service such as Gmail, you can use the same username and password when you sign up for AdWords. But you have to associate your existing Google Account with AdWords before you can use it.

Signing Up for AdWords

It's free to sign up for AdWords, and the program itself is free to use—you only pay cost-per-click fees for the ads you create. Before you get started, you should have at least a rough idea of what you want to advertise and what keywords are typically used by Google searchers to locate products or services like yours. Do some searching on Google for your own products and see which keywords work; also check out the AdWords ads that have already been created for products like yours. It's not a good idea to copy them outright—you want to get more attention for your own ads than your competitors do—but you might get some suggestions for keywords and phrases you can insert into your ad text.

1. When you're ready, go to the *AdWords* page (http://adwords.google.com), log in if necessary, and click the [*Begin*] button.

2. On the ***Choose Edition*** page, click the version you want. Since you're just starting out, this example assumes you click Starter Edition. This is a simplified version of AdWords that is tailored to beginners. The other version, Standard Edition, includes more advanced features such as the ability to start and track multiple ad campaigns at one time; it might be good for an upgrade eventually. Choose the button that indicates whether you have a Web site or not, and click the [Continue] button.

 Note: You need to have a Web site up and running before you start using AdWords. If you don't, you can create a simple Web site with another Google tool, Web page creator, as described in Chapter 11.

3. When the *It's All About the Results*™ page appears, choose the location of the customers you want to reach by selecting one of the options under the heading Where are your customers located?. Then select the language of your site and enter the URL for the site where your customers will go when they click on your ad.

5. Write the ad by filling out the form shown in Figure 5-3.

Writing Your Ad

One of the most creative aspects of working with AdWords is the fact that the success of your ads depends to some extent on your writing skills You are not allowed to go over the allotted character limit—25 characters in the title, and 35 characters in the two lines beneath it—you won't be able to type any more. Writing AdWords ads is a skill that takes practice. It's more difficult than you think to cram the main selling points into such a small space. If you need help, click the *Give me ideas* tab or the *Five keys to powerful ads* link above the form. When you're ready, follow these steps:

1. In the title box, type a 25-character or less title for your ad.
2. In the two boxes beneath the title, enter the rest of your ad.
3. Double-check the URL you previously entered for the destination page—the page you want shoppers to go to when they click on your ad—and make sure it's correct. If not, click edit and change it.

 Tip: You don't have to limit yourself to writing one ad. You can write several variations on a single ad and put them all online. Track them

Figure 5-3. Your ad should be short, focused, and use keywords.

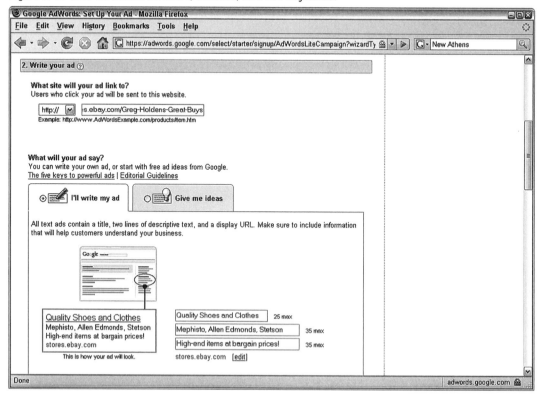

for a week or so, and delete the ones that don't attract as much attention. You aren't paying for ads that no one clicks on, but for the sake of good housekeeping, and to avoid losing money from ads that don't produce, it's a good idea to delete the less profitable ones. Keep the successful one online.

AdWords ads work best when you can target them to people who are already eager to find the product or service you are advertising. If possible, write ads that describe products that appeal to a niche market. Instead of ads for "Women's Shoes," for instance, write an ad for "Coach women's pumps," or "Nike NT Training Shoes." The Web is ideal for reaching dedicated enthusiasts who love—or are even obsessed by—a product or brand. Find a niche market that appeals to you and stick with it. Also make your ads describe items you know well and that you hopefully like yourself. They don't necessarily need to be items you are selling; you'll do better, though, if you know the products and can describe desirable models or brands. Promote a product or service you either know well already or that interests you enough to learn more about it. If you know about it, you'll be better able to choose the keywords and phrases that will encourage visitors to make a purchase or join up.

For instance, when I did a search on Google for sponsored ads for the Olympus C-5060 digital camera I was going to advertise, I found lots of examples. The headings looked like these:

- Sale: Olympus C-5060
- Olympus C-5060 Camera
- C-5060 Olympus Camera
- Olympus Cameras at Staples
- Sale on Cameras

I noticed that no one noticed product reviews that identified this model as a "best buy," so I thought I might play that up to stand out from the others. My ad looked like this:

Best Buy! Olympus C-5060 (21 characters)
Top-rated model—read reviews (33 characters)
Special unadvertised lowest prices! (35 characters)

This particular ad is for a single product for sale. But typically, advertisers sell products that are available in quantity and that they can advertise for weeks or months at a time. Although you can remove an ad within minutes after it's sold, you don't want to spend your time continually creating and deleting ads for individual products. It's much less work to create an ad and track it over a period of time. When you're done writing your initial ad, move down to the part of the form that lets you select keywords.

Google maintains a set of editorial guidelines for AdWords ads that you should review at https://adwords.google.com/select/guidelines.html. Among other things, the guidelines protect copyrights and trademarks. If you use a company's brand name in an ad and the trademark holder has previously informed Google that they do not want their trademark used, Google will prevent you from using it. If your ad violates AdWords' listing policies in some way (by making unsubstantiated claims

> such as "lowest price in the world," for instance), the AdWords form
> will inform you. You'll see a warning message and be instructed to re-
> write the form before it is accepted.

Choosing Keywords

The part of your ad that shoppers don't see, but that is just as important as the ad
copy that appears on Google's search results, is the keyword selection. Enter a term
in the text box shown in the Choose keywords section of the form (see Figure 5-4).

The best keywords are those that uniquely describe the item or service you are
advertising. Use the ones you might enter yourself. Do a search for the item you are
advertising, and scan the search results for likely terms either in the body of the ad
or the title. If you need help coming up with keywords, click Search to view some
suggestions. Enter as many keywords as you can in the box—but keep them as specific
as possible, or you'll get lots of impressions with no clicks or purchases. Such an ad
doesn't cost you anything—you only pay for clicks, not impressions—but it doesn't

Figure 5-4. Select keywords that are likely to produce clicks as well as purchases.

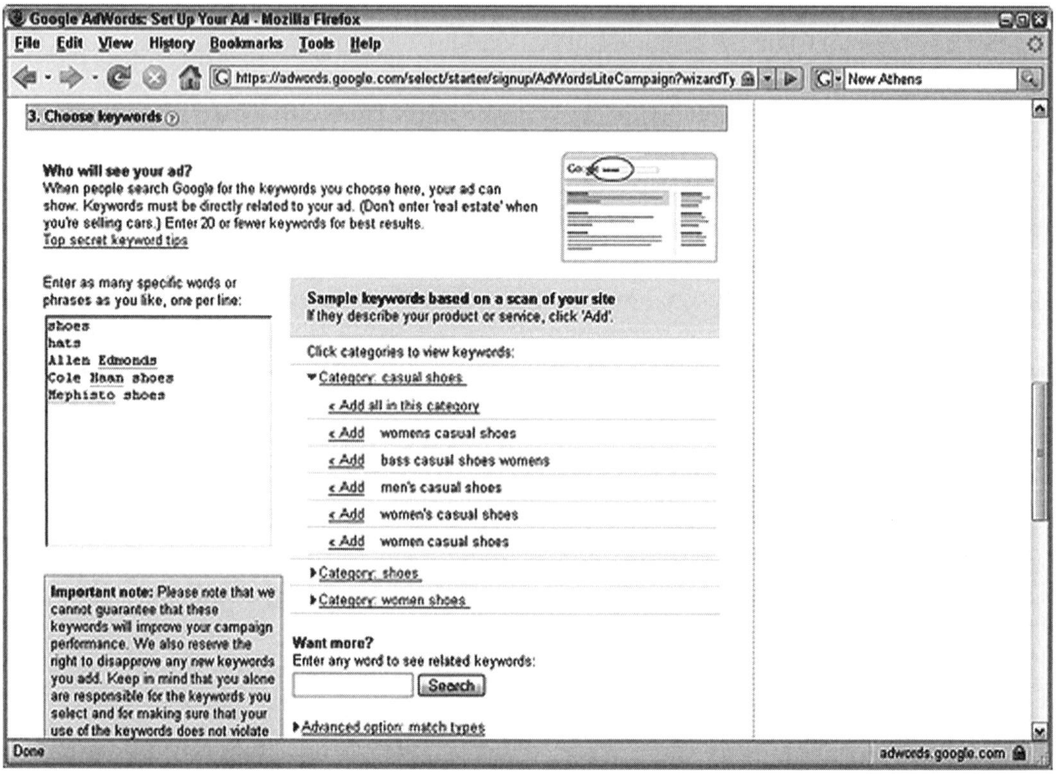

accomplish your goal, either. The keywords can be a single word or a short phrase. The trick is picking words or phrases that are likely to attract people to your ad—and not only that, but get them to follow through with a purchase or registration.

If you click the link Advanced option: match types near the bottom of the keywords section of the page, four examples appear showing how you can use punctuation to control exactly how and when your keywords will match someone's search terms and cause your ad to appear. The first option is not to use any punctuation at all. If you don't add punctuation and simply type the keyword, you attract a "broad match." In a broad match, your ad will appear whenever the keyword is entered. The other three options are:

- *Exact match.* Your ad will appear if someone enters the exact word or phrase you specify, without any other keywords. Enclose the keyword in [brackets]. For example, if you specify [Nike shoes], your ad will appear when someone searches only for that phrase; it will not appear for the search phrase "Men's Nike shoes."

- *Phrase match.* Your ad will appear only if someone enters the exact word or phrase you have specified, whether that word or phrase is alone or with other search terms. You enclose the phrase match in parentheses, like this: "phrase match." For example, your ad will appear if you specify "Nike shoes" and someone enters the phrase "Women's Nike shoes."

- *Negative match.* Your ad will only appear if the specified keyword is not entered. Use this option in conjunction with other search terms, or else your ad will appear more often than you wish. This option narrows your original search terms, for instance: "Nike shoes-trainers" will cause your ad to appear when someone searches for "Nike shoes" but not when they add the word "trainers."

When you're done entering keywords or phrases, scroll down to the next section, where you choose your preferred currency from the drop-down list. Then scroll down to the next section.

 Tip: There's no limit to the number of keywords you can enter, though Google recommends you use 20 or less for best results. A service called Wordtracker (http://www.wordtracker.com) provides search marketers (people who use search services like Google or Yahoo! to market their businesses) with suggestions of keywords that should drive traffic toward the products they are trying to sell. The service is free to try out and will instantly supply you with a selection of keywords based on a product description you submit. If you sign up for a subscription, you get hundreds of keywords for each submission.

Set Your Budget

Next, you scroll down to the *Set Your Budget* section of your form. Click one of the options shown to create a daily budget, the most you're willing to spend in ads in one day on your AdWords ads. For this example, enter $50. It's unlikely you'll spend this much in one day, but in case you do, you'll have a "cap" on your spending so you don't spend more than you want to.

Setting Up Your Account

The next step is to set up your account.

1. When you're done setting your budget, click Continue.

2. The next page, ***Set Up Account***, asks whether you already have a Google e-mail address or account. Select the option that says you do, and a second option that prompts you to use a single Google Account for AdWords and other services. A page appears asking you to wait while your account is created. The Ad Campaign page appears.

3. Review your ad, and if it's OK, click the option to enter your billing information. (If it's not, click Review ad first.)

4. On the next page, you choose your country and time zone and click Continue. Your campaign is started, and your ad begins to run. The campaign summary page lists the keywords you have associated with your ad. Because you just began the campaign, you don't see any clicks or charges on this screen (see Figure 5-5). Return back later in the day or the following day and monitor which keywords get the most clicks.

If you decide to move up to the Standard Edition of AdWords (it doesn't cost anything to do so), you gain more control over your costs per click. Instead of simply setting a maximum daily budget you're willing to spend on "clicks," you are able to specify a cost for each keyword. It's reasonable to start out with a CPC (cost per click) of ten cents to begin with.

Figure 5-5. Return to this campaign screen frequently to monitor your success.

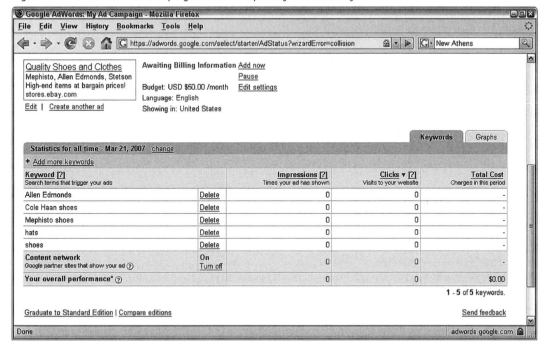

Once your ad goes online, you can check for any page impressions, clicks, or searches by signing in to Google, logging in to AdWords, and immediately seeing your campaign summary. It's unlikely you'll see any page impressions or clicks initially, however. You'll probably see them show up in several hours, or a day.

Tips for Creating AdWords Ads

A successful AdWords ad will attract a certain amount of clicks compared to the number of times the ad is viewed. Simply having an ad that's viewed 1,000 times per day with 0 clicks doesn't result in any success for you. An ad that gets 1,000 views and perhaps 50 to 100 clicks is highly successful, however. To induce those clicks, it's important to select "action" words that prompt shoppers to take the steps that will bring you money. Good action words include "Shop," "Buy!" "Choose," "Try," or "Explore." Bad ones include "Think," "Be," "Wonder," "Consider," or other terms that don't encourage the shopper to actually do something. You have to be careful not to violate a company's trademark, but here, the AdWords ad creation tool will help you; it's "smart" enough to tell you when it thinks you're violating a company's rules.

Also keep in mind the general business principle that, if you want to make money, you first have to spend money. That's as true in cost-per-click advertising as it is selling online. With AdWords, though, your expenses come in a manageable few cents at a time. Before anyone registers or signs up for the product you're advertising, you're going to get some "clickers"—people who click on your ads, take a look at what is being offered, and don't follow through by buying something. These lookers will cost you something each time they click on a link. To keep your expenses from "clickers" from costing you too much, be sure to establish a reasonable budget. You agree to pay a reasonable per-click fee, and you set a maximum for the amount you'll spend in any given day.

It's also important to monitor your ads and adjust the text or the keywords, or both, to get better results. For instance, I got lots of impressions and clicks with the following ad:

Allen Edmonds Shoes
Old World Craftsmanship for Men
Dress Shoes Made in U.S.A.

The ad didn't encourage anyone to buy the shoes because it was too general. It mentioned the entire brand of desirable shoes and didn't prompt a specific action or play up a particular feature. I got better results with:

Allen Edmonds Wingtips
Buy Classic Hand-Tooled Men's
Dress Shoes in Black, Cordovan

On the other hand, don't give up on an ad immediately just because it doesn't get any attention at all. If you see that shoppers clicked on an ad 50 times in a day without buying anything, you can end that campaign and start another. Remember that with AdWords, you are in control.

Deciding on Ad Placement

Where your ad appears on a Web page depends in part on how much you have bid per click, and whether or not you have bid the most in the category. Cost per click advertising enables you to choose keywords that will cause your ad to appear in a set of search results. You place a bid on the keyword; the bid indicates how much you are willing to pay if someone clicks on your ad. The higher you bid, the better placement you have in ads.

Here's an example: Suppose you want to place an affiliate ad for an iPod Nano. This is a popular item, so you can expect to have a lot of competition from other search marketers who want to promote the same product. Suppose you have five other marketers who bid on the keyword "iPod Nano." How can you stand out from the crowd? One option is to be as specific as possible: if the other marketers bid on the keyword "iPod Nano" and you bid on "4GB iPod Nano" you'll distinguish yourself—and attract a more targeted audience. You'll get fewer clicks overall, but the chances will be better that the people who see your ad will click on it and make a purchase of the iPod Nano you are promoting.

Another way to stand out from the crowd is to bid higher than everyone else. Suppose you have five people bidding on the keywords "iPod Nano." When the keywords are the same, the thing that determines placement on a page full of search results is the amount of the bid (see Table 5-1).

Evaluating Ad Reports

Once you have your ad campaigns up and running, you need to keep monitoring the ads and their progress. You can quickly get caught up in obsessively returning to your campaign page on AdWords to see how clicks are coming through. At the very least, though, it's important to track the following basic factors:

- *The clickthrough rate.* Examine the number of times visitors click through the ads you place and actually connect to the Web site you are advertising.

- *Volume.* You need to evaluate the volume of traffic: the number of clicks and clickthroughs.

Table 5-1. Cost Per Click Bids and Placement Results

Number Bid Per Click	Placement
1	.75 #1 in Search Results
2	.50 #2 in Search Results
3	.45 #3 in Search Results
4	.30 #4 in Search Results
5	.15 #5 in Search Results

Affiliate Marketing with AdWords

The most obvious use for AdWords is the promotion of your own Web site or online business. But you can also promote sites such as eBay, Amazon.com, and other big e-commerce sites that pay individuals to send customers to them. When you advertise on behalf of one of these sites, you function as an affiliate. Affiliate advertising brings together several components:

- *A company that wants to promote itself on the Internet and gain new clients or customers.* The company decides to attract users by paying affiliates to function as an independent spokesperson for the advertiser.

- *The search and content network.* In this case, the network is Google. Its AdWords system is among the best-known paid advertising services.

- *The affiliate.* That's you.

- *An advertising network.* A company like Commission Junction (http://www.cj.-com) or AffiliateFuel (http://www.affiliatefuel.com) monitors how many times people view an ad, click on it, and end up making a purchase or registering on the site. An advertising network also brings you lots of opportunities to join affiliate programs; they present you with lists of advertisers who are looking for affiliates, along with their payment schemes and payout rates. If you sign up with an advertising network you don't work with the advertisers directly; you work through the network instead.

The actual preparation of affiliate campaigns on AdWords is the same as advertising for your own business. But the additional requirement of signing up with an affiliate network is different. So is the way you get rewarded. When you advertise for yourself, you are rewarded with more visits and possibly increased business. When you advertise as an affiliate, you typically earn a fee only when someone performs the desired action on the advertiser's Web site:

- *By the purchase.* You earn a fee only when someone clicks on your affiliate ad and ends up making a purchase on the advertiser's Web site (for instance, Amazon.com).

- *By the lead.* You earn a fee only when someone registers for the first time to be an official member of the site (for instance, eBay).

Some sites pay you a commission when the person you send there registers there or downloads some software. In some cases you might earn a small fee every time someone clicks through from your ad to the advertiser's Web site, but this sort of payment system is less common than the other two.

AdWords and AdSense

In this chapter you were introduced to Google's innovative and popular paid advertising service, AdWords. Just as Google's search technology enables AdWords ads to appear alongside relevant search results, AdWords ads themselves are used to provide content for another Google-sponsored advertising program: AdSense. In Chapter 12, you'll discover how AdSense can deliver targeted ads to your Web pages and generate more revenue for you.

PART

Putting Google to Work for You: Google Apps

CHAPTER **6**

Collaborating with Google Apps

Understanding Google Apps

If you're like me, you have spent years purchasing and installing applications for your computer. The centerpiece of those applications has probably been Microsoft Office, the application suite that is virtually ubiquitous and that includes the Microsoft Word word processing application, Microsoft Excel for spreadsheet, PowerPoint for presentations, Outlook for e-mail and communications, and Access for database applications. Every few years, a new version of Office is released, and you have the option of installing it so you can keep up with the people you work with in other companies, who have their own versions of Office, too.

Google Apps is a set of Web and business applications that is aimed at competing with Microsoft Office. What makes Google's offering dramatically different from Office is the fact that the applications are all offered online as Web-based services that you access with your Web browser, not as separate applications you install on your computer. This "software as a service" approach wasn't invented by Google. Lots of other companies give you the ability to store files, keep your financial records, and perform other functions online using your browser. The fact that these applications are being offered by one of the most popular and best-known—not to mention most successful—Web businesses around is what makes Google Apps notable. Google Apps is Google's signal that it wants to shift from being the leader in Web search to a leader (if not eventually the leader) in Web services.

The "Software as a Service" Approach to Work

One big advantage of "software as a service" (also known as Web-based applications) is the fact that the end user does not have to go through the expense of buying the package (or at least paying as much as Microsoft Office or its big brother Microsoft Exchange costs these days). The package was launched in August of 2006 and includes the Google email service Gmail, Google Talk, Google Calendar, Google Page Creator, and Docs & Spreadsheets. The latter two are positioned as competitors to Microsoft Excel and Word. Users: they don't give you all the features of these Microsoft Office applications, but as you'll see later in this chapter, they're quite adequate for basic everyday use, either in the office or at home. You also gain access to Google Analytics, a hosted service for tracking Web site usage and traffic.

 Note: Google Apps won Datamation's Product of the Year award in the Enterprise Email category (http://itmanagement.earthweb.com/cnews/ article.php/3660631).

Google Apps Premier

Buying the premier version of Google Apps increases e-mail space to 10GB per account, adds several new applications such as Gmail for mobile devices, and promises nearly 100 percent uptime for $50 per user per year. This is far less than the $225 per year it costs to use Microsoft Exchange, and the $499 cost to purchase a single standalone version of Microsoft Office Professional Edition 2007. This level also lets you use programming instructions Google Apps recognizes so your company can create custom programs that allow you to customize your service.

Competitors to Google Apps

Google Apps isn't the first player in the field of Web-based business applications. It's got some catching up to do with companies that have paved the way. By knowing who the other players are in the field, you can make a more informed decision about whether or not to sign up for Google Apps yourself, as well as whether or not to choose the Premier version.

Google Apps Versus Office Live

Google's biggest competitor in the field of online computer storage and business applications is undoubtedly Microsoft Office Live. Both Google and Microsoft are offering individuals and small businesses a chance to achieve much of the functionality available to larger businesses. In both cases, documents and data are created by you, the individual user. If your business signs up for Google Apps, the other members of your workgroup will have access. Although you own your data, you store it on servers that are owned by the larger corporation, either Google or Microsoft. In either case, you rely on Google or Microsoft to protect your information. There are, however, significant differences between the two services:

- *Cost*. Office Live Basics is free but doesn't contain any business applications, only Web page and e-mail tools. The two versions that do include applications, Essentials and Premier, cost $19.99 and $39.99 per year respectively. The regular (not Premier) version of Google Apps is free.

- *Interface*. Microsoft limits you to using the ultra-slow Internet Explorer browser to access Office Live. Google Apps supports Firefox and Netscape Navigator as well as other browsers.

- *Another Big Difference*. Both the regular and premier versions of Google Apps can import and export Microsoft Word .doc and Microsoft Excel .xls files. Office Live does let you open and work with Word files, as long as you have Office 2003 or later already installed on your file system: it isn't an online version of Microsoft Office, however.

Salesforce.com

Salesforce.com provides its paying members with a software environment that allows users to access and share applications that everyone in your office can use. This alternative to Google Apps also incorporates the kinds of online applications that Google Apps provides.

Zoho

This company (http://www.zoho.com) includes a presentation tool that is currently missing from Google Apps. Zoho also has a presentation tool that is missing from Google Apps.

The comparison presented in Table 6-1 should give you a clearer picture of what makes Google Apps so special by showing how its features stack up against Microsoft's offering and against the other primary competitor, Salesforce.com.

Pros and Cons

Google offers huge server farms that are capable of handling huge amounts of data. Google has big ambitions that include taking business away from the leader in the desktop software market (Microsoft), so it has a vested interest in continually updating and improving the quality and range of the applications it makes available.

Table 6-1. Google Apps Versus Microsoft Office Live.

Feature	Office Live	Google Apps	Salesforce.com (A CRM [Customer Relationship Management] Application)
Cost	Basics (free); Essentials ($19.95 per month); Premium ($39.95 per month)	Standard Version (free); Premier ($50 per user per year)	Starting at $65 per user per month
Browser	Internet Explorer	All Recent Browsers	All Recent Browsers, but optimized for MS Explorer
Storage (E-Mail)	2GB	10GB	Synchs up with Outlook and other pre-existing email services
Storage (Web Site)	500MB-2GB	200	1 GB
E-Mail Accounts	25–50	200	Links and templates can be added or modified
Domain Name	Free	$10 (one-time fee)	Your workspace is hosted on their site
Number of Users who can have separate accounts	25–50	200	29,800 Customers and 646,000 Subscribers
Shared Calendar	Included with Essentials and Premium	Yes	Yes (Can also be synchronized with MS Outlook)
Business Contacts	Essentials, Premium	N/A	Has preset list views and can be customized
Shared Workspaces	Yes	N/A	Folders and files can be shared or locked from viewing by certain parties

On the downside, Google has run into some security flaws. If you store your business data on its site, you do put a large measure of trust in its company and its servers. In February 2007, just before Google Apps went out of beta, Google discovered a security hole that put its users at risk of having their business information stolen and having their PCs hijacked. There was no immediate evidence that hackers actually took advantage of these weaknesses, but they point out the potential dangers of which you should be aware when you decide to put sensitive business information on servers that are operated by another company. (You can read a summary of the security problem at http://blogs.zdnet.com/security/?p = 45.)

Business Models for Google Apps

Despite the security weakness, companies both big and small already subscribe to Google Apps because of the convenience, the fact that the standard version is free, and for basic services such as word processing, spreadsheets, e-mail, and chat. This shows how flexible the service is. Examples include:

- Pixar Animation Studios Inc. under the Walt Disney Co. (http://www.pixar .com)
- RedOctane-Video game and accessories publisher, creators of Guitar Hero for the PlayStation gaming consoles (http://www/redoctane.com)
- Faculty of Management Studies, Delhi University Business school, located in India (http://www.fms.edu)
- Cambria-Rowe Business College Career training college (http://www.crbc .net)
- 2night Entertainment Worldwide nightlife guide and social network, based in Guatemala (http://www.us1.2night.com/index.asp)

Getting Started with Google Apps

In order to start using Google Apps, you need to have a domain name. You might think of your domain as the virtual equivalent of your house or apartment in the real world. It gives you an address, and it gives you a space within which you can work, communicate, and perform many different functions. Your domain determines the URL by which people will find you on the Web, so it's important not just for gaining access to Docs & Spreadsheets and other business tools but for establishing a viable presence for any online business you want to create within the Web space Google Apps gives you.

Choosing a Domain Name

Before you go to the Google Apps site and start the signup process, give some thought to the domain name you want to use. The concept of Google Apps is built around the idea that Google will give you applications that enable multiple users to collaborate, but only when you first have a domain within which you'll do the work. The first step is obtaining a domain name. If you have a name registered already and want to transfer it to Google, see the section "Verify Your Domain Ownership" later in this chapter. If you don't have a domain, you'll need to register one for a $10 fee with the domain name registrar affiliated with Google Apps: GoDaddy.com. You might well not find the first name that comes to you; you might want to consult friends or business colleagues and compile a number of possibilities so you can see if they're available during the signup process.

To find the domain name that's right for your online business, take a page from the world of psychology and do some free association. Ask customers and colleagues: What's the first thing you think about when you think of our company? Write down the answers and try to get domain names that correspond. Then make sure that no one else already has the name you want. Google Apps itself will make it easy for you to search for available names during the registration process described below.

What's In a Domain Name?

A domain name gives a Web site an alias for its computer addresses that customers can remember easily. It makes your site easy to find—easy to Google, in other words. In order to obtain a name, you pay a fee and "stake a claim" to it by registering it with a company that is an approved domain name registrar. (You'll find a complete list of registrars at http://www.internic.net/alpha.html; Google Apps' registrar, Go Daddy.com, is on the list.)

A domain name consists of two parts: the name itself, and the domain name suffix. In the domain name amanet.org, amanet is the domain name, and .org is the suffix. When you sign up for a Google Apps account, you either specify a domain name that you already own and want to transfer to Google Apps, or you buy a new one. If you choose the latter option, select a domain name that ends in one of five suffixes. Each one is intended to be used by entities that fall into a specific category; in reality, the suffixes are frequently "misused." Many commercial organizations use the .org suffix, which was originally intended for nonprofit organizations, for instance. The five options are:

- .com for commercial organizations
- .net for network providers such as Internet Service Providers
- .org for nonprofits
- .info for general use by any type of organization
- .biz for commercial businesses

Many more types of domain names are available such as .edu for educational organizations, but these are only the five that you can register with Google Apps. If you are set on a name with a different domain name (such as .edu) you'll have to find another Web hosting service. The Internet Corporation for Assigned Names (ICANN, http://www.icann.org) maintains a complete set of domain name suffixes that are currently available.

With the exploding popularity of the Internet, catchy domain names (especially those with the .com suffix) are becoming scarce. The important thing is to pick a domain name for your business that customers can remember immediately without having to write it down and that fits your organization's identity. Also keep it short (ideally, no more than 6–8 letters) and easy to spell. And be sure the name is clearly different than those of your competitors. If the only domain name that fits all of these criteria is in the .biz category, purchase it—as well as similar, alternate spellings that visitors might mistakenly enter. A short and easy to remember domain name ending in .biz is better than a long and complicated one that ends in .com. Also consider buying domain names with alternate suffixes so that competitors can't purchase [your name].biz, [yourname].net, or [yourname].com and thus infringe on your identity. You can purchase them economically through GoDaddy and take advantage of this site's discount coupons, too.

Registering with Google Apps

Even if you have already signed up for Gmail and have a Google Account to use other services, you still need to register for Google Apps. That's due in part to the requirement that you obtain a domain name you can use. When you have identified a primary domain name and some alternate selections, you're ready to register. Follow these steps:

1. Go to the Google Apps home page, http://www.google.com/a.

2. Click the blue "Get Started" button and the "Choose the edition that fits your needs" page appears.

3. Click the "Sign Up" button beneath the name of the version you want. These steps assume you are signing up for Google Apps Standard.

Note: The differences between the three versions of Google Apps (Standard, Premium, and Education) aren't dramatic. Each version gives you access to user accounts, e-mail, Docs & Spreadsheets, a shared calendar application, and a start page.

Google Apps Standard will be adequate for most home and small business users.

Google Apps Education is useful if you are a student or if you work in an educational institution. The Education edition enables schools to conduct virtual conferences online. It gives an institution's IT staff the ability to create programs that customize the way Google Apps looks and feels. It also provides staff with 24/7 support.

Google Apps Premium, which is discussed in more detail in Chapter 20 and carries a $50 per user monthly fee, gives each user five times as much e-mail storage space (10GB versus 2GB per user) as Standard or Education. Premier also guarantees that your email will be online at least 99 percent of the time, and gives you phone support as well as support for any custom applications you or your tech support staff need to create. The Standard and Education versions of Google Apps are reliable, but your email messages could be unavailable if Google's e-mail servers malfunction.

4. Sign in with your Google account. If you don't have a Google account you can click on the "Create an account now" link. Otherwise enter your password in the sign in box and press the "sign in" button.

5. If you only have a Gmail account you still have to sign up for a Google Account. Your existing Gmail account is not associated with a Google Apps account, you'll need to create a separate Gmail username and password for Google Apps. When you click on the link, the "Create an Account" page appears, fill out the required fields.

6. Click on the "I accept. Create my Account" button. Google will send an e-mail to your e-mail account. You need to open that e-mail and click on the link provided to activate your account and verify your e-mail address.

7. A Google Accounts page appears telling you your e-mail has been verified.

8. Return to the Google Apps home page (http://www.google.com/a) and click Get Started. On the next page, click Sign Up under the edition of Google Apps that you want (these steps assume you choose Standard Edition).

9. When the "Choose a domain name" page appears, under the heading I don't have a domain, type the name you want and click Check availability. If the name you want the most isn't available, a page will appear stating that it is already registered. However, you'll be presented with a set of similar names that are available (see Figure 6-1).

10. If necessary, either click one of the suggestions or enter one of your own alternate names and click Continue. Repeat this step until you find a domain name that is currently available.

11. Click Continue to Registration.

12. Fill out the registration information for your domain.

 The check box just beneath the "terms of service" check box is worth noting: you can leave the box checked if you want the domain automatically renewed each year. But you have no way of knowing what the regis-

Figure 6-1. Your first choice might be taken, but you'll be given other suggestions.

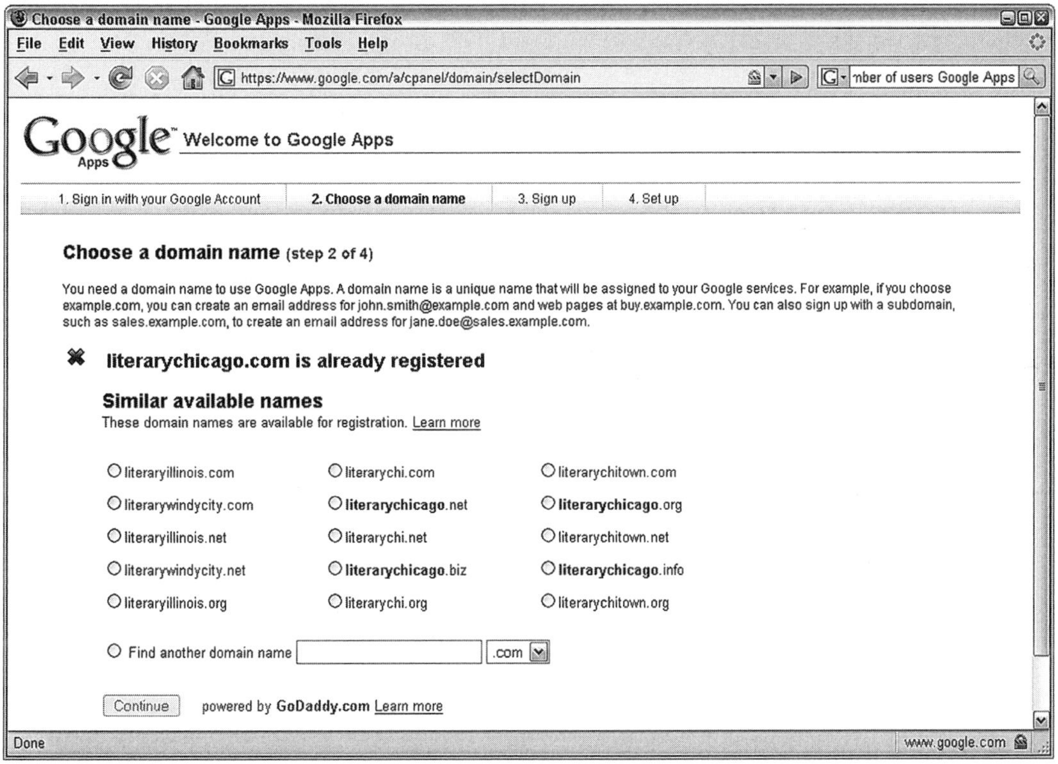

tration fee will be; you agree to pay "GoDaddy's then current rates," according to the Terms of Service. You may not want to check this box; at the end of a year, you'll receive a reminder e-mail to renew the domain name, at which point you might want to lock the name down for a two- or three-year period at a lower annual rate. (Typically, you pay a lower annual rate if you sign up for a two- or three-year period.)

13. Click I accept. Proceed to Google Checkout. A secure checkout page appears.

14. Enter your credit card information and click Agree and Continue.

15. A confirmation page appears; enter your Google Account password and click Sign in and continue.

16. A Review and place order page appears (see Figure 6-2). Pay attention to the two checkboxes; make sure the first box is checked if you don't want your e-mail address to be shared with what Google calls "Sellers." Make sure the second box is unchecked if you don't want to receive promotional e-mail messages. When you're done, click Place your order now.

Figure 6-2. You pay a $10 fee to register your domain name for a year.

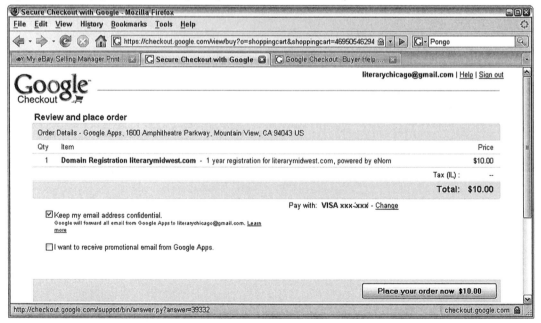

When you're done registering, you get instant results: A notice appears stating that you can now access your Google Apps domain.

1. Click the link "click here" beneath this notice to start working with your domain immediately. A page appears prompting you to "Create your first Administrator account" for your Google Apps domain. As Administrator, you have the ability to create other user accounts and control how the various component applications work.
2. Fill out the form with a username and password.
3. Click the "I accept. Continue with set up" button at the bottom of the screen. You go to the Start Page for your account (see Figure 6-3). After you have first registered, you see the message "Pending Payment" next to the names of the individual apps. Although you can set up user accounts at this point, you have to wait until your payment is processed before you can start working with individual applications. The Start Page (also called the Dashboard) is de-

Figure 6-3. Once you register, you go to your account's Start Page.

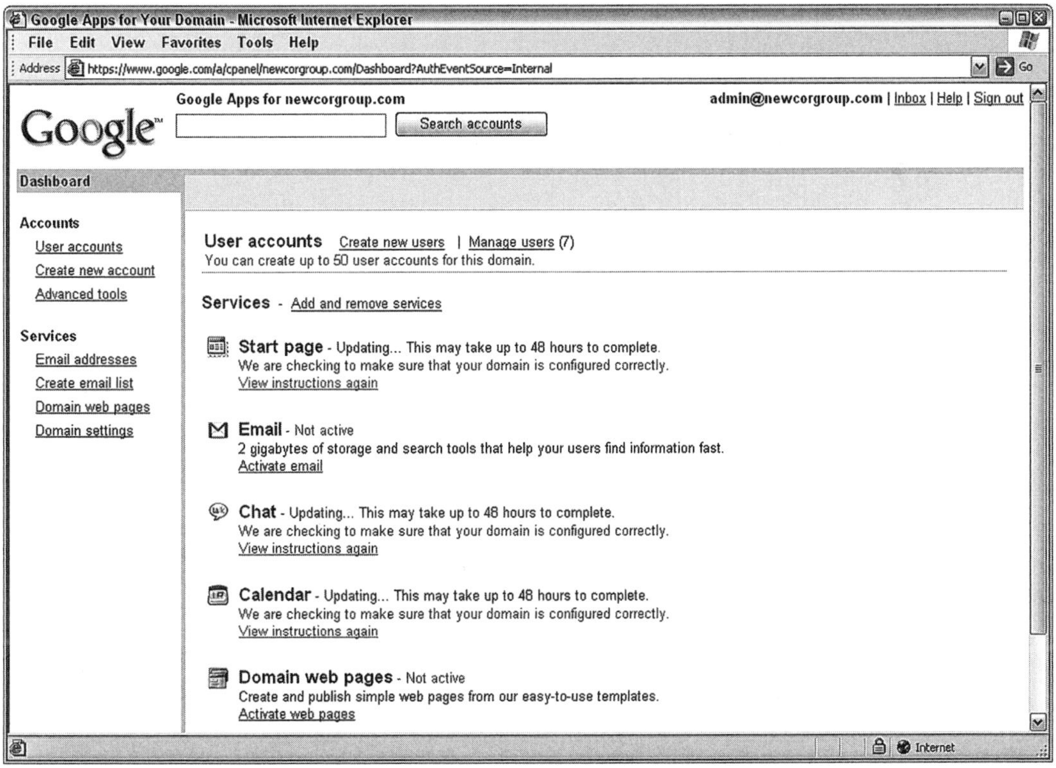

scribed in more detail later in this chapter in the section "Working With Your Start Page."

Verifying your Domain Ownership

If you are moving a domain you already own to Google, you need to verify to Google that you are its legal owner. It's a way of avoiding domain hijacking—the practice of taking away ownership of a domain so it can be misused. It's a form of online identity theft: someone either pretends to be you or steals your domain information, and moves your domain name to their servers.

It's worth remembering that domain hijacking is a serious threat when you're going through the process of verifying your domain ownership to Google. You need to do this before you can start using any of the individual Google Apps services. Yet, I found the process to be less than straightforward. You have two options for telling Google you own the domain you want to use, and you want Google to host your domain rather than your previous hosting service:

- Change the records for your domain so your name "points" at Google's servers rather than the site that currently hosts them.
- Create a simple Web page file (a file that uses HyperText Markup Language or HTML for its formatting) and upload it to Google. That means you save the file on your file system and move it to Google's servers.

The advantage of moving an existing domain name to Google is more than just economic. You do save some money because you don't have to register a new domain name. But you also get to move and make use of any content you've created for the Web site that uses the domain name. And you gain the advantage of using Google's business collaboration applications, too. Once you have the instructions spelled out for you, the process is doable though it just takes me a few minutes. The two options are described below.

 As of this writing, the US version of Google's Web site tells you that you'll find instructions for the two verification methods—changing the CNAME record for your domain or uploading a file—on your Control Panel. There are two problems with this. First, the words "Control Panel" don't appear anywhere on Google Apps. You want to use either

> the Start Page or the Dashboard. Second, I couldn't actually find the instructions—at least not on the Start Page/Dashboard. I did find them on the UK version of Google, at http://www.google.co.uk/support/a/bin/answer.py?answer=48238.

Changing Your CNAME Records

In order to use Google Apps, you need to have a domain name. If you purchase your name through Google Apps, Google handles the steps involved in "pointing" the name from the hosting service that manages your registration information (the domain name registrar GoDaddy.com)

But suppose you already have a domain name that you paid to register. That domain name is in all likelihood being held by another registrar and it may have another Web host that provides you with space to create a Web site as well as e-mail service. You can use your existing name with Google Apps. However, you have to verify that you are the owner, and move your domain registration to Google so you can begin creating Web pages with the domain name.

One option is to change the CNAME records for the domain name you want to use. The term CNAME might sound technical, but it simply denotes an alias for your Web site's real or "canonical" name. The alias is a name like www.mycompany.com. The canonical name is a series of numbers called an IP (Internet Protocol) address. You do this with the domain name registrar that holds your original registration information, not with the Web hosting service where your Web site resides. To begin, you need to do two things:

- Remember where your domain name registration is actually held.
- Obtain your username and password so you can log in to your account with your registrar. If you don't keep good records, you might have to retrieve this. You probably use this username/password pair far less than others, so it's easy to lose.

These two options might not be as simple as they sound if you have owned your domain name for several years and haven't updated or renewed your information for a while. This is the situation I encountered when I wanted to move my domain name literarychicago.com to Google so I could use it with Google Apps. I had to go to the Web site of my registrar, Network Solutions (http://www.networksolutions.com) and retrieve both my username and password.

Note: Domain name registrars and Web hosting services are two different entities. A domain name registrar makes sure the people who purchase a name actually own it and can use it. They also make sure the name you choose is unique and not owned by someone else already. If registrars weren't available, chaos would result on the Web; when you tried to connect to a special URL, you might never know where your browser would end up. Some domain registrars provide Web hosting services as well. A Web hosting service provides space on its name servers where the domain name resides so you can create pages for a Web site that uses the domain name in its URL. In order to create a Web site with the hosting service, you need to tell the registrar to "point" the name at the hosting service's name servers.

The exact steps will vary depending on the registrar you use. Here are the steps I followed for the registrar Network Solutions:

1. I opened the Start Page for the Google Apps account I already established.

2. I clicked the link Verify Domain Information near the top of the page.

3. When the Verify Domain Information page appeared, I chose CNAME from the drop-down list.

4. I highlighted the first part of the subdomain name Google gave me and pressed Ctrl + C to copy it to my computer's clipboard. The name looked like this:
    google05dfe111xsf78.literarychicago.com
    I only copied this part of the subdomain, in other words:
    google05dfe111xsf78

5. I went to the Network Solutions home page and clicked My Account.

6. I logged in with my username and password (which I retrieved through e-mail).

7. I clicked the link View Domain Information List.

8. On the Domain Names List page, I checked a box next to the domain name I wanted to edit, and then clicked Edit DNS.

9. When a page appeared with general information about my registration, I clicked the button labeled Continue in the box that allowed me to change my A, CNAME, or MX records.

Note: If you are only interested in verifying your domain ownership, you need to add Google to your CNAME records. You only need to edit MX records if you are moving an existing e-mail exchange to Google as well. You don't need to worry about A records if you are setting up Google service.

10. In a page entitled Edit DNS, I skipped the options to change the IP Address or Host Alias information for my account and clicked a link called Add Sub-Domain in a section called Mail Servers. This was a potentially confusing step because the Host Alias section displayed a message "No CNAME Records." However, if you read Google's instructions carefully, you are changing your CNAME records, but you are doing so by adding a subdomain to them.

11. On the net page, in a box labeled Mail Servers, I pasted the long and complicated-looking subdomain name Google gave me earlier and that I copied to my clipboard in step 2 in the box labeled Sub-Domain.

12. In the box to the right of Sub-Domain labeled Mail Server, I pasted google .com. This pointed the new subdomain of my domain literarychicago.com to google.com. A third column, Priority, contained a default numeric value and did not need to be changed. Table 6-2 should make this clearer.

13. On the next page, I confirmed my new subdomain by clicking Continue. The last page presented me with my new DNS records and indicated that I had created the following subdomain: google05dfe111xsf78.literarychicago .com. As a final verification, I clicked the link http:// google05dfe111xs-f78.literarychicago.com and viewed my new page.

Uploading a Web Page to Google

Changing your CNAME records is somewhat technical; you might want to call your registrar's tech support staff (as I did) to have them walk you through the process. If

Table 6-2. Pointing a subdomain at Google.com.

Sub-Domain	Priority	Mail Server
google05dfe111xsf78	10	google.com

you follow the steps incorrectly, you can either throw your existing Web site or e-mail account offline and still not have a Web site with Google Apps. As an alternative, you can try the second option for verifying that you own the domain you want Google Apps to host. This option requires you to create a simple Web page, save it on your computer, and then transfer it to Google.

Creating a Web Page

A Web page is simply a text file with a few identifiers that tell a Web browser it was formatted using HyperText Markup Language (HTML) commands.

1. Click on the "verify domain ownership" link.
2. Select "upload an HTML file" from the drop down menu.
3. Instructions for how to finish verifying your domain ownership.
4. Open a text editor such as Notepad and type the following:

   ```
   <html>
   <head>
   </title>test page</title>
   </head>
   <body>
   googleg9rf11176acg6d3d3
   </body>
   </html>
   ```

   The line of code that begins with "google . . ." is provided in the Google Instructions.
5. Save the file with a specific name provided to you by Google in the Verify your domain ownership page: googlehostedservice.html.

As an alternative to working directly with Web page code in a text file, you can use a Web page editor to create your HTML document and save it on your computer in a more user-friendly way. Since you're only creating a test file for verification purposes, I suggest you use a free Web page creation application such as Mozilla Composer. Composer comes with one of the most popular Web browsers, Mozilla Firefox. If you have Firefox, start it up, and choose Composer from the Window menu.

 Note: In order to make use of Composer you need to download and install the full Firefox application suite, which includes Composer, rather than the standalone browser. This might seem like a lot of work just to create one simple Web page, but Composer can help you assemble other Web content in the future.

The Composer window opens with a blank page displayed.

1. Switch back to Google Apps.

2. Log in, go to your Start Page, and click Verify domain ownership.

3. When the Verify your domain ownership page appears, choose Upload an HTML file from the Choose verification method . . . drop-down list.

4. You will see instructions telling you what to name the file, and providing you with a block of characters to include in the body of the file. Scroll across the characters to highlight them and press Ctrl + C to copy them to your computer's clipboard.

5. Switch to the Composer window and click the HTML Source tab at the bottom (see Figure 6-4).

6. Click in the document to position the cursor between the and commands.

7. Press Ctrl + V to paste the text you copied earlier into the page.

8. Choose "Save As" from Composer's File menu. When the "Save As" dialog box appears, you are prompted to enter a title. Enter a title such as Google hostedservice and click OK.

9. Upload the file (in other words, transfer the file from your computer to one on the Internet) to the directory that holds the domain you want to move to Google. The exact method you need to use depends on your Web hosting service. You might use a Web browser to upload files. You might also use an FTP program (as I do) to upload the googlehostedservice.html file to your server as shown in Figure 6-5. You locate the file on the left side of the window, which displays the contents of your local file system, and you move it to your Web server on the right side of the window.

 Tip: Several easy-to-use and affordable FTP programs are available if you need to upload your Google page or other Web page files. WS_FTP is available from Ipswitch Software (http://www.ipswitch

Figure 6-4. Paste Google's code into the source code for your page.

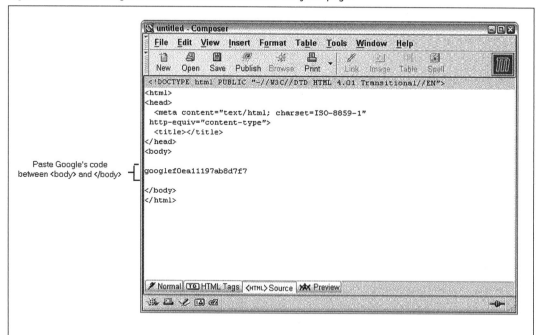

.com/Products/WS_FTP). You can purchase it for $39.95. CuteFTP by GlobalSCAPE is available for $59.99 at http://www.cuteftp .com. For Macintosh users, Fetch is available for free from Fetch Softworks at http://www.fetchsoftworks.com.

Customizing Your Start Page

Your own Windows or Macintosh computer gives you access to many different applications, which you find through various menus and applications. Google Apps has its own set of applications, but where do you find them? You log in to Google Apps by following these steps:

1. Go to http://www.google.apps/a/.
2. Click the "Returning user, sign in here" link near the top of the page.
3. Enter your domain name and choose "Go to Start page" from the drop down menu to the right. (See Figure 6-6.)
4. Click the "Go" button.

You can also access your Google Apps Start Page through the Control Panel. You get to the Control Panel page in one of three ways:

Figure 6-5. You may need to use FTP software to upload your HTML file to use an existing domain.

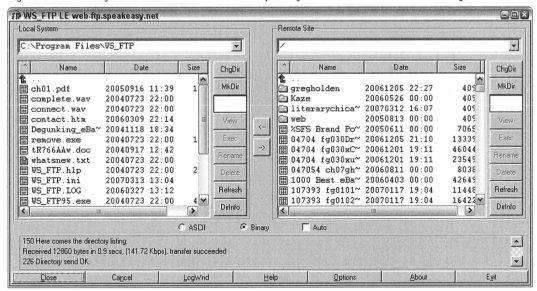

Figure 6-6. Fill out this simple form to go to your start page.

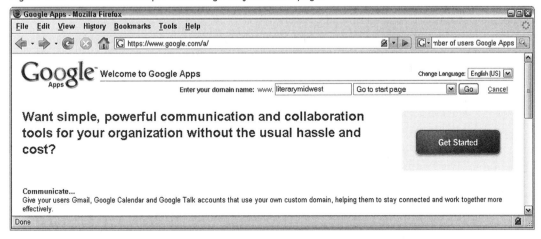

- You go directly to the URL https://www.google.com/a/[yourdomainname]
- Your login access "times out" due to inactivity, and Google prompts you to log in again.
- You log in with one of your domain's e-mail accounts to check your e-mail.

Once you are logged in you can access other services that are available to you, such as the Calendar, by clicking the tiny links to them at the top of the Gmail page (see Figure 6-7).

Figure 6-7. You can move from Gmail to other Google Apps by clicking these links.

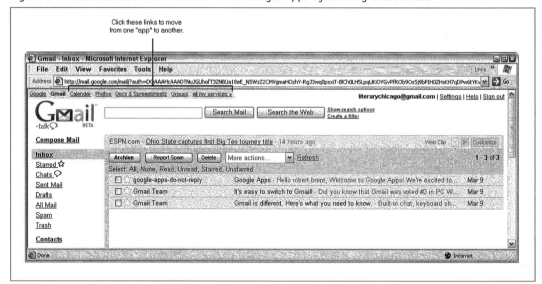

No matter how you arrive there, the Control Panel page has a misleading name—it's simply a login page. Sign in with your Google Apps e-mail address and password and click Sign in to access your Start Page. If you have just signed up for Google Apps, it takes 24 to 48 hours for your domain registration to be processed (possibly longer on a weekend). Until it is processed, you'll see a generic "Not Found" notice. Return to the Google Apps login form periodically and keep trying. When the registration goes through, you'll see a start page like the one shown in Figure 6-8.

Like a dashboard, the page gives you and your employees or colleagues access to your Gmail inboxes, shared calendars, and other services. Once you have signed in to the service and have obtained a domain name, you can access the start page at any time through a URL that has this form:

http://start.[yourdomainname].com.

For instance, if your domain name is mycompany.com, your dashboard page URL would be http://start.mycompany.com. The Start Page performs another important service: before you can actually start using any of the component services, such as Docs & Spreadsheets, you need to activate it from the Start Page. You can't simply start working on it.

Once you gain access to your Start Page because your domain registration has been processed, you can start working with it to create accounts.

Figure 6-8. The Start Page gives you access to Google Apps user accounts and services.

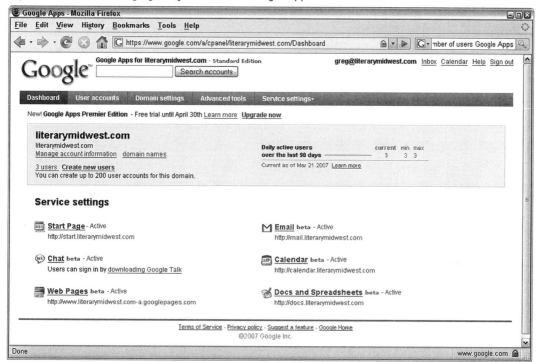

Creating User Accounts

Even if you obtain a Google Apps account just for your own personal use, you still need to create a user account. The service, though, is ideally set up for allowing coworkers and others into your Google Apps domain so you can view shared calendar information and exchange documents. First, you create your Administrator account by filling out the form shown in Figure 6-9.

To open your domain to those you want to have access, you need to create user accounts for them. Each Google Apps domain can have as many as 200 accounts. With that many usernames available to you, you can consider creating some "generic" names that can be accessed by more than one individual in your workgroup, such as:

- admin@mydomain.com
- purchasing@mydomain.com
- webmaster@domain.com

Not only can you create generic usernames, but you can also create accounts that are specifically dedicated to customers, business partners, or others outside your organization:

Figure 6-9. The first account you need to create is for yourself as Administrator.

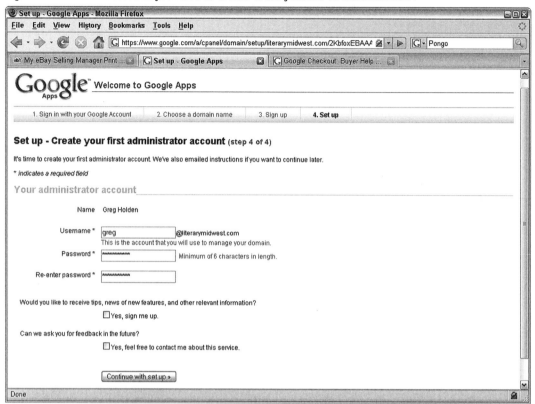

- customerservice@mydomain.com
- press@mydomain.com
- supplier@mydomain.com
- accountant@mydomain.com

Start page is a landing page from which your employees or visitors can easily jump to other parts of your Google Apps domain. It also provides visitors with the current weather and news headlines. It isn't your Web site home page, however. You create that page using Web Page Creator, a tool described later in this book.

 Note: If you do give "outsiders" access to your Google Apps domain, make sure you tell them to protect their registration information carefully. After you assign them a temporary password as described below, they'll have the opportunity to assign a custom password. Tell them to convey that password to you so you can keep it in your records. You can then change or delete the password if you discover their account is being misused by unauthorized individuals. Also tell them to observe basic security measures—for instance, not writing down your password on a sticky note and attaching it to their computer where everyone in their office can see it.

Once you have determined how many user accounts you need initially, you can create them as follows:

1. In the Dashboard click the "Create new users" link in the blue box near the top of the page. (This box also indicates how many user accounts you have created currently.)

2. When the Create a new user page shown in Figure 6-10 appears, type the user's first name and last name. Then assign a username.

Figure 6-10. Use this form to create user accounts.

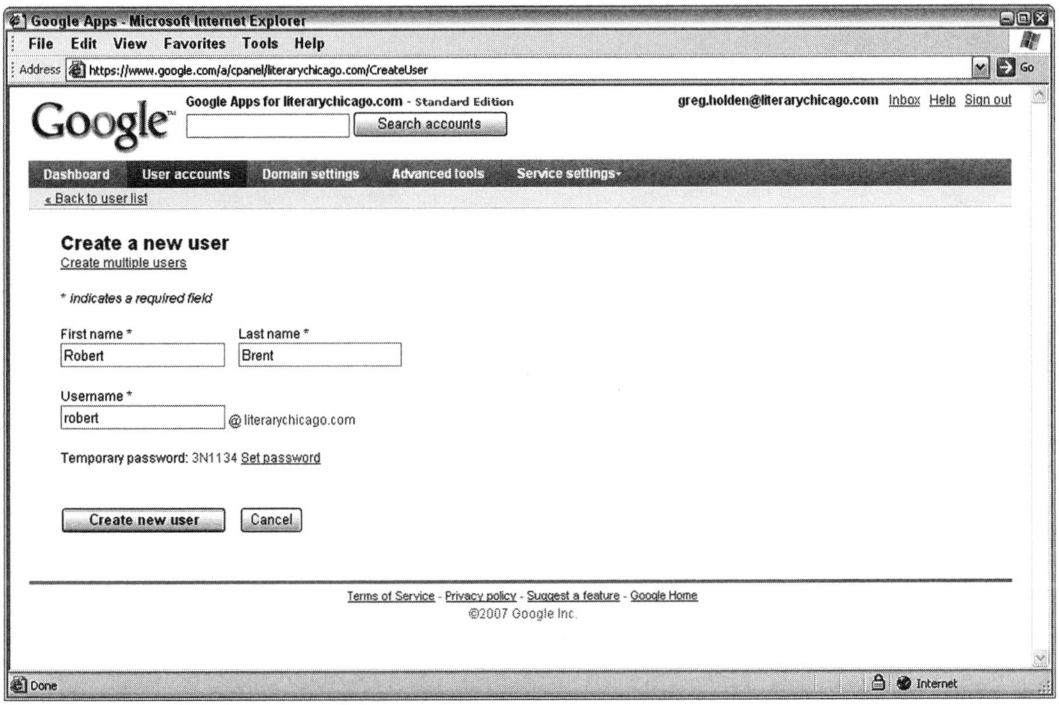

> **Tip:** The username you assign should be short and clear as well as unique. It will be part of the user's e-mail address, so it needs to be easy for anyone to type in Gmail or another e-mail program. The address will look like this: username@[mydomainname].

3. Write down the temporary password shown at the bottom of the screen. You'll need this password to convey to the individual whose account you are creating. A temporary password gives the end user the ability to create his or her own password at a later time. If you want to create the permanent password to begin with, click Set password. Two boxes appear to let you enter and then re-enter the permanent password you want to use.

4. Click the "Create new user" button. A page appears with the user's name at the top. This page provides you with the temporary password, if one was used, and the user's e-mail address. In addition, a small gold box near the top of the page notifies you (and other individuals who are currently logged in to the site) that a new user account has been created, as shown in Figure 6-11.

Figure 6-11. This page confirms a new user account and lets you print out details for your records.

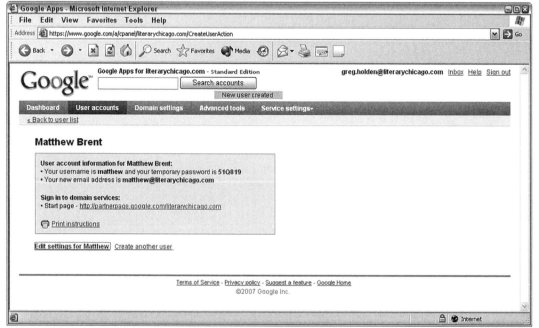

This page confirms a new user account and lets you print out details for your records.

5. The link "Print instructions" at the bottom of the gray confirmation box is useful if you want to print out the temporary password and e-mail address for your files or to hand to the user him- or herself. The user can then access the account with the temporary password you have created and go on to assign a permanent one.

At any time you can click User Accounts to view this and other accounts that have been created for your Google Apps domain. The User Accounts screen lets you control and change other aspects of user accounts, as described in the sections that follow.

Managing User Accounts

By the time you have 20, 30, 50, or more user accounts associated with your Google Apps domain, you have a management challenge before you. To face the challenge, you click the "User Accounts" tab to open the User Accounts screen for your domain (see Figure 6-12).

As you can see from User Accounts, the screen tells you the last time the individ-

Figure 6-12. You can adjust access privileges and add or delete users from the User Accounts list.

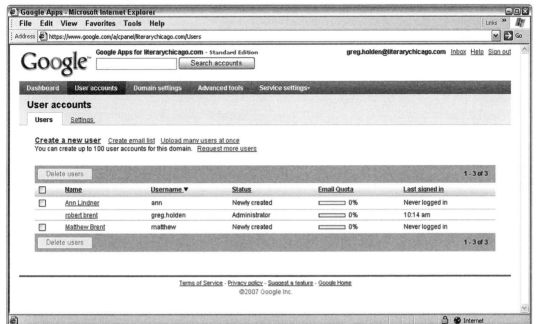

ual has logged in, and the amount of e-mail storage space that individual has used. To add someone to the list, click Create a new user and follow the steps presented in the preceding section. To delete a user, check the box next to his or her username and click the Delete users button. Once you delete a user, you can "recycle" his or her username; you can either add the username immediately to an e-mail list you are creating with your Gmail account (see Chapter 9), or you can wait five days until the original record is purged from Google's servers, at which point you can re-use it.

 Tip: Even if you're the administrator for your domain and plan to use the administrator account, you'll probably want to create an account for your personal use. That way you'll be able keep your personal e-mail and other information separate from your communications as "admin."

The number of accounts you see listed in the User Accounts window isn't necessarily the same as the number of e-mail accounts you use in your domain, however. You also create e-mail addresses based on nicknames, and e-mail addresses for mailing lists. Addresses like announcement-list@mydomain.com won't be recorded in User Accounts. To view all of the e-mail addresses in your domain, click Dashboard, click Email, and then click Email addresses.

When you need to edit a user account—for instance, if someone needs to change a password or add a second e-mail address (called a "nickname")—you only need to open the User Accounts page and click the person's username. Scroll down the page and make the changes you need. When you're done, click Save Changes.

 Tip: It might seem like 200 users is enough accounts for any organization. But Google has big plans in mind for Google Apps. They want to be a presence in enterprises and large organizations across the country. If Google Apps is used to give a university e-mail service, hundreds or even thousands of e-mail accounts might be needed. If you run out of accounts, click the link Request more users on the User Accounts screen to ask for more. You go to a page where you fill out a simple form specifying how many more user accounts you need and explaining why you need them. You submit the request to Google, where it is evaluated and either approved or denied.

Protecting Your Passwords

Using File Encryption Software

If you manage a domain in which, say, dozens of individuals each have unique passwords, as administrator for that domain you are faced with a question: do you allow individuals to manage their own passwords and keep them secret from you? Or do you want to take a more "hands on" approach and maintain a list of the passwords? If you keep a list, you can retrieve passwords if an individual loses them. You can also "get into" that person's account if he or she leaves or is fired.

But writing down the passwords for your entire office or recording them in a text file goes counter to the notion of good password security. In an ideal world, everyone will choose a complex and secure password and be able to remember it all the time: a phrase like I Belong To Sand String Incorporated can translate to the password Ib2SsI, which is a fairly secure password that is also easy to remember.

It is a good idea to record passwords, but you should protect them so unauthorized individuals can't access them. You have several options:

- Try password management software like Password Officer by Compelson Labs (http://www.passwordofficer.com), which can help you generate, store, and protect your passwords.
- Store your passwords online with a secure password storage such as pins.steganos.com (http://www.steganos.com) or PasswordSafe (http://www.password safe.com).
- Store your passwords in a text file. You can then encrypt (turn the file into unreadable code that only you can decode) using your computer's built-in file encryption utility. You don't need to encrypt your password list, but encryption is one option for protecting your passwords so unauthorized individuals can't obtain and misuse them.

The file encryption system for Windows is simple and effective. Once you have saved your passwords in a Microsoft Word or Notepad file, follow these steps to encrypt it:

1. Choose "Save As" from the File menu.
2. When the "Save As" dialog box opens, click Tools and choose General Options or Security Options (the menu option differs depending on the version of Windows you are using) as shown below.

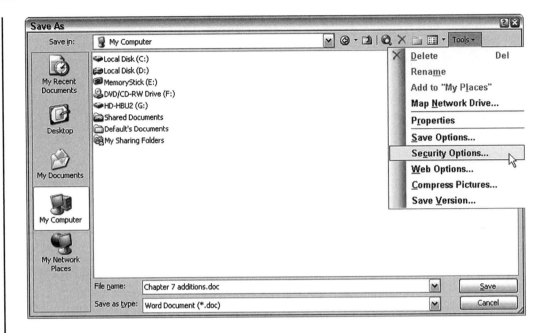

3. When the Save or Security dialog box appears, type a password in either or both the Password to open and Password to modify boxes, as shown below. Password to open requires someone to enter the correct password to open the file; Password to modify requires a password to type or otherwise edit the file.

4. Click OK to save the file with the passwords.

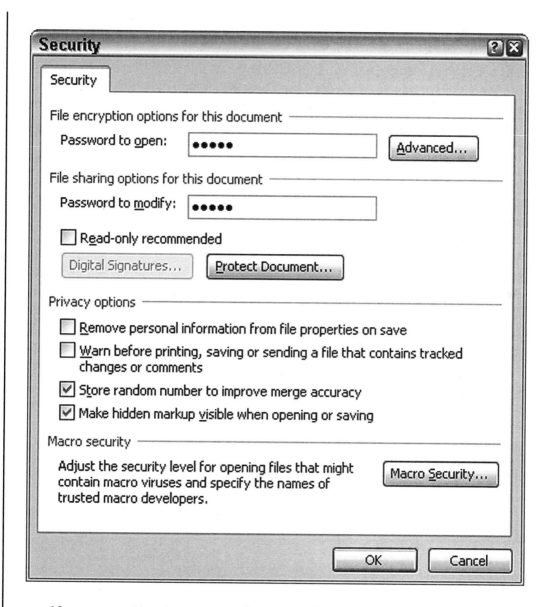

Of course, you then have to save the password that you just created to save all of the other passwords for your workgroup, but you will probably be OK if you write it down and save it in a secure and non-obvious location.

Changing Access Privileges

If you want to change access privileges for an individual, click the user's name in the User accounts list of names. By default, a new user is considered a "standard user." The potentially confusing thing is that the words "Standard" or "Standard User" don't actually appear in the Status column of User Accounts. The Status Column is where the user's access level as well as other status criteria are listed. The available designations are shown in Table 6-3.

To change someone from a Standard user to an Administrator, click the user's name. When the detailed user settings page for that individual appears, check the box next to Privileges. This allows the person to administer your domain. Anyone who has a user account can be an administrator, but you want to limit the number of administrators you have for reasons that should be obvious. If two, three, or more people have the power to create or delete user accounts it will be difficult for those who manage your employees to keep track of who is an administrator, who is not, and who has been assigned a user account in the first place.

 Tip: If someone in your organization forgets his or her username or password, they'll have to come to you, the administrator who originally set up the account. Even if you have two or more users with administrative privileges, you'll be listed as "admin" for the domain

Table 6-3. Google Apps User Account Designations.

Status	Designation	What It Means
Standard	None; Status is empty	The user has standard, not administrative, privileges
Administrator	Administrator	You can manage user accounts for this domain
New	Newly Created	The account has just been established
"On Probation"	Abusive	If someone has misused privileges Google will give you this designation
Suspended	Suspended	If someone misuses office resources you can suspend him or her; the user will need to re-enable this account

and users will probably come to you. (They could also go to the other administrators if you aren't available.) When you first assign someone a username and password, you might also tell those users to click the link Forgot your username or password? on their login page if they run into this trouble. They'll see a message displaying your contact information. You'll need to retrieve their information from the list of nicknames and passwords, which you presumably have stored in a secure location.

Uploading Multiple Account Files

As I said before, Google Apps is targeted at businesses with multiple users, and the more users, the more successful service is, from Google's standpoint. If you need to create dozens of user accounts at one time, this can be a tedious process. Google Apps provides businesses with a bulk upload tool for creating many accounts.

Go to User Accounts, and click the link "Upload many users at once," provided you already have a list of users saved in a spreadsheet or CSV (comma separated value) format. "Comma separated" normally means the elements within each account (name, e-mail, and so on) are separated by a comma. But to use the bulk upload tool, you need to save the names in the form of a table or a spreadsheet. There should only be four fields:

1. Username for Google Apps
2. First name
3. Last name
4. Password for Google Apps

If you keep your personnel file in Excel format, be sure to choose Save As from the File menu and save the file in .csv format. Your own personnel file probably has a variety of other information already in it (office number, phone number, and so on) so you'll have to edit those other fields out and save the file with only the four fields Google Apps specifies. But if you perform this relatively painless task, you'll save lots of time in the long run. An example is shown in Figure 6-13.

1. When the Bulk account update window appears, choose one of the three update options. The first option is preselected and you cannot deselect it, which means Google will perform this action by default: it will create new accounts for any individuals who have not yet been assigned usernames. The second

Figure 6-13. You can save your account information in CSV format and upload it in bulk.

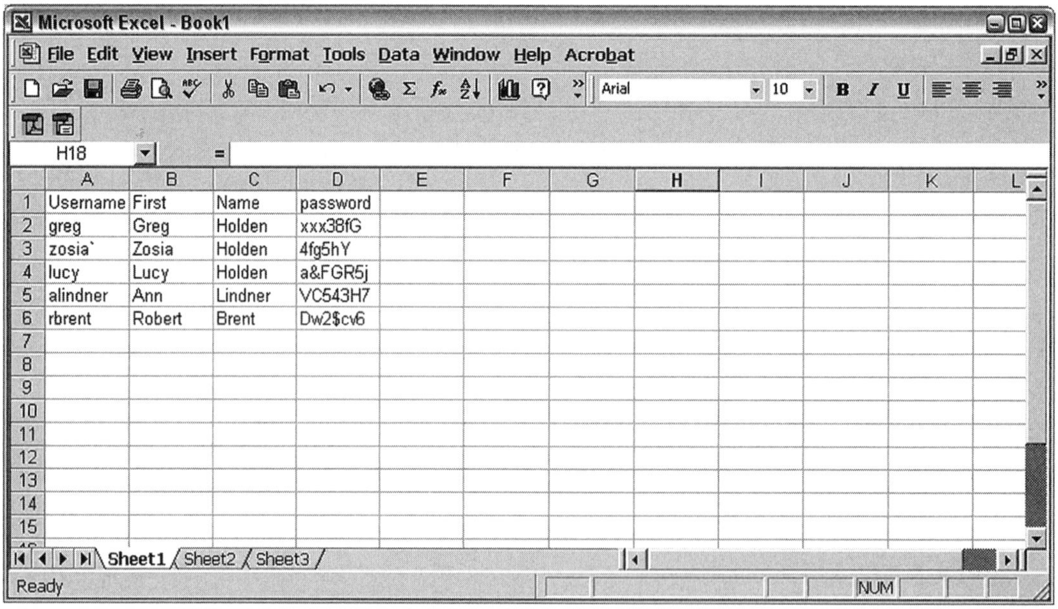

	A	B	C	D
1	Username	First	Name	password
2	greg	Greg	Holden	xxx38fG
3	zosia`	Zosia	Holden	4fg5hY
4	lucy	Lucy	Holden	a&FGR5j
5	alindner	Ann	Lindner	VC543H7
6	rbrent	Robert	Brent	Dw2$cv6

option will cause you to update existing accounts. The third option will require new users or those whose account information has been changed to change their passwords. In either of the last two options, you check the box next to the appropriate item to select it.

2. Click Browse, locate the CSV file and select it.
3. Click the "Upload and Continue" button to add your files to Google Apps.
4. Then press the "confirm and run update" button. When your files have been uploaded, you'll see either a list of new users or an altered list of existing users. Scan the list to make sure the changes took effect and are accurate.

Suspending a User

Every office has (or should have) some consequences for misbehavior. When you are working with shared resources, you need to respect one another's virtual territory. Consider a university or other educational environment where many students have respective e-mail accounts. If someone hacks into someone else's account or steals a password and is able to intercept e-mail, you don't want that person on the network any longer.

In the lingo of Google Apps, when you need to temporarily disable access to an account, you can suspend the user. When an account is suspended, no e-mail can be sent, and any messages addressed to that individual will also be blocked. Here's how to suspend a user if you need to do so:

1. Click User accounts in the Control Panel, the Dashboard, or in the links at the top of the Google Apps screen you are viewing currently.
2. When the User Accounts window appears, click the username of the person who needs to be suspended.
3. When the user's account details page appears, click "Suspend user" link.
4. Click on "Suspend user and e-mail" button.
5. The screen refreshes with a notice that says "this user has been suspended" and offers you the option to click on "restore user" link.

A suspended user cannot sign in until you restore access privileges. If you need to restore a user who has been suspended to Standard or Administrative privileges, open User Accounts, click the person's username, and click Restore user. When prompted, confirm that you want to restore account access by clicking Restore User. You'll need to let the individual know that access has been restored by sending an e-mail message or other means; the person doesn't automatically know his or her status has been changed.

Sharing User Accounts

As administrator, you get to see all the usernames and e-mail addresses for everyone in your Google Apps domain. But those individual users won't be able to see the others unless you have contact sharing enabled for your domain. When you enable contact sharing, you populate each user's Contacts list with all users at your domain. To enable contact sharing, you need to:

1. Open the User Accounts page.
2. Click the settings link (which appears immediately beneath the User Accounts heading).
3. Click Enable Contact Sharing.
4. Click Save Changes.
5. It's worth noting that contact sharing means your users' contact information isn't shared outside your domain, however.

If, on the other hand, you disable contact sharing, you won't affect existing users. This means that the Contacts lists of existing users will continue to have all the addresses that you shared by enabling the feature in the first place, the names don't simply go away. Your existing users will retain their current contacts lists but won't include new users at your domain.

Adding Nicknames

A nickname is a word or two that functions as an alias—an alias for an e-mail address you can use in addition to your regular Google Apps e-mail address. If you're going on the road, or if you just want to route your incoming Google e-mail to a second address in addition to your Google apps address, assign yourself a nickname as follows:

1. Click User Accounts in the Control Panel or any other Google Apps page.
2. Click the name of the user to whom you want to assign a nickname.
3. When the user account detail page appears, scroll down to the section labeled Nicknames and click the Add a nickname link.
4. When the box shown in Figure 6-14 opens under the user's regular e-mail address, you can add the second name in it.

Figure 6-14. You can create a nickname to identify users on the network.

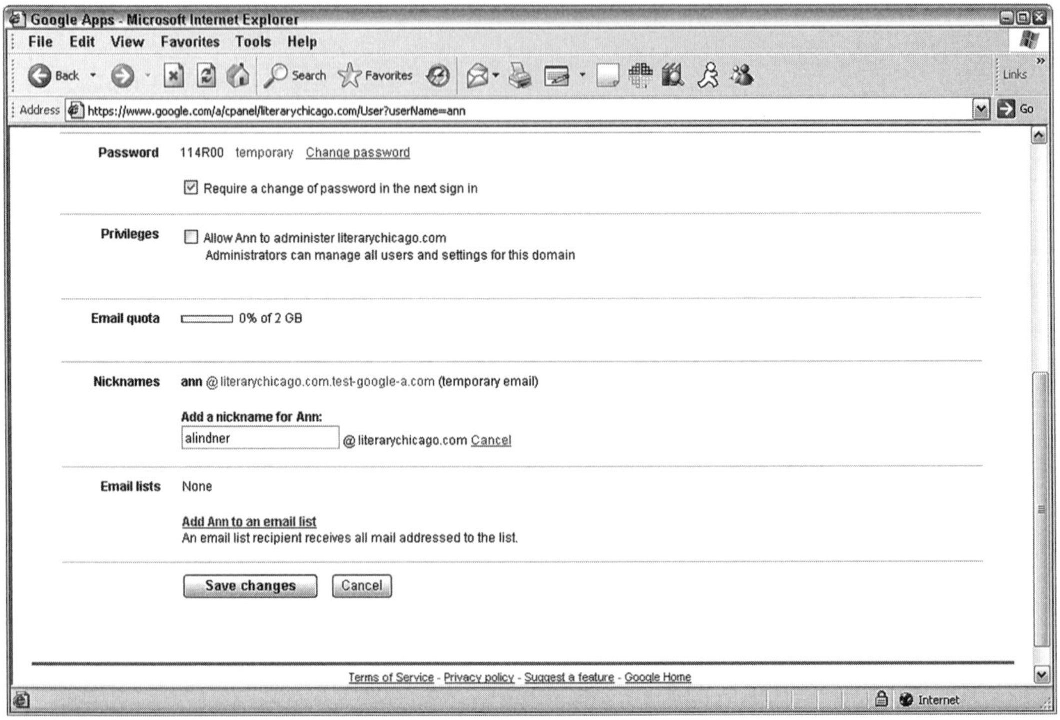

5. Click Save Changes.

Once you've defined a nickname, you can't create a new user with that same username. The user will receive messages addressed to his or her original username and the "nickname" e-mail address included in the account. You can send e-mail from either your nickname address or your primary one as described in Chapter 9.

 Tip: Usernames may contain letters (a–z), numbers (0–9), dashes (-), and periods (.). Passwords may contain any combination of characters, with a minimum of 6. First and last names may contain spaces, letters (a–z), numbers (0–9), dashes (-), forward slashes (/), and periods (.).

This chapter presented detailed examination of Google Apps, a set of applications that has the potential to change the way businesses work. Instead of (or as an additional option to) installing expensive applications on each of your workstations, you can create administrative and individual user accounts for you and your colleagues. A Google Apps account includes a domain name you can use for your office's e-mail addresses, and for a Web site you create with one of the individual applications, Page Creator (see Chapter 11). In the next chapter, you'll explore one of the most important and practical file sharing components in Google Apps: Docs & Spreadsheets.

CHAPTER **7**

Working with Docs & Spreadsheets

If there's anything an office needs to share, it's memos, reports, and other word processing files. While I was writing the book you are reading now, in fact, two assistants helped me. Matthew and Robert Brent and I had to share files, while making sure we were working on the latest version of any one file and that we were not duplicating each other's efforts by trying to edit a document that someone was already revising.

My coworkers and I found that, while Docs & Spreadsheets isn't quite as full-featured as Microsoft Word and Excel, the two components (one for word processing and one for spreadsheets) were quick to load, easy to use, and perfectly functional. The level of functionality you get with such programs is surprising considering that you can use them for free. Like other Google Apps applications, Docs & Spreadsheets comes either in a version you can access if you have a Gmail account or as a component of Google Apps. The Google Apps version gives you tools for sharing, publishing, and even conducting real-time chats while you and your colleagues review files. This chapter assumes you are using the Google Apps version.

Making a Business Case for Docs & Spreadsheets

The idea behind doing word processing and working with spreadsheets on Google Apps, using software that Google provides rather than your own office productivity software, is a revolutionary one. Ever since personal computers became popular in the 1980s, Microsoft and other companies have competed to develop software that needs to be purchased, installed, and updated on them. Unlike Word and Excel, Docs & Spreadsheets doesn't need to be bought, installed, or updated. (At least not by you; Google installs updates as necessary.)

Students who already live much of their lives online will naturally be attracted to keeping their term papers and other reports on Google Apps so they can view and edit their documents from any place with an Internet connection. But for small business owners or managers, it's not an obvious step forward. An overwhelming number of businesses have some sort of word processing and spreadsheet software already installed on each of their workstations. Chances are you have some form of Microsoft Office already installed even before you had a Web browser or Internet connection. And if you have a bigger office you might well have to make a case to the managers in your office for using Docs & Spreadsheets. What can you do with this innovative service that you can't already do with your existing software, and what are the advantages and limitations? Some of the primary benefits as well as drawbacks are listed in Table 7-1.

That last drawback, which might involve instruction sessions with employees, and which certainly involves depending on workers to back up their files and handle data safely, is made irrelevant if you sign up for Google Apps Premium, which guarantees virtually 100 percent "uptime."

 Note: There are browser restrictions for using Docs & Spreadsheets. It only works with Internet Explorer 6 or later for Windows (but not version 6.0.26), Firefox 1.07 or 1.5.0.6 or later, Mozilla 1.7.12 or later, and Netscape Navigator 7.2 or 8.0. Google says the service may not work on Safari, Netscape 4, or Opera.

Getting Started with Google Apps

The Google Apps user documentation indicates that you need to activate Docs & Spreadsheets before you can use it, but as soon as my domain was active (see Chapter 6 for a detailed description of how to activate a domain), Docs & Spreadsheets became available. (Other Google Apps applications like Page Creator did need to be activated, however.)

Once you are able to access Docs & Spreadsheets (whether you have to activate it or not), you open it in one of several ways:

- If you obtain Docs & Spreadsheets through Google Apps, you access it via the Google Apps Dashboard

Table 7-1. Pros and Cons of Docs & Spreadsheets.

Pros	Cons
Mobility	*Features*
You don't need to be at your own computer or carry around your own laptop. You can access your files with a Web browser from any computer that has access to the Internet.	The programs used in Docs & Spreadsheets are hardly as powerful or full-featured as Word or Excel. In fact, they're pretty minimal.
No Need for Storage Devices	*Reliability*
You don't have to use floppy disks or memory sticks	If Google or its servers go down, your files become inaccessible.
Before D&S, you might need to save a few files to a floppy disk and carry it around with you to access that information from a different location. Since many people now have laptops to mobilize their information, the floppy disk is already seldom used. But with D&S, forget the floppy disk because all you need is an Internet connection.	*Access*
	If you need to edit a document or spreadsheet in a hurry, you need to be connected to the Internet to do it. Otherwise you need to download or export your file to your computer.
No E-Mail Attachments	*Security*
Forget Word and Excel attachments Instead of emailing your colleagues a Word or Excel attachment, just invite them to view your document or spreadsheet online. Collaborators will be able to make edits to your documents without saving a new copy to their hard drive and emailing the revised version back to you.	If you put critical business files online, you are trusting in Google's servers to handle them securely.
Improved Collaboration	*Education*
Forget being in the same room to edit the same document at the same time You can invite people to your documents/ spreadsheets and everyone can make changes together at the same time.	Perhaps the biggest drawback is the need to develop new habits. You and your coworkers have to adjust your behavior and get used to working online.

- You go directly to the URL http://docs.google.com/a/[mydomain]
- You go directly to the URL http://docs.[mydomain]

In either case, you'll need to replace [mydomain] with your domain name. You'll be prompted to log in, and create and share documents and spreadsheets.

There's another option that's worth mentioning: although this book emphasizes the use of Google Apps for business collaboration, and encourages you to sign up for Google Apps, you can get Docs & Spreadsheets without Google Apps. If you sign up only for Gmail service, when you open your Gmail inbox you see several links in the upper left-hand corner of the page. The Calendar link takes you to Google Calendar, and the Documents link takes you to a page where you are asked to sign in to use Docs & Spreadsheets. It's the same version as the Google Apps Docs & Spreadsheets.

 Note: If you use the Google Apps version of Docs & Spreadsheets, you can exercise some control over whether or not individual users can send or receive word processing files or spreadsheets outside your domain. You may not want to share your company's sensitive files with the outside world. You can specify that documents created inside your domain cannot go outside your domain. The version of Docs & Spreadsheets you use with a conventional account doesn't contain such controls.

General Considerations

Docs & Spreadsheets is actually two separate programs that appear within a single interface. You could refer to the two as Google Docs and Google Spreadsheets. Each program has separate functions and a different interface. Still, some features are common to both, and this section addresses issues and concerns that are shared by both Docs & Spreadsheets.

Viewing Lists

When you first open Docs & Spreadsheets, you go to the Docs & Spreadsheets home page. If you have never used Docs & Spreadsheets, you see a list of things you can do with the program. Once you have created some files, this page will instead present you with a list of your documents and spreadsheets (see Figure 7-1).

 Note: If you have been away from Docs & Spreadsheets for a month or more, you won't see your files. Don't be alarmed. Google has automatically archived them for you. Click the All Documents link to display these files. (You might need to click Browse Docs & Spreadsheets and then choose All Documents from the drop-down list that appears.)

Figure 7-1. The Docs Home page lists both word processing "docs" and spreadsheets in the same list.

The two types of files (word processing "docs" and spreadsheets) are contained to-gether in the same list. Because you can view both types together, the list can easily get lengthy. You can narrow it down by grouping the contents in four different catego-ries:

- Active
- All
- Tagged
- Starred

You can quickly "star" an item by clicking the dimmed-out star icon next to its name. When you do so, the star "lights up" and becomes more easily visible. To choose one of these designations from the Docs & Spreadsheets interface, you check the box next to one or more file names to select them. Then select an option from one of the drop-down lists at the top of the document list. You can select Star or Un-star from the Actions drop-down list, for example.

Tip: Keyboard shortcuts that you are used with Word, Excel, and other files in a Windows environment work with files in Documents & Spreadsheets. Press:

- **Ctrl + Z** to undo the last action;
- **Ctrl + Y** to redo the last action;
- **Ctrl + X** to cut something to your computer clipboard;
- **Ctrl + C** to copy it to the clipboard; and
- **Ctrl + V** to paste something that has been cut or copied previously.

Working With Documents

With some collaboration services, like Office Live, you work with a Document Library, but you create Microsoft Word documents. Office Live also limits you to using Internet Explorer. With Google Apps, you don't have to have Word or another word processing application present on your computer.

Uploading Files

Uploading a file is different from simply opening it. If you create a document from scratch on Docs & Spreadsheets, you can simply open it. If you have a document already on your computer and you want to work with it and share it on Docs & Spreadsheets, you move it from your computer to your Docs & Spreadsheets space on Google, and that process is called *uploading*. It's easy and convenient to upload a file from your computer to Docs & Spreadsheets—so easy, in fact, that you might well be left wondering whether it is actually possible for Google to connect to your computer and look right into your files. (It can't do this, by the way.) Before you upload your document, you need to make sure it's in one of the formats that Docs & Spreadsheets can actually handle:

- HyperText Markup Language (HTML) files, which have the .htm or.html file extension Plain-text files (.txt)

- Microsoft Word (.doc) files
- Rich Text Format (.rtf) interchange files
- OpenDocument Text file (.odt)
- StarOffice (.sxw) files
- Comma Separated Value (.csv) files
- Microsoft Excel (.xls) files
- OpenDocument Spreadsheet (.ods) files

If you try to upload a file other than the ones listed above you'll see a dialog box stating that Docs & Spreadsheets doesn't support it. It would be helpful if you could use your Docs & Spreadsheets page to upload image files or other documents, or if Google Apps provided you with a storage space where you could store such objects; but you are limited to the word processing and spreadsheet options shown above. If you want to share images or other files, you'll need to e-mail them.

When you're ready to upload your files, connect to the Docs & Spreadsheets Docs Home page. You can get to Docs & Spreadsheets in several ways. Earlier in this chapter, I listed two URLs you can enter directly in your browser window. Here are two more options:

- Go to http://docs.google.com/a/your domain.
- Go to http://www.google.com/a, click Returning user, sign in here, enter your domain, choose Go to Documents from the drop-down list, and then click Go.
- If you're currently in another one of your "apps," such as Gmail or Calendar, click Docs & Spreadsheets at the top of the page.

Either one of these options should take you to the Docs & Spreadsheets page. To start a new document, click the New Document link. Once you have a file created and saved (you'll find out how to do this later in the chapter), you can click any one of the file names and it opens in its own window. A typical word processing "doc" is shown in Figure 7-2. It looks just like a word processor, and you are able to type, cut, and paste text just as you would with a word processing application, but the program operates within the Web browser window.

Figure 7-2. The Docs & Spreadsheets word processor appears and operates within your browser window.

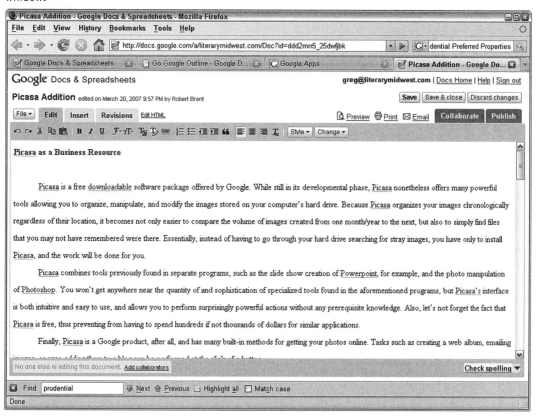

 Note: At some point, when you log on to your start page as described in the preceding bulleted list and attempt to go to Docs & Spreadsheets, you'll be asked to choose the default URL before you actually connect to the service. You see a page with two options: http://docs.[mydomain] or http://docs.google.com/a/[mydomain]. Choose one of the options and then click Continue. You can also click the link Change URLs for all domain services if you want to use the same form for Gmail and other Google Apps services. The change happens immediately. You should change the URL only if you want something shorter and easier to remember than you have already, in my opinion.

You can click the Upload link near the top of the page to locate the file you want to upload. When the Upload a File form page shown in Figure 7-3 appears, your first task is to locate the file you need.

Figure 7-3. You can upload a file or a Web page object.

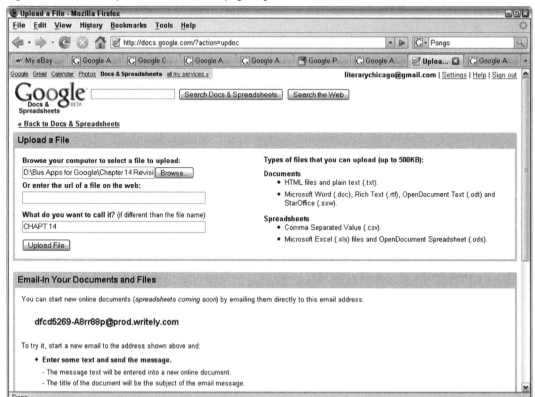

You have two options for locating and uploading a file: If the file is on your local file system or your local network, click Browse. If the file is already on the Web, you can transfer it from one Web server to another.

To upload a local file, click Browse, locate the file in the File Upload dialog box, select the file, and click Open. File Upload closes and you return to the *Upload a File* page, where the path leading to the file appears in the box next to the Browse button. Press the "upload file" button.

To upload a file that is already published on a Web site you own, enter its URL. This is ideal for Web page files you want to back up on your Google Apps site. The document's file name must end in .htm or .html for an HTML file, or .txt for a plain-text document. The file name that will be listed in Docs & Spreadsheets is not the actual file name, but the first line of the text. The file is transferred instantly—you aren't prompted to enter the username or password you are normally prompted to type when you upload files to your site.

In fact, the ability to upload a file based on its URL isn't limited to a Web site you actually own and operate yourself. You can upload *any* file from *any* site that is already on the Web. Is this a violation of copyright? It's an open question: when you view a Web page in your browser window, you essentially copy the page from the Web server to your computer so your browser can display it. You can quickly view the source code for the page, where you can copy and paste it into a word processing document. When you copy someone else's Web page to Docs & Spreadsheets, you are doing much the same thing. If you start re-using some of the contents on your own Web site, you're almost certainly violating copyright, however.

 Tip: You can change the name of any file you upload. The name that is listed in the Active Docs & Spreadsheets column doesn't have to be the document's file name, or the Web page's first line of text. It can be shorter and more understandable. Since other people who didn't originally create the document might end up working through the Google Apps site, it's a good idea to edit the name by entering it in the "What do you want to call it?" box in the "Upload a File" page. Do this before you press the "upload file" button.

You have a third option for uploading files, and it's explained to you at the bottom of the Upload a File page, under the heading Email-In Your Documents and Files: you can e-mail a message to the complicated-looking e-mail address shown (the address differs your e-mail message) or attach a word processing document to the e-mail message using your e-mail software. The file you e-mail will now appear in your document list.

 Tip: The e-mail address you are told to use to upload a file is one of several places where you see references to "Writely" when working with Docs & Spreadsheets. Writely is the original name that was given to Google's word processor. The name was eventually dropped in favor of Docs & Spreadsheets.

Creating New Files From Scratch

Suppose you're on the road and you are able to connect to the Web using a workstation in a library. You need to start drafting a report that has to start circulating around your office before your return. Or you're at a computer in one of your campus lounges and you want to start your term paper. Normally, you'd have to be concerned about what sort of word processing program the workstation had. If you have Google Apps, you don't need to worry about available software: you can use Docs & Spreadsheets to create a new file, name it, and save it on Google Apps. Just click the "New Document" link just beneath the Google logo on the Docs & Spreadsheets main page.

A new blank page labeled "Untitled" appears. At the top of the writing/editing page, you'll see three tabs:

- Edit lets you type in a document or make formatting and editing changes.

- Insert lets you insert special content: an image, a hyperlink, a table, a bookmark (a record of a URL), a line or other separator, or a comment box.

- Revisions lets you track any changes that have been made to the document since it was last opened. You can compare two or more revisions—revisions made in the current editing session, the previous session, and the one before that.

Cutting and Pasting Files

If you are unable to upload a file, you can also create a new document (see the section "Creating New Files from Scratch" immediately before this one). You can then cut and paste the text from the document you wanted to upload into the new file. Follow these steps:

1. Make sure the file you want to copy is open and press **Ctrl + A** to select all of its contents.
2. Press **Ctrl-C** to copy the text to the clipboard.
3. In Google Docs & Spreadsheets, click New Document.
4. When a new blank file opens, press **Ctrl + V** to paste in the text.

Typing, Editing, and Saving

The basic process of editing and saving text is the same in the Docs & Spreadsheets word processor as it is in Microsoft Word or another text editor.

Typing Text

You enter text, backspace, and type to the end of a line as you would normally, using the vertical text cursor to position where the letters appear. You can also break a page at any time.

Page Breaks

To insert a page break in your document, just follow these steps:

1. When you are working in the Edit window, click the Insert tab, which highlights that tab and makes the insert tab tool bar visible.
2. Click to position your cursor where you'd like the page break to appear.
3. Click Separator at the top of the page, and choose Page break.

Spell Checks

It's always important to perform a spell check when you're working on a word processing file. The Docs & Spreadsheets spell check utility is easy to find: just click the Check Spelling link in the bottom right corner of the current window. After clicking on Check Spelling, all misspelled words will be highlighted in yellow. You can then perform three actions:

- To see a list of suggested spellings, right-click on the highlighted word.
- A window will pop-up with suggested spellings; click one to choose it.
- If you want to recheck your document after making corrections, click Recheck.

Deleting Files

The process of uploading and importing files is discussed separately in the Working with Documents and Working With Spreadsheets sections later in this chapter. But the process of deleting files is the same:

1. In any one of the documents and spreadsheets lists (Active, Tagged, All, or Starred) check the box next to the document or spreadsheet you want to delete.
2. Click Delete in the row of four buttons found either at the bottom or top of the page. The document will now be moved to the "Deleted Docs & Spreadsheets" page, otherwise known as the Trash.

 Tip: You can empty the "Deleted Docs & Spreadsheets" page by clicking on the "Browse Docs & Spreadsheets" and selecting "Deleted (Trash)" from the drop-down menu. From here, click "Empty Trash." Until you go through the process of emptying the Trash, you can still

> retrieve a file you have deleted: Open the Deleted Docs & Spread-
> sheets page, check the box next to the name of the file you want to
> retrieve, and click the Undelete button. The file is moved back to
> your Docs & Spreadsheets list.

Finding and Replacing Text

Search and replace is one of the sophisticated functions that users of Microsoft Word and other word processors take for granted. While Docs & Spreadsheets also lets you "find and replace" terms in documents, the feature is still in its experimental stages. At the time this was written, the following limitations were in effect:

- At this writing, "Find and replace" could only be used to "replace all," not to selectively replace certain terms in a document.
- Undo doesn't work with this feature; after you find and replace all, you can't "go back."

The "Find and replace" feature is one of many useful options on the File drop-down list, which appears when you click the File button just above and to the left of an open document. Follow these steps:

1. Click File and choose "File" and choose "Find and replace."
2. Enter the term(s) to find in the Find what field, and the terms to replace them with in the Replace with field.
3. Click the "Replace All" button.

The find and replace limitations mentioned above are significant, to be sure, but the find and replace feature will probably be improved by the time you read this. And because you're using software as a service (not to mention free software as a service) rather than software you install, improvements aren't something you need to worry about: you don't need to install "patches" or updated versions of the software. Google will make improvements in the background and you'll be able to use the improved versions right away.

Adding Hyperlinks

Because the word processing files you are working with are actually part of a Web browser window, you can add clickable URLs to those files. If you need to add a clickable URL, position the cursor where you'd like the link to appear, click the Insert tab to bring it to the front, and click Link.

When the link window appears, select URL from the Link To options along the top of the window. Then type the URL into the box titled URL. Press the "ok" button.

You can also add a clickable URL by turning a word or phrase in your document into a hyperlink. For example, you might embed a link to your home page, www.my-homepage.com, using the phrase Visit our home page. If someone clicks on the phrase Visit our home page, www.myhomepage.com will open automatically in a separate browser window. To designate a piece of text as a link:

1. Select the "link" tab to bring it to the front.
2. Type the desired text into the box labeled Text.
3. Select Link from the "insert toolbar."
4. Enter the URL that you want the hyperlink to send the viewer to in the "URL" field.

Once you have created a link, you can add a popup message called a "flyover" to it. This small popup will appear whenever someone mouses over your link. For instance, if you create the link Special Offers to promote some items you have for sale, you might cause a popup window to appear with a message "Check out our latest deals!" or something similar. To create a flyover, click the Insert tab and click Link. When the Insert Link dialog box shown in Figure 7-4 appears, enter the text of your choice in the box titled Flyover. Click OK to close Insert Link. When you pass your text cursor over the link you just created, the flyover message will now be visible in your document. To make sure the link actually works, press the Ctrl key and click on the link.

Linking to Specific Locations—Bookmarks

If you have created Web pages at all, you know that you can create links to Web pages on your own site, Web pages on other sites, and specific words or phrases in a document. This last kind of link is called a *bookmark*. Since the word processing "doc" you are editing is something you are viewing in a browser window rather than an application like Microsoft Word, it's actually part of a Web page. Because you're working on a Web page, you can create bookmark links within that file as well. Bookmarks can prove useful when you need to make a table of contents, or when you want to jump from one part of a long document to another without scrolling. To create a bookmark in your document, follow these steps (see Figure 7-5):

Figure 7-4. You create a link by typing the link text and the URL in this dialog box.

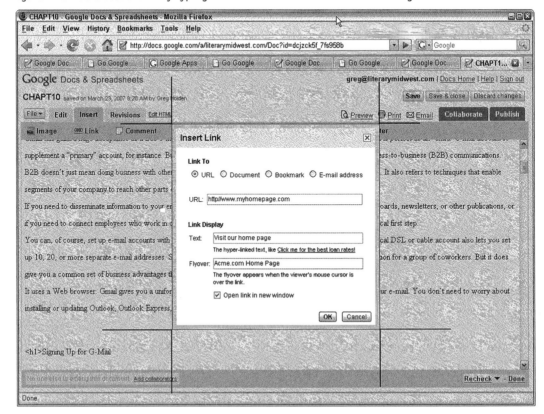

1. Click to position the cursor at the location within the document where you want to place the bookmark.

2. Click the Insert tab.

3. Click Bookmark in the Insert tab's toolbar.

4. When the Insert Bookmark dialog box appears, type the name of the book-mark in the New Bookmark field.

5. Click OK.

However, a bookmark is only useful when you can link to it. Creating a link means you provide some highlighted text that, when clicked, jumps to your bookmark. To create a link to a bookmark, follow these steps (see Figure 7-6):

1. Highlight the part of your document that you'd like to turn into a link. (You're not creating the bookmark—you did that in the previous set of steps—but you're

Figure 7-5. You need to name your bookmark so you can link to it later.

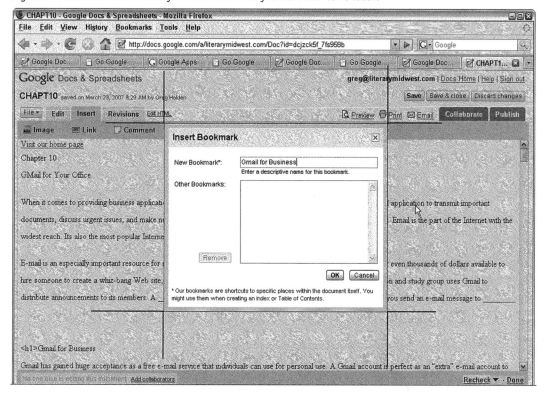

highlighting the text that will cause a browser to jump to your bookmark.) Alternately, you can just click on a blank space in your document and have the link created there.

2. Click the Insert tab.

3. Click the Link icon in the Insert tab's toolbar.

4. When the Insert Link dialog box opens (see Figure 7-6), in the Link To section, select the Bookmark option.

5. In the Bookmark section, choose the bookmark you want.

6. Click OK.

Although you'll be able to see the new link in your document while in Edit mode, you can't immediately click the link and have it jump to the bookmark so you can test it out. To test it you put your cursor over the link and right click. Select Open link in this window or Open link in new window. Or click Preview: that way you can preview the page in order to try the link out. Once in Preview mode you can click the link and have it jump to the bookmark.

Figure 7-6. Once you create a bookmark you can choose it in this dialog box.

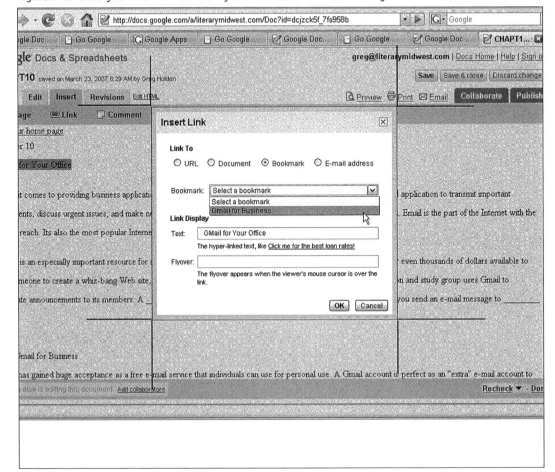

Formatting

The toolbar along the top of the Edit tab lets you perform many of the standard formatting functions you're probably used to with Word and other documents. For instance, you can change the font or the text size quickly, without opening the Document settings window.

1. Select the text you'd like changed.
2. Click either the font icon or the text size icon (which is indicated by two, differently sized Ts).

By default, a D & S document is presented in a single column. To format your document in columns, you can create a table. Place your cursor where you want to begin the table. Select table from the Insert menu in the document editing window. When the Insert Table dialog box shown in Figure 7-7 appears, specify that this table have one row and as many columns as you'd like. Click OK. You'll need to select your text and paste it into the table cells. When you publish or print this document, the borders of this table won't be visible, and your document will be formatted in columns.

File Menu Options

The File button just above the text you are editing lets you perform general functions of the sort that the File menu in Microsoft Word lets you perform. Most of the options in the drop-down menu that appears when you click File (and that is shown in Figure 7-8) are self-explanatory. But a few bear explanation.

- *Save*—Docs & Spreadsheet files are saved automatically by Google, but if you want to "force" a save without closing the file (for instance, if you need to log out or publish your file), choose this option.

- *Rename*—The option allows you to enter a new name for your document.

- *Save as*—This enables you to save the file in HTML, RTF, Word, or other common formats.

- *Count words*—This option tells you how many words, sentences, and characters in the current document.

- *Document settings*—Use this option to change your file's general settings. When you choose Document settings, the dialog box of the same name opens (see Figure 7-9). You are only able to change two settings, however: the font and the line spacing. You aren't able to adjust margins or the page layout, for instance.

Once you're done working with your file, you simply click elsewhere to get out of it. You don't need to save your changes; they are saved automatically by Google when you do so.

Working With Google Spreadsheets

Spreadsheets tend to be the domain of those few who are adept at juggling numbers and who enjoy keeping track of data and performing calculations. Programs like Microsoft Excel are great for accountant types. But for the rest of us who don't need

(*text continues on page 120*)

Figure 7-7. You can divide text into columns by creating a table without visible borders.

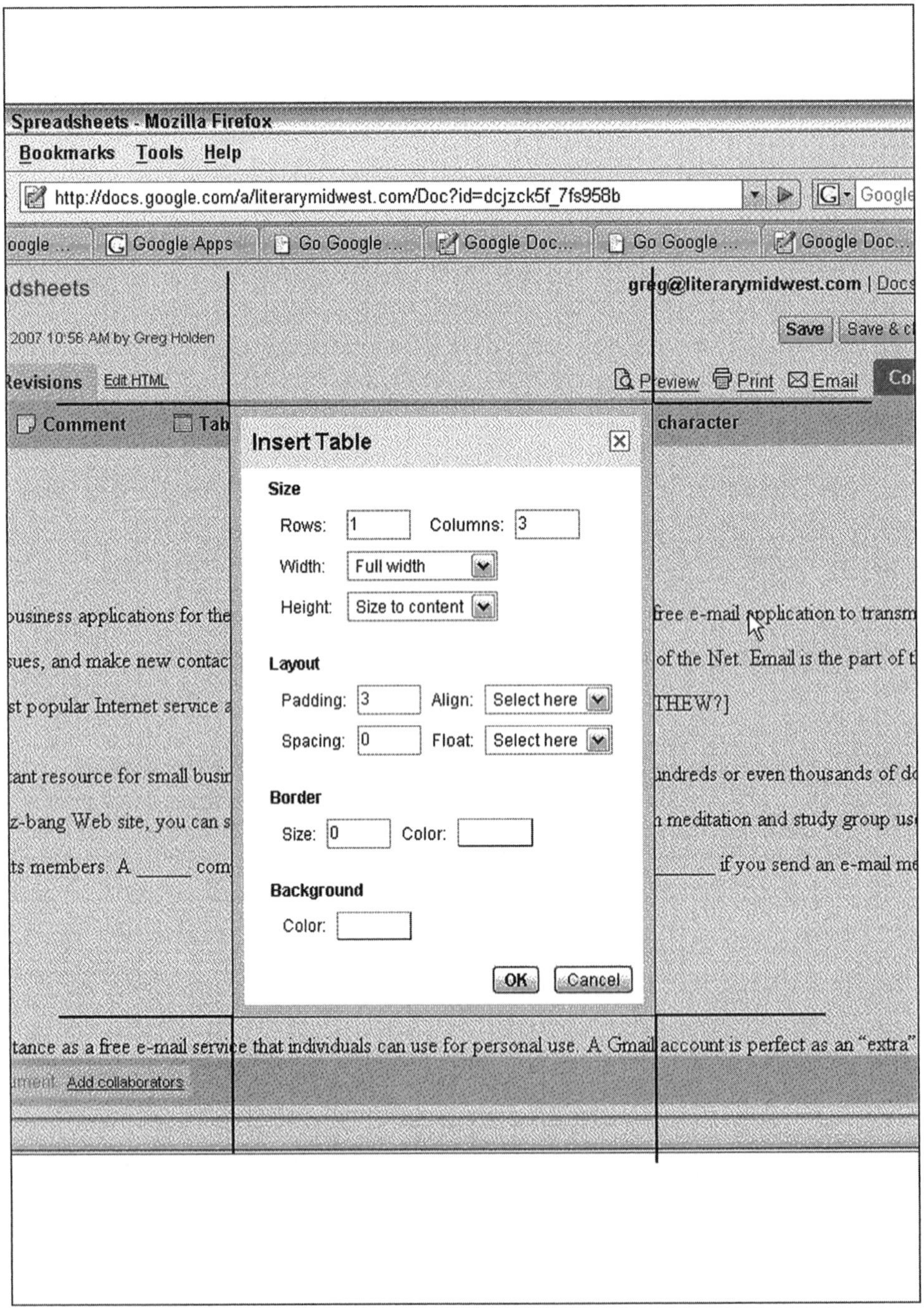

Figure 7-8. The File menu lets you edit and manage your document.

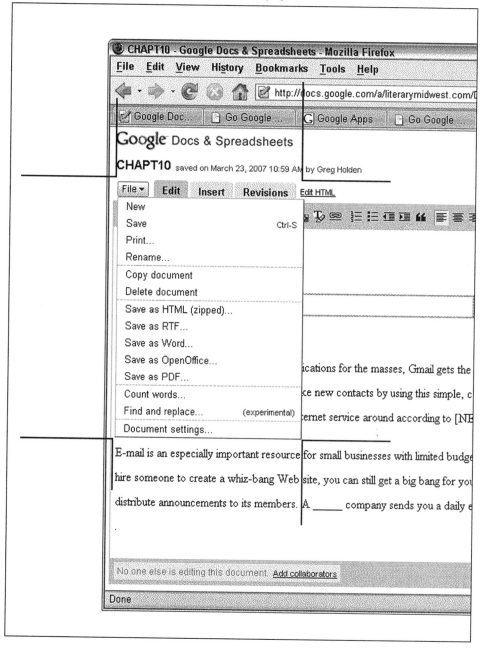

Figure 7-9. This dialog box only lets you change minimal settings related to the current file.

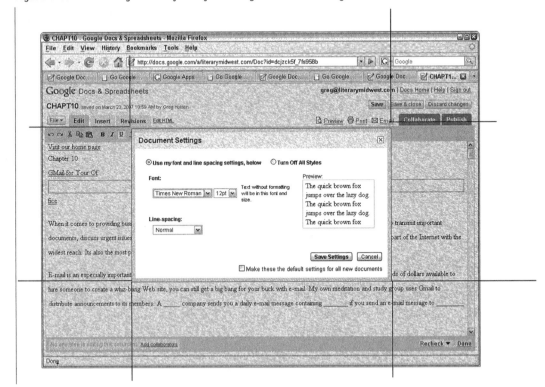

to work with complex spreadsheets all day, such applications are far more powerful than we need. Google Spreadsheets brings basic spreadsheet functionality to the masses with a basic level of functionality—for free. This last point is worth pondering for a moment. Instead of paying hundreds of dollars to purchase Excel or paying a monthly fee for an online spreadsheet application just so you can do your taxes once a year, you can sign up for Google Docs & Spreadsheets and start keeping your financial records in much the same way as you would with a "real" spreadsheet application. It may not have all the bells and whistles of professional applications like Excel, but you might be surprised at how much you can do with the program and how easy it is to learn.

Once you're used to working with the "docs" part of Google Docs & Spreadsheets, you'll have no problem moving to this part of the online service. The same basic controls used to upload files, create new documents, save or archive, or collaborate with others apply here, too. And you'll probably find many more uses for Spreadsheets than just crunching numbers. You can keep track of names and addresses, schedule meetings, and prepare lists of reports, too.

To get started with Google Spreadsheets, go to docs.google.com/a/[yourdomain]

.com or http://docs.[yourdomain].com). Then Log into Docs & Spreadsheets with your Google Account. Docs & Spreadsheets main page opens with a list of your active files (see Figure 7-10).

Most of the tools in the toolbar above the spreadsheet give you standard controls for cutting, pasting, and formatting text. One, though, is specific to the spreadsheet. When you select two or more adjacent cells in the same row, the Merge Cells button "lights up" and becomes active. Click it, and the separate cells are merged into one. When you select the merged cell, the button turns into Break Apart. You can click Break Apart to separate cells that have previously been merged.

The tabs behind the spreadsheet on the left provide you with different views of the data contained within it. They are different from the tabs that appear in the same area when you are working on a document:

- *Edit*—This tab is the one that opens by default and it's the one that lets you view and edit your data.

Figure 7-10. The toolbar above your spreadsheet helps you format data.

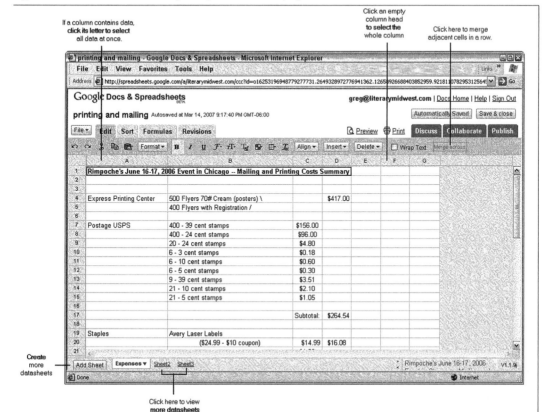

- *Sort*—This allows you to sort data within the spreadsheet.

- *Formulas*—This tab lets you create formulas that let you perform functions on the data in the spreadsheet. (See "Using Formulas" later in this chapter.)

In addition to these spreadsheet-specific controls, you'll also find some useful tools under the File menu on the left side of the window. When you click the File button you see the options shown in Figure 7-11.

Figure 7-11. The File menu contains several options specific to spreadsheets.

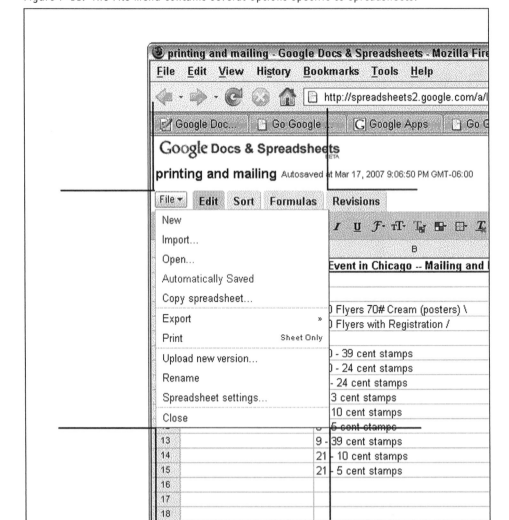

Export, for instance, lets you export the spreadsheet to an Excel (.xls), Web page (.html), or Portable Document Format (.pdf) document. Exporting is a fancy way of saying you save the document in a different format on your computer. Spreadsheet Settings opens a window that only contains two settings: the country where you are located and your time zone. These settings affect any currency-related data you want to handle and any time-sensitive functions. The two other buttons on the spreadsheet toolbar (which appear on the right side of the window when you are editing an open document) contain more useful functions:

- *Save*—Initially, this button is called Save. Not long after you start working with a new spreadsheet, a pop-up message will appear in the lower right-hand corner of the spreadsheet prompting you to save the file so you won't lose any change. Once you do save the file, the Save button changes to Automatically Saved. Once you see Automatically Saved, you don't have to do anything; the spreadsheet application itself will save the file for you.

- *Save and Close*—If Automatically Saved is not displayed, this button lets you save the file before you close it so you don't lose any changes.

Other controls that appear in the spreadsheet editing window include:

- *Format*—This option lets you format a variety of data, such as percentages, currencies, dates, and the like (see Figure 7-12).

- *Align*—This controls the alignment of data within table cells. You not only get to choose flush-left, flush-right, or centered, but top, center, and bottom as well.

- *Insert*—You can insert a row or column, either to the right or left of the currently selected row or column.

- *Delete*—When you select a cell, you can click Delete and choose an option to delete the row or column in which the cell is contained, or just the cell itself.

Besides the buttons and tabs, the other navigation items you see on the typical spreadsheet screen are the links Preview and Print; Preview lets you view the document in its Web browser window without the Docs & Spreadsheets controls being visible. Print lets you print it. Spreadsheet files have the square icon with the grid on them next to their name.

Working with New Spreadsheets

You can create a new spreadsheet at any time. If you have a spreadsheet open, you can choose New from the File menu. If you are on the main Docs & Spreadsheets

Figure 7-12. Use these options to adjust the way different sorts of data are formatted.

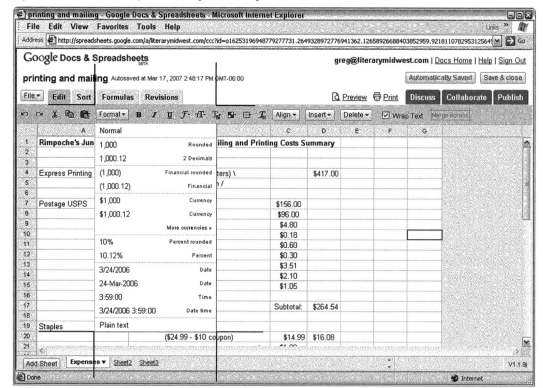

page, click New Spreadsheet. In either case, when you click New Spreadsheet your existing spreadsheet remains open, and you can still access it by returning to the main Docs & Spreadsheets page. If you already have a spreadsheet open, you can return to the main page by clicking the Docs home link near the top of the window.

 Note: If you use Internet Explorer and click New Spreadsheet, the new file opens in a new browser window. If you use Firefox, when you click New Spreadsheet it opens in a new tab.

Opening an Existing Spreadsheet

If you have other spreadsheets contained within Docs & Spreadsheets and you want to open a new one, click the File button and choose Open. The Open a spreadsheet dialog box shown in Figure 7-13 appears. Choose a spreadsheet by clicking it once; the dialog box closes and the spreadsheet appears.

Figure 7-13. This dialog box allows you to open an spreadsheet you have previously created.

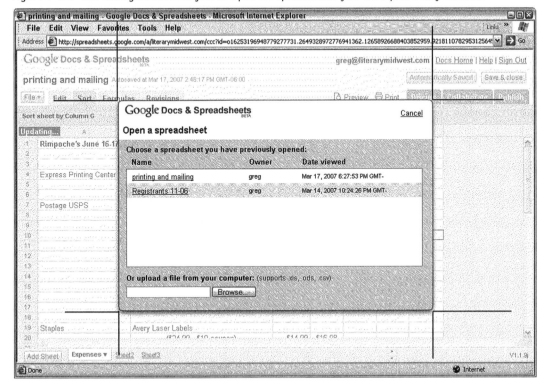

Uploading Spreadsheets

The process of uploading a spreadsheet is the same as a document: you open the main D & S page, click Browse, locate the spreadsheet on your file system, and click Upload file. Three formats are supported: Excel (.xls), OpenDocument Spreadsheet (.ods), and Comma Separated Value (.csv).

If you are already working with a spreadsheet and you don't want to have to jump back to the Docs & Spreadsheets opening page, you can click File and choose Open. When the Open a spreadsheet dialog box appears, click the Browse button at the bottom.

When you upload your spreadsheet, its file name (or any "alias" name you as-signed to it) is listed alongside your word processing documents. If the file extension (for instance, .xls) doesn't actually appear in the file name, the only way you and your coworkers know for sure whether a file is a word processing document or a spreadsheet is by the symbol next to the name. The two symbols are shown in Figure 7-14.

There are limits to the size of any individual spreadsheet you upload to D & S,

Figure 7-14. You can tell docs and spreadsheets apart by their file icons.

and to the number of spreadsheets you can upload in total, but they seem generous: each user can upload a total of 200 spreadsheets, and each one can contain as many as 10,000 rows, or 256 columns or as many as 50,000 cells, or 20 sheets—whichever limit is reached first.

When you upload an Excel spreadsheet to D & S, it takes a few seconds for it to open in your browser window. When it does open, you'll likely be very impressed with the similarity to the Excel interface.

 Tip: In order to work with spreadsheets, your browser needs to have JavaScript enabled. That means it needs to be able to process content formatted using the Web page programming language Java-Script. The exact instructions vary depending on the browser you are using. For Internet Explorer 6 or later, choose Internet Options from the Tools menu, click on the Security tab, click Custom Level, Scroll down to the Scripting section, and click Enable under the heading Active Scripting. For Mozilla Firefox 1.5 or later, choose Options from the Tools menu, click Content, click Enable JavaScript, and click OK.

Creating a new spreadsheet is the same as writing a new document: you go to the D & S main page, click New Spreadsheet, and a new document titled Unsaved

Spreadsheet appears on screen. You can start entering text in cells just as you would in a spreadsheet application.

Editing and Formatting Spreadsheet Data

Most of the controls for formatting the data in a spreadsheet are found in the Edit toolbar. It includes buttons for bold, underline, italics, font color, cell color, font family, and font size. You can also change cell alignment, merge cells, wrap text, insert or delete rows and columns, or add borders.

If you need to change the dimensions of a cell, you can do so by clicking and dragging one of the cell's borders:

1. Position the cursor so that it rests on the dividing line between the name of the row or column you'd like to change and the next row or column. The cursor turns into a double-sided arrow. (Note that the arrow only appears when you position the cursor above the grid of rows and columns, in the list of column names—A, B, C, and so on.)

2. Click and drag the arrow in the direction you want your row or column to enlarge or contract.

 Note: Google Spreadsheets supports a lengthy list of keyboard shortcuts that help you get around a file. Here are a few of the most useful ones.

- **Tab** to move to the next cell in a row
- **Shift + Tab** to move to the previous cell in a row
- **Enter** to move to the next cell in a column
- **Shift + Enter** to move to the previous cell in a column
- **F2** to edit the active cell
- **Shift + Spacebar** to select an entire row
- **Ctrl + Spacebar** to select an entire column. You might want to print out the complete list from the Spreadsheets Help files. Search for the topic "What keyboard shortcuts can I use with my spreadsheets?" or go to http://docs.google.com/support/spreadsheets/bin/answer.py?answer=40606&topic=8839.

Sorting Spreadsheet Data

When you click the Sort tab above the spreadsheet you're currently viewing, you access a set of options that let you reorder the information you're working with so you can focus on information that you want to highlight, or interpret the information more easily.

As with Microsoft Excel, you begin by selecting the data before you do a sort. First, select the parts of the Google spreadsheet that you want to sort. You can select a cell, a group of cells, a row, or a column. Then, click the Sort tab and select either the A->Z option or Z->A option. A->Z sorts in ascending order, and Z-> arranges in descending order.

If you want to "freeze" the contents of up to five rows at the top of the sheet (in other words, keep their contents and position constant so they're not sorted), choose a number from the Freeze header rows drop-down list at the top of the Sort tab (see Figure 7-15).

If you plan to do calculations using a currency other than the dollar, pound, Euro, or Yen, check the Help files to make sure your chosen currency is supported. Only nine currencies are supported at this writing; more may be included by the time you read this.

Figure 7-15. You can "freeze" the contents of rows at the top of a sheet.

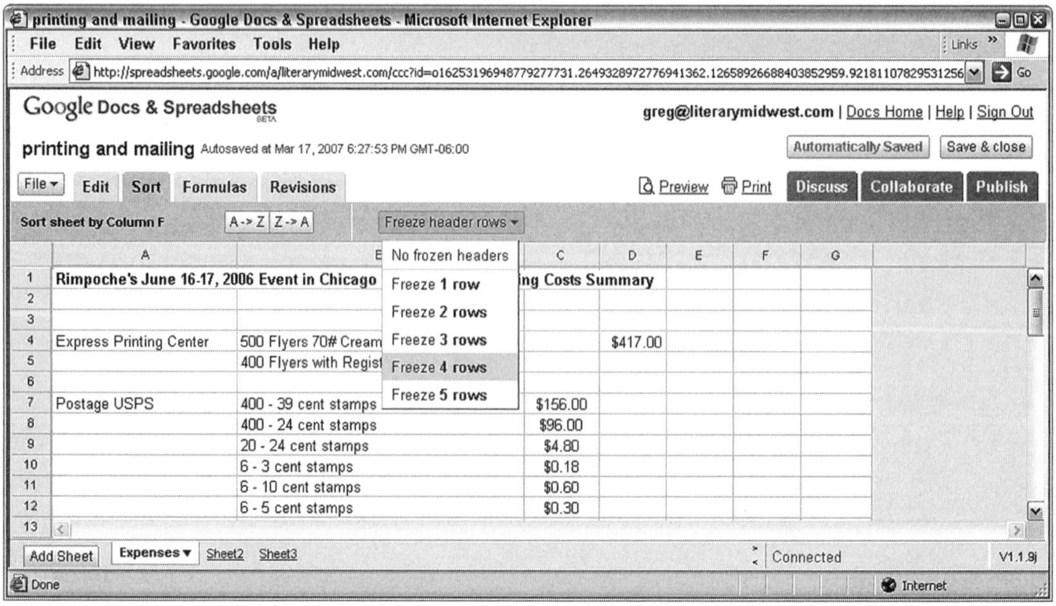

Making a Business Case for Google Spreadsheets

Some of the advantages of working with Google's spreadsheet application have already been mentioned. But if you suggest to your office manager or other supervisor that they start using this online service, you may meet with some resistance. For one thing, accountants and other financial officers are probably already using a spreadsheet application. Then there's another concern: security. It's likely many of the records stored in your office's existing spreadsheet applications are confidential in nature. You probably have names, addresses, and phone numbers of your own staff people, for one thing. For another, you might use spreadsheets to store your company's financial records and customer records, including credit card numbers that are sent to you in the course of doing business.

The security concern is a valid one. Google protects your account with passwords, but if you use Google Docs & Spreadsheets as part of a domain, you may conceivably give password access to as many as 100 or more users. It's up to those users to manage their passwords carefully and avoid giving them out to unauthorized people. As Google says in its Help file page on security and privacy (http://docs .google.com/support/spreadsheets/bin/answer.py?answer = 37615&topi c = 8836), all spreadsheet files are private by default, and if you never give out the URL of a spreadsheet to anyone or never give another user access to a spreadsheet, no one will see it but you; spreadsheets cannot be found by searching for them on Google.

If you do plan to store sensitive information online using Google, you might want to either limit access to it to as small a number of individuals as possible, or instruct those people to guard their passwords as closely as they can.

The other concern—the fact that your financial officers might already be using other software—isn't necessarily negated by Google Docs & Spreadsheets. It's not an either-or situation. The "professionals" can still use Excel or other applications, but other staff people can use Google for sharing estimates, schedules, and other data. The same advantages presented by other Google "apps" also apply:

- The ability to access information from anywhere
- The familiar spreadsheet interface, which looks uncannily like Excel
- The fact that the application is available for free
- Because you're using an online service, you don't have to download the program or upgrade it as new versions come out
- Storing data online means you use up less disk storage space on your office's servers

Besides that, your coworkers will find that Google Spreadsheets is accessible to anyone because it has a very easy-to-climb learning curve. You can learn how to perform the basic functions quickly and with a minimum of technical expertise.

Applying Formulas to Data

Formulas are one of the most popular features in Google Spreadsheets. A formula is used to perform calculations on the data contained in specified cells and display the result in the currently selected cell. You begin by selecting the cell in which you want the result to be displayed. You then choose the formula you want to use and specify the cells to which the formula should be applied. For instance, if you want to total the numbers contained in cells A1 through A7, you would select an empty cell and enter the formula = Sum(A1:A7). Then press Enter or click Sum, and the sum appears in the cell where you typed the formula. But you don't have to memorize formulas or type them from scratch. Instead, follow this example. Suppose you want to add up the numbers included in cells C7 through C15 as shown in Figure 7-16. The sum will appear in the highlighted cell, D17.

1. Double-click the empty cell where you want the results to appear. The cell borders appear to expand slightly and a cursor appears within the cell.
2. Click the Formulas tab. In the blue bar just above the spreadsheet, you see D17 = on the left, and six formulas listed on the right: Sum, Count, Average, Min, Max, and Product (see Figure 7-17).

Figure 7-16. Google Spreadsheets can apply formulas quickly for you.

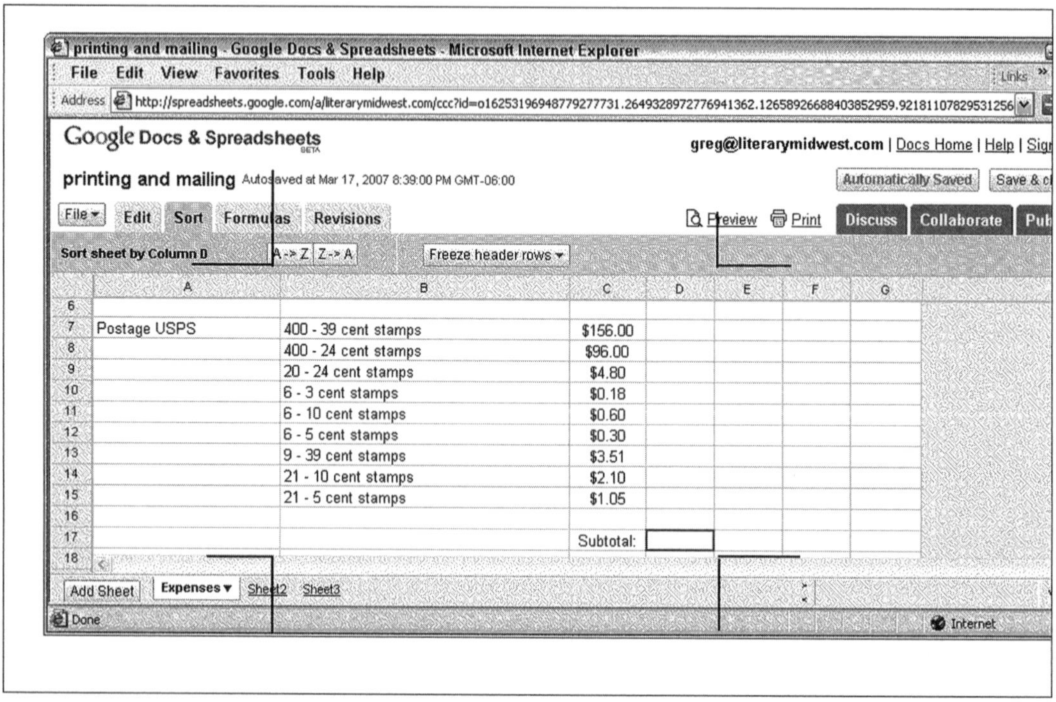

Figure 7-17. Six formulas appear initially, but many more are available.

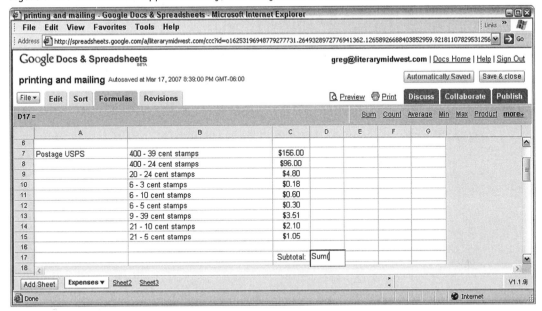

3. Click Sum. The beginnings of the formula, "Sum(", appear in the cell.

4. Select the first cell of the cells you want to add up.

5. Press Shift and click the last of the cells you want to add up.

6. Press Enter. The sum appears.

The six commands initially displayed in the Sort tab (Sum, Count, Average, Min, Max, Product) are only a few of the ones available. Click more to view a much wider selection of possible formulas.

Sharing Files

When you use Docs & Spreadsheets as part of a Google Apps domain, you gain the ability to share files with your coworkers. You can also control how freely files are shared with those who aren't part of your Google Apps domain (in other words, who don't have user accounts that you have set up in the domain). The general options are described below.

If you are the administrator for your domain, you can manage your domain's sharing options, including those specific to Docs & Spreadsheets, in your control panel. You access the control panel by entering the URL http://www.google.com/a/

[yourdomain. Sign in with your username and password, click Sign in, and you go to the start page for your domain. Click Service Settings+ in the blue toolbar near the top of the page and choose Docs & Spreadsheets from the drop down menu. Choose one of the three buttons in the Sharing Options sections of the page shown in Figure 7-18.

- *Users cannot share documents outside this domain*–This options means that users aren't allowed to invite people from outside your domain to view their files, or view documents and spreadsheets created outside your domain.

- *Let users receive documents from outside this domain*–If you check this box, users still aren't allowed to invite people from outside your domain to view their files, but they can receive invitations to view files outside your domain.

- *Users can share outside this domain, but will receive a warning each time*–If you choose this option, individual users can share documents and spreadsheets, but will receive a pop-up warning message when they try to share a file with someone outside your domain. The warning appears to remind you that you

Figure 7-18. Choose these options to control general sharing properties for all Docs & Spreadsheets created within your domain.

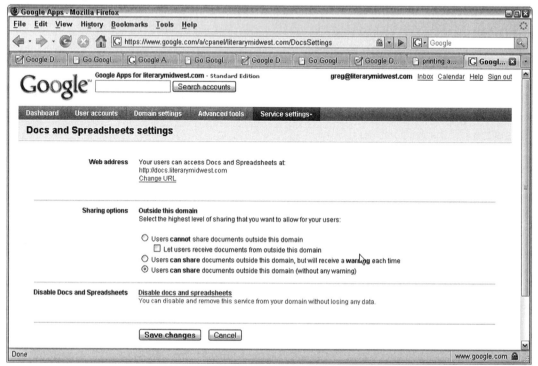

are in danger of sharing sensitive company information with people outside
your company.

- *Users can share documents outside this domain, without any warning*—This option lets your workgroup users share files freely.

The aforementioned sharing options control all of the documents created within your
domain. If an external domain shared a document with one of your users, your user
will be able to collaborate and view that document. You can, however, share individual files with others in your domain by following the steps described in the next
section.

Sharing Docs & Spreadsheets Files

Your Docs & Spreadsheets content is private by default: that means only you can
view the documents you have either uploaded or created on Google Apps. You might
have your own set of documents, but your coworkers can't see them by default;
instead, they'll see their own set of documents that they've been working with. These
two sets of files remain separate until you take steps to share them. If you'd like to
share your documents or spreadsheets with others, you can. When creating a document or a spreadsheet, you have the option to collaborate with everyone at your
domain, or to allow all the users of your domain to view your files. To enable domain
level sharing:

1. Create a document or spreadsheet at http://docs.google.com/a/your_domain
   .com.
2. Do one of the following:
   - If you want everyone in your domain to view the file, click Publish, and click
     the Publish Now button. This makes the file available to all user accounts.
   - If you want to invite selected users to view the file, click Collaborate and
     invite them as described below.
3. Click Allow anyone to view or Allow anyone to edit to grant all your users
   access.
4. Or, enter the name of another one of your domain users in the box and click
   the Invite user button shown in Figure 7-19.
5. When you click Invite User, an invitation window pops up with a stock message you can send to the other person: "I've shared a document with you . . .
   to open this document, click the link above."
6. Click the Send Message button at the bottom of the window. The recipient
   will receive an e-mail inviting him or her to view the file. However, that person

Figure 7-19. You can invite other domain users to view the file along with you and chat about it.

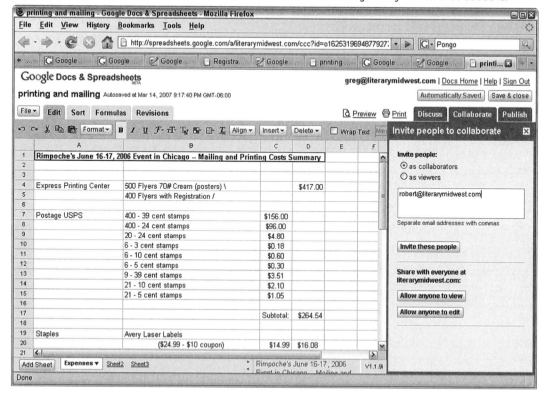

can already view the document without receiving the mail or clicking the link. If you are the recipient, and you log in to Docs & Spreadsheets, click the owner/Collaborators/Viewers link just above the list of files. The document that the other team member has decided to share with you appears with the message: View-only from [other user's name], as shown in Figure 7-20.

Once the other person you are inviting clicks on the name of the file, the Discuss-Collaborate-Publish window opens on the right side of your browser window, with the Discuss tab in front. The Viewing now heading shows who is viewing your file currently. You and the other participants can type a message in the bottom of the screen and press Enter to send the message to the others who are logged in.

The advantage of chatting is that you don't have to burn your long-distance or cell phone bills; you can also make changes to the document at the same time you are chatting about it.

 Note: Once you do receive the link to the document or spreadsheet, you can distribute this link so that other users can access your file. If you

Figure 7-20. You can see a file someone has invited you to share with them.

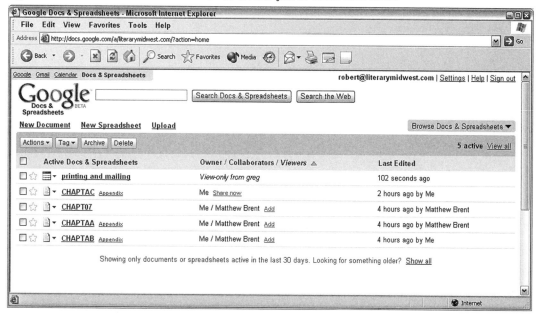

would like to stop sharing the document with everyone at your domain, click Stop allowing anyone to view or Stop allowing anyone to edit.

Discussing Files

Google Talk, one of the standard "apps" that comes with Google Apps, gives you the ability to type chat-style messages with others who have access to your domain. You can also chat within Docs & Spreadsheets. When you use D & S in an Apps domain, you can click the Discuss tab at any time as shown in Figure 7-21 and open up a discussion with someone else in your workgroup.

"Checking Out" a File

One of the nice features of many collaborative applications, such as Microsoft Office Live, is the ability to visually "check out" a file so you can work on it and indicate (by means of a visual icon such as a check mark) that you are working on the file and no one else should work on it until you are done.

Google Apps doesn't include a visual "checking out" feature, unfortunately, but it does give you other ways to know when a file was last edited, who worked on it, and even to track how it was revised. Presumably, you can contact the person who last edited the file by means of Google Talk or—shudder—an old-fashioned telephone.

Figure 7-21. You can hold a chat session to discuss a Docs & Spreadsheets file.

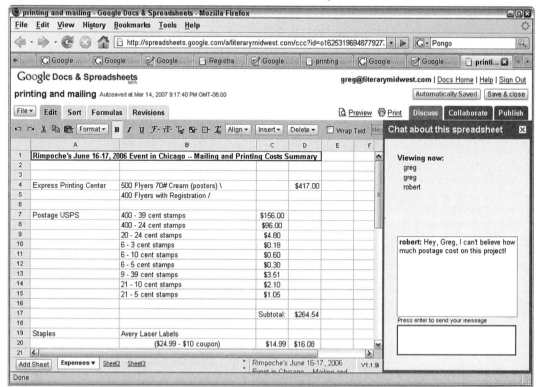

What You *Can't* Do With Docs or Spreadsheets

If you're used to using Microsoft Word, Excel, or other professional word processing or editing applications, you'll be looking for certain features that you're used to and take for granted when you start using Google's services.

Limitations of Docs

When I was working on the Docs portion of Docs & Spreadsheets, I longed for a feature that would allow me to change margins and track the number of pages in a file. You don't have any control over the page setup settings. The Find and replace feature was not well developed and prevented me from changing words on an individual basis.

Limitations of Spreadsheets

You can't spell-check spreadsheets unless you use Google Toolbar. You can't insert an image into a spreadsheet.

In either case, you are limited by the ability of your Web browser to process and publish information. While Word and Excel have sophisticated printing features, for instance, the average Web browser's Print feature is relatively limited and you need to be online in order to edit and review files that are held on Google's servers; if you leave a file open overnight and your Internet connection is interrupted for service needs or other reasons, you'll open your file in the morning and see a dialog box asking you if you want to discard your previous changes and disconnect. It's always a good idea to save your changes or click Save and Close before you quit working on a file for the night.

This chapter presented a detailed examination of Google Docs & Spreadsheets. This set of applications presents you with a powerful and sophisticated set of tools for editing and manipulating files. It's the most powerful set of tools in the Google Apps suite, and the one that's most likely to be of immediate benefit to small business—unless, that is, you take into account the Google Calendar scheduling application, which is also sure to be of use to virtually every small business. Calendar is ideal for a hosted application environment, and it's the subject of the chapter that follows.

CHAPTER **8**

Working with Google Calendar

If you work in an office and are tasked with getting people together at the same time for a meeting, you know how difficult it is to get everyone on the "same page." Google Calendar, one of the standard apps that comes with Google Apps, won't be able to give you more than 24 hours in a day or get everyone in the same physical location in order to have a meeting. But it can give participants a place to look in order to verify that the meeting is occurring. It's one of the simplest Google applications to implement and one of the most rewarding. And it's absolutely free: you get all the functionality mentioned in this chapter for absolutely zero monthly fee. Microsoft Outlook does have a more powerful scheduling tool, but you have to pay $100 to $200 to either upgrade or purchase Microsoft Office just so you can use it! And it isn't Web-based. Another competing program, Microsoft Office Live, also has a calendar tool, but you have to pay $20 to $40 per month to use it. Google's calendar program might not have all the bells and whistles of its commercial competitors, but it's a quite sophisticated program nonetheless.

There are lots of other shared calendar applications on the Web. In fact, calendars are one of the most popular Web-based applications around. But Google's is free, it's exceptionally easy to use, and it offers a more powerful set of features than many of its competitors. Not only that, but you don't actually have to do anything to sign up for Calendar or set it up; if you have signed up for Google Apps you are already signed up for the Calendar application, and your default calendar is created automatically for you. Even if you don't sign up for Google Apps, you still get access to the Calendar when you sign up for Gmail e-mail service.

 Note: I just said this, but since it's potentially confusing, I'll say it again. Google Calendar comes to you as part of two different groups of Google applications. If you plan to use many different business applications, including the word processing and spreadsheet application Docs & Spreadsheets, sign up Google Apps. Calendar is included as one of the "apps." If you don't need many collaborative business applications and are primarily interested in e-mail, sign up for a Gmail account. Calendar comes with Gmail as well. When you go to your Gmail inbox, you'll see the link Calendar near the top of the page. Click it to access Google Calendar. Calendar's features are the same in the versions that come with both Google Apps and Gmail.

Navigating Through Your Default Calendar

The biggest single advantage of using Google calendar is that it is a Web service, which means you can access it from any computer that is connected to the Internet, and you can use virtually any Web browser to access it. You can connect to Google Calendar in several ways. In any case, you get the same level of functionality:

1. at http://calendar.google.com;
2. by connecting to your Google Apps start page and clicking Calendar; or
3. by going to http://calendar.[mydomain].

Once you have the Calendar open you'll find that it's easy to move from one day or month to another and to find your way around the current time period you are viewing. It's as easy as navigating a printed calendar, in fact:

- To jump to a particular date, click a number in the miniature calendar displayed on the left side of the screen (see Figure 8-1).
- To move ahead or back a month, click the left or right blue arrows.
- Click on the *Today* button on the top left of your calendar whenever you want to jump quickly back to today's date.
- To add an event:
  1. Click the rectangle located at the date and the time you want.
  2. Type the meeting event in the "What:" pop-up box that appears on the screen.
  3. Enter the event in the box.
  4. If you are finished, press the "create event" button.
  5. The time will default to the half hour you select from the calendar. If you

Figure 8-1. A miniature calendar on the left controls the content displayed in the main calendar.

want to change the time or other details about the event you are entering on the calendar, click on the "edit event details" link in the popup box.

6. Here you will have the option to adjust the time for the meeting, indicate if it is all day, indicate whether or not the meeting repeats, add location, add descriptions, and add a guest list.

7. Press the Save button at the bottom of the box.

The two blue buttons that contain arrows at the top left-hand corner of the main calendar box, next to the *Today* button, enable you to move in different increments depending on your current calendar view. If you're in monthly view, they let you move forward or back a month.

Changing the Default View

When you first connect to the Calendar, you may be asked to choose your time zone. (If you have already specified your time zone as part of working with another Google application, you won't be prompted to do so again.) When you specify your time zone, you open the Calendar, which appears to you in the default weekly view. (The current week is displayed by default.) To move to a different view, click one of the tabs in the upper right-hand corner:

- *Day*—This shows all of the hours in the current day, or another day you move to.

- *Week*—This displays a week's worth of days.

- *Month*—This shows the traditional month's worth of days.

- *Next 4 Days*—Click this tab, and you view an hour-by-hour grid for the current day and the next three days.

- *Agenda*—Any events or appointments you have recorded, either in the future or the recent past, are presented in list form.

You have the ability to change the default view of the calendar. When you first open the calendar, it probably appears in either one month view or one week view. You can customize the default view as well as the configuration for Next 4 Days tab. To customize the view:

1. Click the Settings link next to Help in the upper right-hand corner.

2. When the Calendar Settings page shown in Figure 8-2 appears, scroll down and change the settings as needed. Most of the options are obvious. Some that aren't so obvious include:

   • *Country*—Choose a different country if you expect to schedule appointments for a different time zone. If you only expect to schedule meetings occasionally in a different time zone, you'll probably want to create a custom calendar for that time zone and keep your primary calendar in your own time zone.

   • *Week starts on*—Your calendar doesn't have to start on a Sunday. If you want to concentrate on a work schedule, you can start it on a Monday. You can also click No next to Show weekends if you want to view only Monday through Friday events.

   • *Changing the view*—The Next 4 Days tab lets you see the next four calendar days by default. But it can be changed to next 2 days, next 5 days, next two weeks, or one of many other options.

   • *Show weather based on my location*—Some events, like a sporting event or picnic, are weather dependent. By default, you don't see the weather displayed for your area. You can view the weather by first specifying your location in the Location box and then clicking either the Celsius or Fahrenheit option.

   • *Sharing and creating calendars*—The Calendars tab, one of three under Calendar Settings, displays any calendars you have created, along with your default calendar. (You might want to create one calendar for business

Figure 8-2. You can customize the Next 4 Days tab as well as other calendar settings.

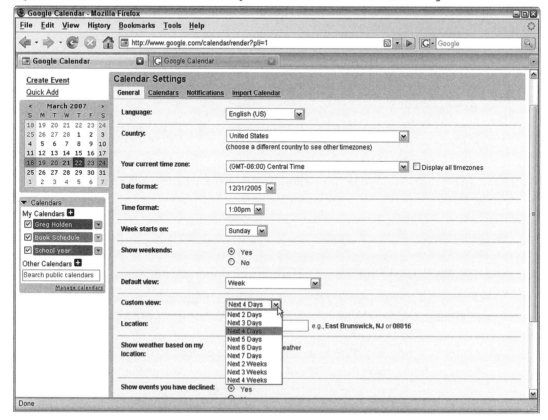

appointments, one for personal use, one for a club, and so on.) Click Share this calendar to set up sharing, and click Create new calendar to make a custom calendar.

- *Notifications*—Calendars aren't any good if you record an event and then forget to attend it. This link in the Settings tab of Calendar Settings controls how soon you are sent a reminder, and how you receive it (e-mail, SMS text message, or pop-up window).

Tip: If you created another calendar in one of two formats used for electronic calendars, iCal or Comma-Separated Value (CSV), you can import all of that calendar's events at once. Click the down arrow next to Add in the calendar box on the left side of the main Calendar page. Choose Import from the drop-down list. The Add Other Calendar page appears with the Import Calendar tab in front. Click Browse to find the calendar file you want to import. Choose the calendar that you want to contain the new data and click Import to complete the process.

Creating Custom Calendars

One attribute that sets Google Calendar apart from other scheduling applications is the fact that you aren't necessarily limited to a single calendar. Rather, you can copy calendars for different purposes: one can be for one workgroup, another for personal use, another for your entire office, and so on. You can also view all of your calendars together on the same Web page, which gives you an instant overview of all your upcoming appointments and deadlines.

Creating a Personalized Calendar

Creating a new calendar doesn't mean you delete your old one. Rather, you add a new calendar to your account. Having several different calendars makes it easy to control who views a particular set of scheduling information. You can share one calendar with family members and friends so they can keep track of your personal and work schedules. You can share a work-related calendar with your coworkers so they can track your appointments, business meetings, and deadlines.

To create a personalized calendar in addition to your default one, click the plus sign (+) next to the My Calendars box on the left side of the calendar window, as shown in Figure 8-3. You'll see all of your calendars listed there. It's a colorful list; each calendar you create isn't assigned its own color, in fact, so you can tell them apart more easily. If you check a box next to a calendar's name, it means that you have the ability to see a quick overview of all of the appointments you have created in that calendar.

You might not want to check every box next to every calendar, however. The reason has to do with "information overload." If you have, say, ten calendars and each one has some appointments that include you, you can quickly get overwhelmed. You might want to remove non-critical calendars by unchecking them. That way, they'll be removed from your calendar view.

Figure 8-3. Personalized calendars you create for different purposes are listed in My Calendars.

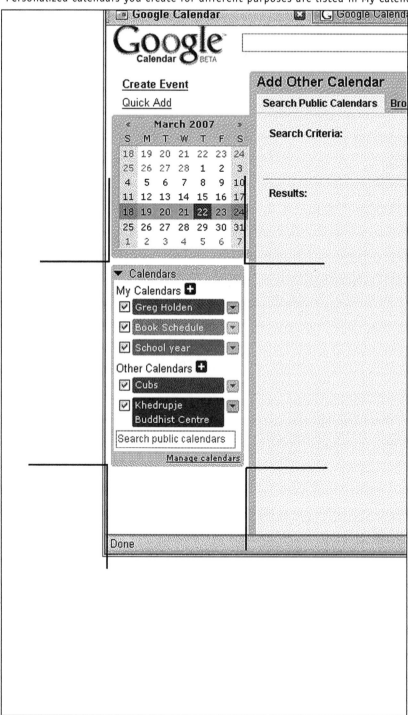

Clicking the plus sign opens the Create New Calendar page. Fill out the form displayed on this page (and shown in Figure 8-4) to name your calendar and type a brief description of it. You also need to enter a time zone so all times displayed are accurate. You also need to choose one of three sharing options:

- *Do not share with anyone.* Choose this option only if you want to keep calendar information private.

- *Share all information on this calendar with everyone.* "Everyone" means not only the users who are in your Google Apps domain but anyone outside your domain who connects to http://calendar.[yourdomain] (provided you are using the Google Apps version of your calendar rather than the standalone version).

- *Share only my free/busy information (hide details).* If you want to make your calendar public, you may well want to choose this option rather than the preceding one. It lets anyone find your calendar easily but they only see

Figure 8-4. Create a new calendar with this page.

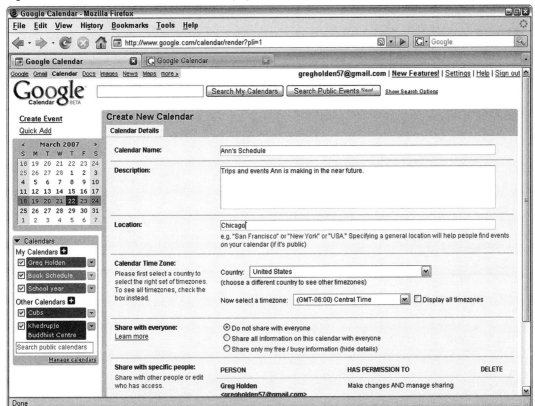

whether you are free or busy at a particular date or time. They can't see who you're meeting, where you're going, or what you'll be doing.

If you want to share your calendar only with certain individuals, such as the registered users you have added to your domain, add their e-mail address to the Share with specific people box shown in Figure 8-5. Be sure to select a permissions level for that individual, too: you can choose one of the three options from the drop-down list. Then click Add Person to give the individual access to your calendar.

 Note: If you do share a calendar, you won't have to worry about whether all times are accurate. Even if your collaborators are in different time zones, Google will automatically adjust times shown to your respective time zones.

Figure 8-5. You can make your calendar visible to everyone or to a selected few.

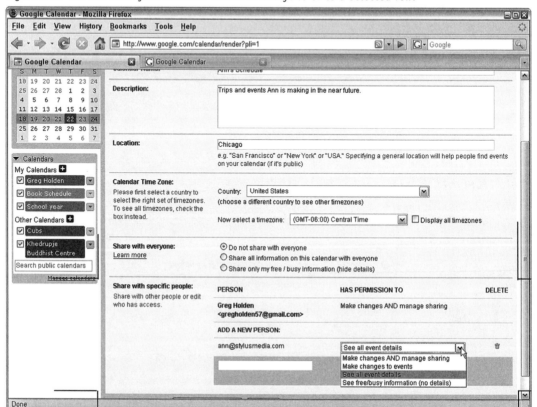

When you're done configuring your calendar and adding people with whom you want to share it, click Create Calendar. When you do this, Google checks to see whether or not the individuals already have Google Accounts that include access to Google Calendars. If they do not, you see the warning message shown in Figure 8-6.

If you click Invite, Google sends an e-mail message to those people who have Google accounts. You'll receive an e-mail telling you the invitation was sent. If you click Don't Invite, the persons are still added to your sharing list. They just won't be invited automatically by Google. You'll need to send them an e-mail invitation to tell them they can view your calendar and let them know where to find it. They'll need to accept the invitation in order to actually view your calendar. After the invitation step, the calendar is added to your list in My Calendars.

Other Google Calendars

Beneath the My Calendars list, you see another heading called Other Public Calendars. These aren't calendars that you create yourself. Instead, they're either calendars

Figure 8-6. If one of your users has a Google account, you can send an invitation to them to access your calendar.

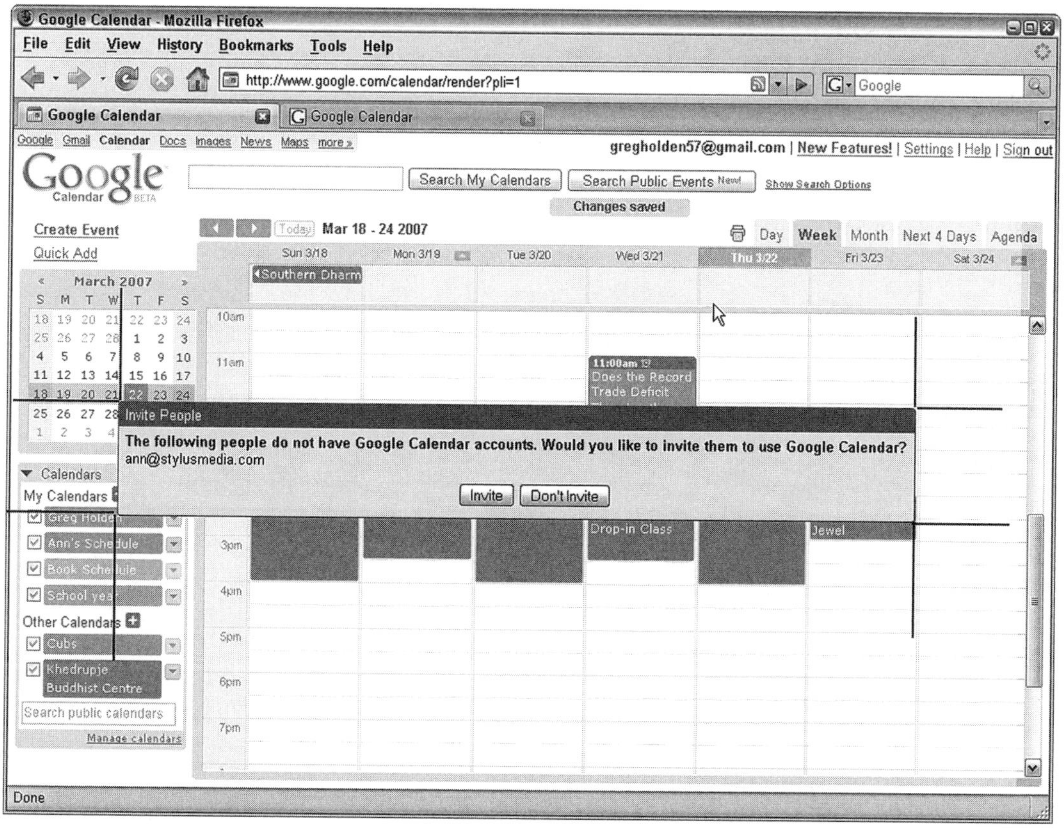

that other Google Calendar editors have made public and that you can access, or a "stock" holiday calendar that contains dates you can add to your own calendars. It's worth exploring the list of "other" calendars to see what's available.

For instance, I live a mile or so from Wrigley Field, where the Chicago Cubs baseball team plays. Knowing the Cubs' upcoming schedule is important to me for traffic reasons. I can search for the Cubs' schedule and add it to my list of calendars. Click the plus sign next to Other Calendars and browse your options in the Add Other Calendar page (see Figure 8-7). You have three options:

- *Public Calendars*—These are calendars that other Google customers have created and made public. If you're ever wondering when your particular politician was born or a particular event happened, enter a search term in the box that appears when you click Search Public Calendars. You'll find calendars with birthdays of U.S. presidents, or many other types of information. A list of calendars appears. Click Preview to view a preview of the calendar without actually opening it. If you find a calendar with dates you like, click Add Calendar, a link that appears just to the right of the description. The calendar will be added to your Other Calendars list.

Figure 8-7. You can add other people's calendars or a holiday calendar to your list.

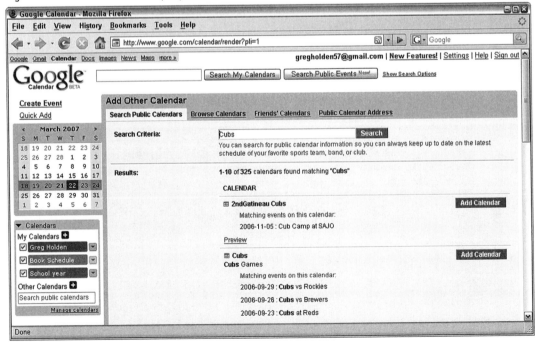

- *Friends' Calendars*—If you're ever wondering if a friend or acquaintance has created a calendar, you can search for them by clicking Friends' Calendars and searching for someone you know. You enter his or her e-mail address. If that person has made a calendar available, you'll see it in the list that appears. Even if you know the person you're looking for has a Google Account, and even if they have a calendar, you might not see them in the search results. They'll only appear if they have at least one calendar that they've made public. If the person you're looking for doesn't have a Google Calendar account, a dialog box will appear prompting you to invite the individual to use Google Calendar.

- *Public Calendar Address*—This isn't a type of calendar, exactly, but it is another option you see when you're looking through the Add Other Calendar screen. Click this option, and you view a page where you can enter the address of another calendar you want to add to your list. You have to have a calendar address beforehand, in other words. You can get such an address if someone specifically sends it to you and invites you to share their calendar. Or you can get it if someone who is authorized to have access sends it to you, with or without the calendar owner's permission. To add an address to your Other Calendars list, either type or copy and paste the address into the box provided and click Add.

Creating an Appointment or Other Event

Google Calendar is integrated with other Google applications, which makes it easy to add appointments and other events. The first option is to open the calendar, click the date on which the event occurs (or starts), and fill out the form that appears. Clicking in the box causes a balloon to pop up above the date, providing you with space where you can type a brief description of the event that is to occur on that day (see Figure 8-8).

 Tip: Only a word or two of your event text appears on the Calendar when you have it in Month view. In Day view, you have more space for your event description. But you have lots of space in which to type a detailed description: I typed more than 100 characters in the balloon and could still type more. Even if you don't see the entire text of the description on the calendar, you can click it to open the balloon. Then you can edit the details or simply read them as a re-

Figure 8-8. Click a date and type details in the balloon that appears to set an upcoming event.

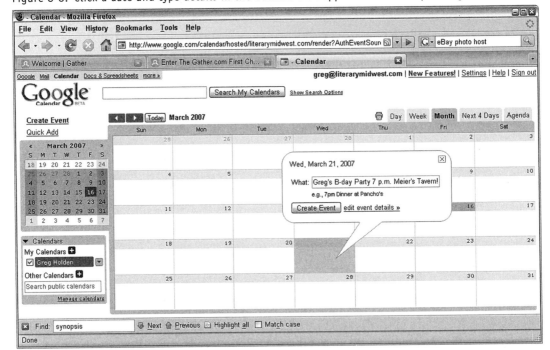

minder. Better yet, click Add Event Details if you need to add a detailed description.

When you are done typing your description, click Create Event. An orange notice appears near the top of the calendar to let you know that the event was added to your calendar space on Google's servers. If you want more space to type information, click Add Event Details next to the Create Event button. When you do so, you view a new form that lets you set a time frame, record which guests are coming, and type a more detailed description (see Figure 8-9). The form gives you the chance to make the event private or public—in other words, even if you make your calendar publicly available, you can make an individual event private.

The Guests column of the detailed information form gives you the chance to invite people to the event you're recording (or announcing, if this is a shared or public calendar) The individuals you invite don't have to be on Gmail or have a Google Calendar. When you click the Add guests box in the Guests column, you can

Figure 8-9. You can add more detailed information about an event or appointment using this form.

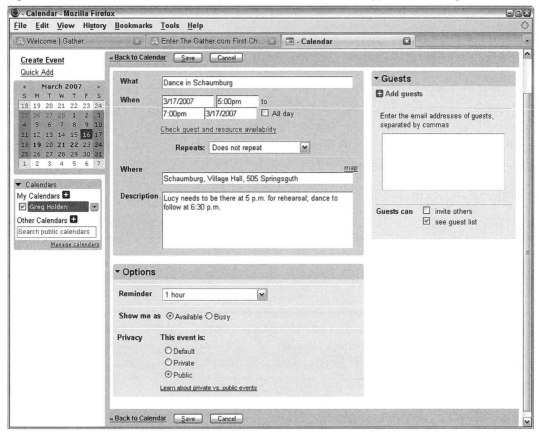

then type the e-mail addresses of those you want to attend. Click Send, and Google sends invitations to the event to the individuals you have listed. The invitation is a stock message, but it gives all the basics. Recipients can choose one of three responses: Yes, No, or Maybe. Clicking any of the three opens a Web page where they can leave comments. They can use this chance to raise questions or solicit more information from you before the meeting takes place. An example is shown in Figure 8-10.

Other Options for Adding Events

Clicking in a calendar box is only one way to add an event. You can also add an event and save a little time by clicking Quick Add. This is one of two links found just beneath the Google logo on your calendar page. Click it, and the box shown in Figure 8-11 appears where you can add a brief message about the event you want to create. Press Return, and the event is added.

Figure 8-10. Google can send invitations to the e-mail recipients of your choice.

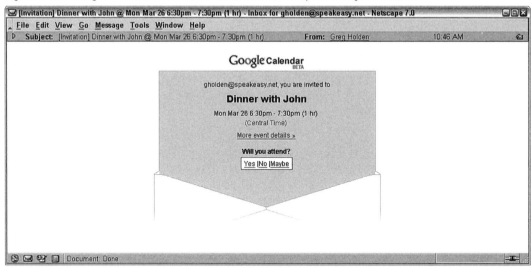

Figure 8-11. Click Quick Add to create a one-line event entry.

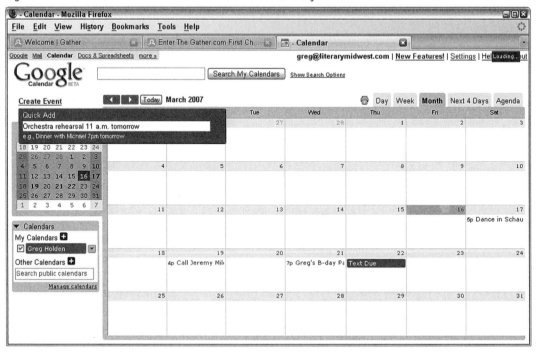

The link found just above Quick Add, New Event, also enables you to add an appointment or other event to your calendar. When you click this link, you immediately go to the detailed event information form described earlier. Type the information about your event in the appropriate boxes and click Save. The advantage of using Quick Event is that, when you have a complex event that you know will require a detailed description, you skip the step of opening the event bubble and go directly to the detailed form.

If you use Gmail, you can add events directly from your inbox to the Calendar. Often, notices of meetings and other events come to you through e-mail—through Gmail, if you're a dedicated Google user. When you get an e-mail message that tells you to be somewhere at a certain time, open the message. Then follow these steps.

1. When the open message is displayed on screen, click the down arrow next to More actions and choose Create Event. (The Create Event menu option doesn't appear when you are looking at a message list, only when an individual message's contents are open.)

2. The familiar event details form appears on screen. Enter the information about your event's date and time and description. (This isn't entered for you automatically, unfortunately.)

3. Click Save. The event is added to your calendar.

 Note: You must be responding to an invitation to an event you receive through Google Calendar or through another shared calendar application in order to create the event from the Gmail interface.

The connection between Calendar and Gmail goes the other way, too: once you create an appointment in the Calendar, you can have a reminder e-mailed to your Gmail inbox—or via SMS, or as a popup message on the calendar itself. Here's how:

1. Click the Settings link at the very top of the Calendar screen, next to Help.

2. When the Calendar Settings screen appears, click Notifications. The Notifications tab jumps to the front.

3. Check the appropriate box (E-mail, SMS, or Pop-Up) in the section labeled "Choose how you would like to be notified." You can also adjust the default 10-minute reminder time in the Event Reminder section. In the Notify me on

my cell phone section, you need to fill out a phone number and choose your cell phone carrier if you want to receive reminders sent to your cell phone.

4. Click Save.

 Note: You can only send yourself reminders for events you have recorded on your primary calendar, not any custom calendars you may have created.

Embedding a Calendar in a Web Page

It's very common for blogs, such as the ones discussed in Chapter 13, to include calendars right on their home pages. For people who visit your blog or Web site on a regular basis, a calendar lets them know about upcoming events. If you create a Web site to serve as an online "gathering spot" for your wedding, for instance, a calendar can let attendees know about wedding showers, parties, and the event itself. Google Calendar gives you the ability to include a miniature version in a Web page or blog you've created. You have to use the calendar's "configuration tool" to add the code. The tool, in turn, requires you to work with the HyperText Markup Language (HTML) code. If you have some rudimentary knowledge of HTML (and you probably do, if you are creating and editing your own Web pages) this should not be difficult. Follow these general steps:

1. Under Calendars in the left column, click on the down-arrow next to the appropriate calendar.

2. Select Calendar settings. (Alternatively, you can click Manage Calendars under Calendars in the left column, then click on the name of the appropriate calendar.)

3. In the Calendar Address section of the form, click on the HTML icon. A pop-up window with your calendar's private URL is displayed.

4. Click on the Configuration tool link in the popup.

5. Follow the instructions on the configuration tool page.

Keep in mind that you can change the amount of information available on your calendar's address by clicking on the "Change sharing settings" link in the "Calendar Address" section.

The more you delve into Google calendar, the more surprised you're likely to be at how many features the service contains. It's just as surprising to realize that the tools are provided to you free of charge. Several of Calendar's features work because of the service's integration with Gmail. You'll learn more about Gmail, another full-featured and free application that can help both personal and business users, in the next chapter.

CHAPTER **9**

Gmail for Your Office

When it comes to providing business applications for the masses, Gmail gets the job done. You can use this free e-mail application to transmit important documents, discuss urgent issues, and make new contacts. And just because Gmail is free doesn't mean it isn't full featured. E-mail has permeated every aspect of modern life, creating both a new, ubiquitous lexicon, and tacit rules of communications etiquette that constantly evolve as e-mail becomes both more widespread and more entrenched. According to Nielsen/NetRatings' data from Mar. 5 to Mar. 11, 2007, approximately 50 percent of all ads placed online were done so through email. The second-place communications method, General Community Web sites, had only 13 percent of all ad placement. Simply put, effective email use is essential for your business.

E-mail is an especially important resource if you have limited budgets. Even if you don't have hundreds or even thousands of dollars available to hire someone to create a whiz-bang Web site, you can still get a big bang for your buck with e-mail. Here are some goals to consider when you're getting ready to set up an Internet e-mail system:

- Save money and time by corresponding electronically rather than using snail mail. Give customers another way to contact you.

- Stay in touch with the office when you or other staff members are on the road. Respond automatically to e-mail requests by sending specific documents.

- Meet colleagues in your field and help research prospects by participating in mailing lists

My own meditation and study group uses Gmail to distribute announcements to its members. Google reports that companies ranging from the video game developer RedOctane (http://www.redoctane.com) to the Chicago-area real estate firm Prudential Preferred Properties (http://www.prupref.com) use Gmail for corporate communications.

Gmail for Business

Gmail has gained huge acceptance as a free e-mail service that individuals can use for personal use. A Gmail account works well as an extra e-mail account to supplement a primary account, for instance. But Gmail is much more than that. It's a tool that also promotes business-to-business (B2B) communications. B2B doesn't only mean doing business with other companies or giving access to individuals outside your organization. It also refers to techniques that enable segments of your company to reach other parts of that same company—B2E or business-to-employee communications, in other words.

If you need to disseminate information to your employees through the Web, enable staff to share ideas through bulletin boards, newsletters, or other publications, or if you need to connect employees who work in different locations where they might not have access to their e-mail through a specially designated e-mail application, then establishing Gmail accounts for them is a logical first step.

You can, of course, set up e-mail accounts with just about any service that gives you access to the Internet. The typical DSL or cable account also lets you set up 10, 20, or more separate e-mail addresses. So there's nothing exclusive about using Google as an e-mail application for a group of coworkers. But it does give you a set of business advantages that you should take into account:

Advantages of Gmail Over Other Services

- *It uses a Web browser.* You can use any Web browser to get your e-mail, which enables you to use any computer connected to the Internet. You don't need to worry about installing or updating Outlook, Outlook Express, Thunderbird, Netscape Messenger, or other e-mail programs.

- *You get a huge amount of storage space.* Google continually increases the amount of space it gives to users. The amount may well be larger by the time you read this. But currently you get 2.8 GB of free storage, which is more than many individuals have on their home computers. The storage space gives it an edge over other free e-mail services such as MSN Hotmail or Yahoo! Hotmail.

- *It can check for e-mail that arrives at multiple accounts.* Not only can you forward e-mail from other accounts to a single Gmail address, but Gmail can be configured to check for incoming mail at up to five other accounts and open them in a single Gmail account.

- *It provides you with search-based organization.* Rather than grouping your sent, incoming, or deleted mail into folders, Google uses its own sophisticated and familiar search technology to help you find what you want in your e-mail "archives." By entering search terms in the Gmail search box, you can locate many different types of information. For instance, if you want to find all the messages from a particular individual, enter a search query such as this:

from:bill_g@mydomain.com

This will retrieve all messages sent to you from the user with this particular e-mail address. You can also use "in:" to search a particular folder, or one of the following to search for e-mail addresses by date:

before:date (yyyy/mm/dd)
after:date (yyyy/mm/dd)

These will retrieve all e-mail messages sent either before or after a particular date, for instance.

Gmail has a lot of good points and it covers most if not all of the basic features you need from an e-mail program. But even devoted Gmail users complain about one problem: spam. Gmail has spam filters like other e-mail services, but they are far from perfect. You can expect this problem to be the same, if not worse, when you sign up for Gmail as it is with your current provider.

Signing Up for GMail

It's free to sign up for Gmail, just as it is with other Google services. Gmail used to be a "closed club" that you could join only if you were invited by a current Gmail account holder. That's not true any more. You get a Gmail account automatically if you sign up for Google Apps. But if you don't follow this route, you can also sign up by following the steps:

1. Go to the Google Home Page (http://www.google.com).

2. Click Sign in, which is displayed in the upper right hand corner.

3. Below the blank fields for entering Email and Password, click on the link that prompts you to Create an account now. you are provided with a blue box that contains the message "Don't have a Google Account? Create an account now" and with a second option to Sign up for Gmail. Click the link that applies to you. Since it's likely that you already have a Gmail account, this would be the option to Sign up for Gmail.

4. Fill in the appropriate fields, and click the "I accept. Create my account" button at the bottom of the page.

5. You should now be able to sign in to your account at the Google Home Page (http://www.google.com), or at the Gmail page (http://www.mail.google .com). As stated in Chapter 2, creating a Gmail account automatically signs you up for a Google Account that you can then use to obtain other Google services.

The Gmail interface is the same whether you sign up for Gmail as a standalone service or whether you obtain an e-mail account as part of your Google Apps domain name.

Gmail for Your Domain

Suppose you have signed up for Google Apps and you have obtained your own new domain. How do you get Gmail up and running for you and your colleagues? It's easy: first, you establish an account for an individual:

1. Go to the Google Apps login page, http://www.google.com/a, and click Returning user, sign in here.

2. In the box labeled Enter, type your domain name (for example, mydomain. com) in the box provided.

3. Choose Manage this domain from the drop-down list next to the domain name box and click Go. You go to the Dashboard page for your domain.

4. Click Create new users.

5. When the Create a new user page appears, fill out the form provided. The text you enter in the Username box becomes the first part of that user's e-mail

address. For example, if your domain name is mycompany.com and you enter "fred," the user's e-mail address will be fred@mycompany.com.

6. Continue filling out the form by assigning a new password and then clicking the Create new user button.

Once the user's account has been created, he or she automatically has e-mail set up through Google Apps. For example, if the user fred@mycompany.com needs to check his e-mail, he first needs to sign on to the domain as described in steps 1 and 2 in the preceding set up steps. Instead of choosing Manage this domain from the drop-down list, Fred would choose Email and then click Go. When the login page appears, Fred would simply enter "fred" in the username box and the appropriate password in the password box, and then click Sign In. Fred would then be taken to his Gmail inbox, which looks and operates exactly the same as Gmail for someone who has a stand-alone Gmail account.

Tip: Suppose you have a standalone Gmail account and an e-mail account through Google Apps as well. You may want to forward your mail from the standalone account to your Google Apps account so you don't have to log in with two separate username/password pairs and scan two separate inboxes. You can move your mail from Gmail to Google Apps using a system called Mail Fetcher. Log in to Google, click Help, and search for the question "How can my users migrate mail from Gmail to Google Apps?"

Reading Your E-Mail

Gmail makes scrolling through e-mail correspondences intuitive and simple by listing every e-mail response back and forth as a "conversation" so you're never left scratching your head trying to figure out exactly why you sent the response you did. Not only that, but a wide variety of applications, such as Google Talk, are already built right in to the interface, so you can communicate not only with multiple people at once, but in multiple ways simultaneously within Gmail.

The primary Gmail controls are located to the left of your Inbox (see Figure 9-1). They give you the ability to see messages in your Inbox, "star" messages to make them stand out in the list, look at drafts, and the basic functions you're used to with other e-mail applications. They aren't the only controls that affect how you see mes-

Figure 9-1. Gmail's main controls for handling e-mail are on the left and just above the message list.

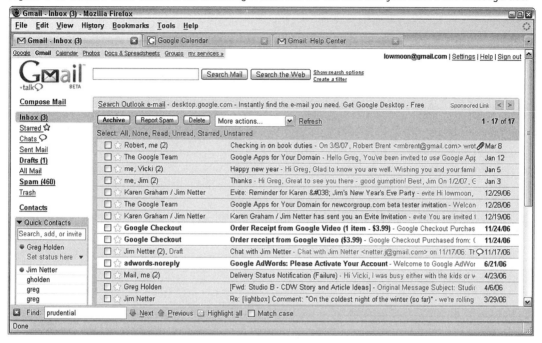

sages, however. For instance, you can also star messages in your inbox, and then choose to view only starred messages. A set of buttons above the message list lets you perform common functions on a message that you have selected by checking the checkbox next to its subject line: you can Archive the message, Report Spam if you think the message is unwanted spam and you want Google to know about it so they can hopefully block similar messages in the future, or Delete the message by sending it to your Trash folder.

One of my favorite Gmail features is that if a message arrives while you are in the middle of writing a response to another one, you can go ahead and head straight for your Inbox. You don't have to worry about losing the draft, because Gmail automatically saves what you've typed in "Drafts" on the left-hand toolbar.

Gmail also provides you with a number of keyboard shortcuts that are quickly learned, and will having you navigating Gmail in style. The shortcuts I use are primarily these:

- Press G + I to go back to the Inbox

- Press P to see the previous message, and N to see the next message

- Once you are in a conversation, press U to scroll backward and K to scroll forward.

These are just a few of the commands available to you. You can find the full list of keyboard shortcuts by clicking Help at the top of the Gmail window and then searching for "keyboard shortcuts." You can also go to http://mail.google.com/support/bin/answer.py?answer = 6594

 Tip: E-mail doesn't work unless you check it periodically. Assign someone from your business to check any generic e-mail accounts you create to receive general inquiries, such as info@mycompany.com.

Receiving Notification of New E-Mail

Gmail comes with a wide selection of basic tools for sending and receiving e-mail. But one basic feature it's missing is a notification feature. If you receive e-mail in your Gmail inbox you have no way of knowing it's there unless you check the inbox visually. With other programs like Outlook Express or Thunderbird, you are notified of new e-mail by an envelope icon that appears in your Windows system tray. Gmail also has a notification utility; it's called the Notifier, and you have to install it separately after you have Gmail up and running. Follow these steps:

1. Go to the Gmail Notifier for Windows home page (http://toolbar.google.com/gmail-helper/notifier_windows.html). A version for Mac users is available at http://toolbar.google.com/gmail-helper/notifier_mac.html.

2. Click the Download Gmail Notifier for Windows button. When prompted, save the file on your desktop and then double-click the file to open it.

3. Follow the steps involved in subsequent screens to accept the license agreement and install the software. When you're done, a Gmail Notifier Setup dialog box appears, prompting you to log in with your Gmail username and password.

Once you have logged in, the Notifier starts working immediately: you see an envelope icon in your system tray if you have unread e-mail in your inbox. In addition, a popup window appears above the system tray notifying you of the subject line of any unread e-mail messages. (If you have multiple unread messages, the popup window appears, sinks back into the system tray, and then pops up again with a new e-mail message subject line, and repeats this action until you have been notified of all your unread e-mail.)

If you ever need to uninstall the Notifier, open your Control Panel, double-click Add or Remove Programs, highlight the Notifier in your list of applications, and click Remove.

Sending E-Mail

Responding or sending email in Gmail is slightly different from sending e-mail with other providers. Because e-mail exchanges are organized as conversations, it is somewhat redundant to include text from an e-mail in your response, although, as described later in this chapter, many still consider it a courtesy—especially if they are using another e-mail service that does not organize sets of messages as Gmail does. Secondly, it is important to always keep track of who, exactly, you are responding to, especially when multiple parties are communicating through the same conversation. I once had a somewhat awkward moment when I responded to a conversation with a message that was intended for everyone present . . . except for the original sender. Once you have typed your message, it's a good idea to read it over or click the Check Spelling icon at the top of the message window. When you're ready, click the Send button to send your message on its way.

When adding text in the text editor, you have several tools familiar to anyone who's used a word processing program. You can add bold, underline, italicize, change font size, type, color, highlight, add links, bullet, number, indent, change alignment, remove formatting, and check spelling.

Learning E-Mail Lingo

In order to use e-mail successfully on the Internet to help your small business, you have to figure out how to speak the language. This applies whether you use Gmail or any other e-mail software. If you use e-mail long enough, it begins to seem like a world unto itself, where people you only know by their first names or e-mail addresses throw around strange terms like these:

- *Flaming*—The exchange of hostile and/or humorous disparaging remarks via email or forum. Flaming can also be image-based (in other words, individuals have been known to embed offensive images in e-mails), and on many forums, the practice has been elevated to surprisingly creative heights.
- *Spam*—Electronic spam takes its name from a Monty Python sketch where the lunch meat, Spam, constitutes everything the eye can see. In email terms, spam thus refers to the unavoidable and constant bombardment of unwanted solicitation that has become de rigueur for any email account.

- *Phishing* —The practice of sending fraudulent e-mail designed to induce the recipient to give out personal information such as credit card numbers.
- *SMTP*—Simple Mail Transfer Protocol, which performs the task of delivering e-mail to the address you have specified.
- *POP*—Post Office Protocol, version 3 (POP3), which allows a mail server to retrieve and route incoming e-mail messages.
- *IMAP4*—Internet Message Access Protocol, version 4, which allows you to manage your e-mail messages when you're traveling and not at your own computer. Because IMAP stores your old as well as new messages on your e-mail server, you can view them all from any location, even if you downloaded and read them previously on your main computer. You can leave your messages on a mail server and organize them into folders without having to download the mail to your computer.
- *LDAP*—Stands for Lightweight Directory Access Protocol, which enables you to access individuals listed in a White Pages address book.
- *Digest*—The distribution of electronic mailing lists where multiple messages are amalgamated and distributed together as a single unit. In other words, instead of receiving 6, 8, 10, or more messages throughout the day from list members, you receive a single message at the end of the day. That single message, called a digest, contains all of that day's individual messages within it.
- *Mailing List*—A series of e-mail messages circulated between subscribers who discuss topics of common interest.
- *Signature File*—A bit of text, or possibly an image, that a user places at the bottom of all e-mails he or she sends.

Remember that many of the individuals with whom you correspond have been on the Net for many years. In order to create a good impression, take a few minutes to understand the language and workings of e-mail so you, too, can talk about sig files and digests and sound like an expert.

Quoting a Previous Message

When you respond to an e-mail message, it's considered courteous to quote some of the original message you received. You don't have to do this every time you reply, but it can be a nice extra touch. This reminds the sender what he or she was talking about in the first place, and it can be helpful if some time has passed between the time the original message was sent and your reply.

Gmail handles quoting differently than most other e-mail programs. It automatically provides you with a running record of previous back and forth messages, which are presented above the text box where you type your new message. The series of messages appear if you are replying to a previous message or if someone is replying to *your* previous e-mail. An example is shown in Figure 9-2. The previous message from my friend Jim Netter appears above the text box where I can type my reply. It also appears below the message you type so you can see it easily.

You can, however, manually format text as a quote. If you click Compose Mail to begin a new message rather than replying to one, you can cut and paste some previous text into the message entry box. Select the text to highlight it, and then click the Quote text button (the one that looks like a set of quotation marks) in the toolbar to format it as a quote. When you click the button, the text is indented to the right, and a gray vertical line appears in the left margin next to all of the lines you selected. The gray lines mark the selected text as a quote. The toolbar only appears when you actually click in the message entry box so you can type your reply.

Forwarding Your Outgoing E-Mail

Any e-mail program enables you to forward a message you receive so that someone else can read it. The only confusing thing with Gmail is that, when you forward the

Figure 9-2. Gmail automatically quotes previous messages when you type a reply.

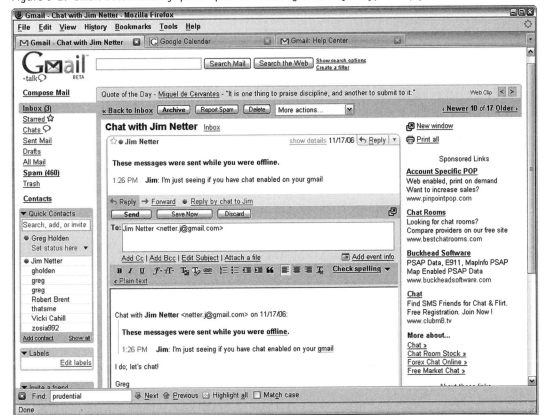

message, the text of the message you're sending does not appear in the message composition window. Instead, the forwarded message is sent as an attachment and you type a message in the composition window that enables the recipient to know what you're sending: "I'm forwarding this message I received from the Human Resources Dept.," and so on. When the recipient receives the forwarded message, the series of e-mail exchanges appears beneath the most recent one.

To forward an outgoing e-mail message, first click anywhere in the message's title line in your Inbox to open the message. Choose the down arrow next to the Reply label in the upper right-hand corner of the message window (see Figure 9-3). It's one of the options in the drop-down list that appears (the others are Reply to all; Print; Add [Sender] to contacts list; Delete this Message; Report Phishing; Show Original; and Message Text Garbled.

 Tip: Choose the last option, Message Text Garbled, if the message you have received contains foreign characters or others that don't

Figure 9-3. You can forward or print a message by accessing this drop-down list.

Search Mail   Search the Web   Show search options
Create a filter

inks six-year, $48M deal with Texans · 2 hour ago   Web Clip

Archive   Report Spam   Delete   More actions...   ‹ Newer 6 of 17 Older ›

for Your Domain for newcorgroup.com beta tester   New window
Print all

Team <apps-noreply@google.com> show details 12/28/06   Reply

gle Apps for Your Domain!

help you offer email accounts and other comm

has been automatically accepted for this ser
w administrative account for your domain -- so
up.com. This admin account gives you acces
nel (https://www.google.com/a/newcorgroup.c
ild log in to the control panel to set up your us
activate those services. The control panel also lets you add additional
adjust a variety of domain settings. If you get stuck, you can always
enter (https://www.google.com/support/a).

Previous   Highlight all   Match case

Reply to all
Forward
Print
Add Google to Contacts list
Delete this message
Report phishing
Show original
Message text garbled?

Sponsored Links

Provisioning Made Simple
The only Provisioning solution you can install and implement yourself.
www.FischerInternational.com

Free CRM Evaluation Guide
Get 100+ Questions CRM Consultants Get Paid To Ask
Entellium.com

Enterprise Desktop Mgmt
Remote Config, Desktop Sharing, S/W Installation, AD Reports, &

display correctly. Choose Report Phishing if you receive an e-mail message in which someone attempts to solicit personal information from you; a dialog box appears that prompts you to report the message to Google.

Attaching a File

Attaching a file to an e-mail message is a quick and convenient way to transmit information from place to place, and it's one of the more useful things you can do with e-mail. Attaching means that you send a document or file as part of an e-mail message. Attaching a document enables you to include material from any file on your hard disk. Attached files appear as separate documents that the recipient can download to his or computer.

You can attach as many files as you want (up to approximately 6 to 10 megabytes, depending on the file type). If you are exceeding the permissible size, Gmail will warn you that the email might not be successfully sent. Even MP3's can be attached and played from an attachment using Gmail's built-in Flash player. This requires you to have Adobe Flash Player installed on your computer, which can be obtained at: http://www.adobe.com/shockwave/download/download.cgi?P1_Prod_Version = ShockwaveFlash

Using Bcc and Cc

Google makes it easy to send mass emails in confidence by providing separate fields for listing recipient addresses, carbon or courtesy copy (Cc) addresses, and blind carbon copy (Bcc) addresses. Typically, the Cc field is used to include the email addresses of recipients who are not expected to respond, such as a supervisor who merely needs confirmation that the email was sent. Any email addresses entered in the Bcc field will not be visible to other recipients. There are many instances where this would be appropriate, such as when you are sending out a newsletter to a list of unrelated clients whose email addresses should not be mutually disclosed.

Creating a Gmail Mailing List

E-mail also gives you a way to access one of the Internet's great resources: mailing lists, which are self-selected groups of individuals who are interested enough in a topic to want to discuss it with others on their computers. Participating in existing mailing lists can help you research your market; starting your own mailing list can help you become an Internet resource and boost your credibility and marketability.

Gmail calls a mailing list a Contact Group. By gathering a set of contacts into a single group, you can quickly send messages to a number of people at once. Here's how to create a Contact Group:

1. Log in to Gmail and click Contacts in the set of links on the left side of a Gmail page.
2. Click the Groups link, and click the Add a Group link.
3. Type a name for your contact group in the Group name field.
4. Type the contacts you'd like to include in the Group in the Add contacts field. Use a comma to separate each address. Gmail's auto-complete feature suggests addresses from your Contacts list as you type (see Figure 9-4).
5. Click the Create Group button.

Setting Up a Signature File

A signature file, commonly called a sig file, is a useful tool for marketing with e-mail on the Internet. The sig file is a text file that's automatically appended to the bottom

Figure 9-4. Gmail suggests names from your Contacts list as you enter them to a group.

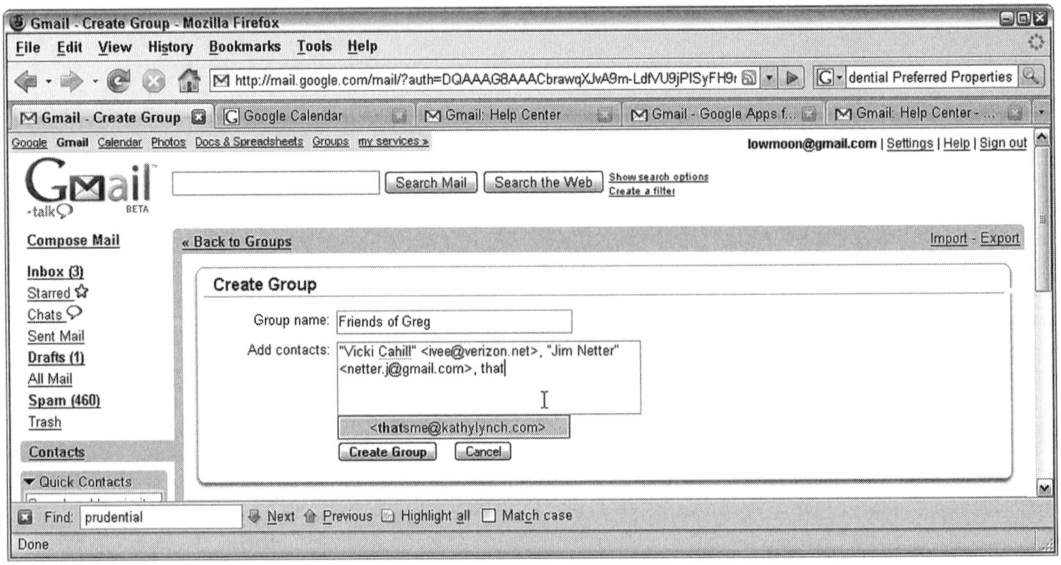

of your e-mail messages and newsgroup postings. It tells the recipient(s) who you are, where you work, and how to contact you. Gmail gives you the ability to create a signature file that it automatically adds to all of your outgoing messages:

1. Open your Inbox page, and click Settings near the top-right of the page.

2. In the Settings page, click the General link if needed and scroll down to the Signature section shown in Figure 9-5.

3. Click on the button next to the empty box in the Signature section. Then type the signature as you want it to appear in the field box.

4. Click the Save Changes button when you are done.

If you change your mind later and don't want to use your signature file, click No Signature.

Figure 9-5. Gmail can automatically add your signature file to yur outgoing messages.

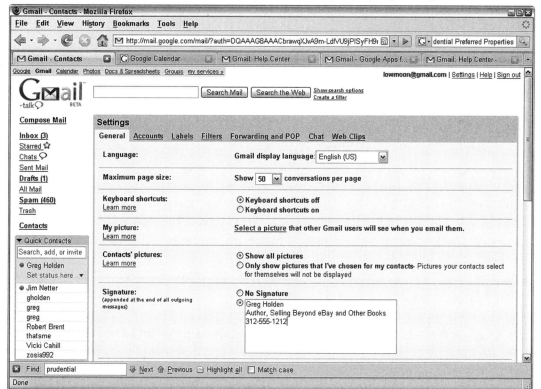

Setting Up Gmail for Your Office

The many services to which you gain when you obtain a Gmail account make Google's e-mail application is a powerful and versatile tool for setting up an office environment. Simply have each employee set up a Gmail account for work purposes, plus a common Gmail account for your office, and before you know it, you essentially have an office intranet system set up on Google's servers. You can have documents uploaded to the Docs & Spreadsheets interface for the common Gmail account, which can be accessed by multiple computers at once, essentially creating an online workspace for you and your coworkers. (See Chapter 7 for more on Docs & Spreadsheets.)

Since the Google Talk chat option is built right in to Gmail, you can also communicate instantaneously with others in your office, or even with coworkers who are in remote locations. Facilitating interoffice communication will help you to foster and maintain an organized business structure, and with Gmail, you can take advantage of these features for free.

Filtering Your E-Mail

Gmail has many of the advanced features that business users like, including the ability to automate e-mail handling by setting up filters. Filters are sets of rules that enable an e-mail program to recognize particular types of e-mail and automatically file, delete, or otherwise handle them. A rule is a directive that you give to your computer, as though you're giving instructions to an assistant. Basically, you're telling your e-mail program, "If you get mail from the president of the company, file it in the folder called Jones." Another kind of filter, called a "bozo filter," is a set of rules that automatically recognizes and deletes e-mail coming from someone you just don't want to hear from (such as, a "bozo").

To create a filter, click the Create a Filter link at the top of your Gmail page. It's to the right of the "Search the Web" button if you can't find it. The Gmail page refreshes and a gold box labeled Create a Filter appears at the top (see Figure 9-6). Then follow these steps:

1. The Create a Filter box contains options that Gmail uses to recognize the mail you want to handle. Choose the box that enables you to specify what part of the incoming message you want Gmail to recognize:
   • If you want Gmail to act on the name of a particular sender, fill in the name, or just the first or last name, in the From box.

Figure 9-6. You can filter e-mail messages using these options.

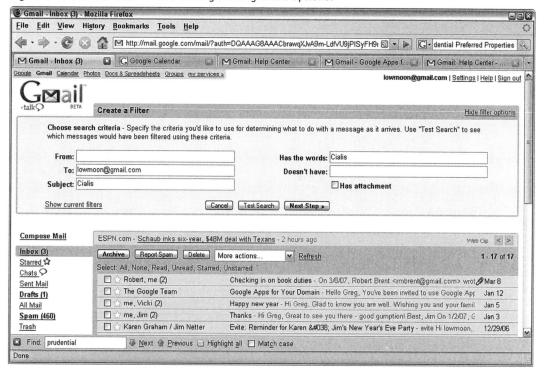

- In the To line, you might want to enter a name that spam mail senders use to send you mail.
- If you want Gmail to recognize a word in the subject box of the e-mail messages, enter that word (or a phrase) in the Subject box.
- If you want Gmail to match a word or phrase in the body of the e-mail message, enter it in the box labeled Has the words.
- If you want Gmail to match a word or phrase that is not present in the body of the e-mail message, enter it in the box labeled Doesn't have. So this would prevent you from getting e-mails that contained a certain term.

 Note: The Doesn't have box will match most, if not all, of your e-mails unless you enter some very non-specific text. Doesn't have is best used in conjunction with other filtering criteria in order to narrow down the results. For instance, you might want to filter all messages that contain the word "Viagra" in the subject line. On the odd chance that someone is sending you a legitimate e-mail message about Viagra, you might want to add a word such as "pharmacy" in the Doesn't have box. You would, of course, filter any legitimate messages you received about Viagra—but you could retrieve them from the folder you designate to store them.

2. Click Test Search to test the effectiveness of your filtering criteria. Gmail will search your incoming messages on a test basis so you can see how many were filtered out.

3. When you're done, click the Next Step button. A set of possible actions Gmail can perform on the filtered messages appears in the Create a Filter box (see Figure 9-7):

   • Skip the Inbox is a good choice for spam. It routes spam away from your Inbox and places it in Gmail's archive area. You can review it later and throw it out if you wish. Star it is a good choice for mail that is the opposite of spam—in other words, mail you have been waiting for and that you need to read immediately.

   • The Apply the label option lets you mark the message with a label so you

Figure 9-7. Choose one of these actions for the messages you want to filter.

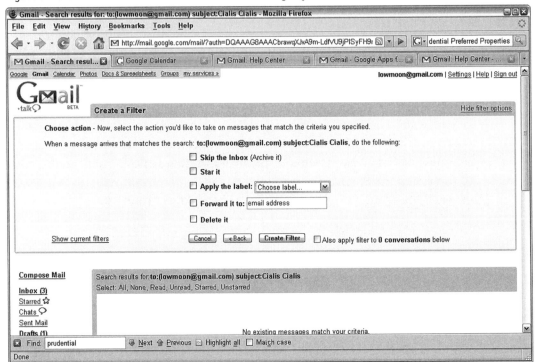

know something about it just from seeing the subject line in the Gmail inbox. Once you have created a label, it appears next to the subject of the message. You have to create your own custom labels. You might create designations such as Urgent, Office, Financial, or Personal, for instance. To create a label, choose New label from the Apply the label drop-down list. When the Explorer User Prompt dialog box shown in Figure 9-8 appears, enter the label you want to create, and then click the OK button.

- Enter an e-mail address in the "Forward it to" box if you want to automatically route filtered e-mail to another e-mail address. A message about technical issues might go automatically to your technical support staff person, for instance.
- Delete it. This option is likely to be a frequently used one if you are trying to filter out spam.

4. Click Create Filter. The page refreshes, and you see the criteria that you have applied to your filter. You also see labels you have created in the Labels box on the left-hand side of the Gmail window (see Figure 9-9).

You don't always need to filter out unwanted e-mail. For instance, if you want to filter any messages from your CEO Mr. Smith, you may enter the word Smith in the From box. Simply specifying Smith rather than Chairman Smith or Peter B. Smith makes it more likely that you will match all the e-mail you receive from Chairman Smith, unless you know the exact form of the name that appears in the *From:* field in all of Chairman Smith's e-mail messages.

Administering Your Gmail Account

One way you can manage the messages you receive with Gmail is the fact that you can check a message and click "Report Spam" above the inbox interface, and the

Figure 9-8. You can create custom labels to mark incoming mail that matches your filtering criteria.

Figure 9-9. Filters you create are listed in the Settings screen, where you can edit them if needed.

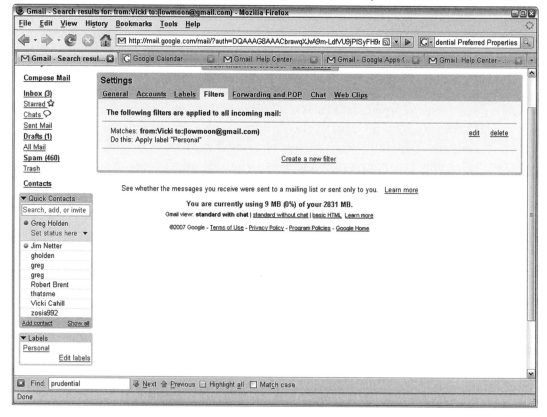

reported sender will never be viewed again in your inbox. If your curiosity gets the better of you, however, you can always scroll through the sometimes humorous emails that were filtered out under the "Spam" link on the left-hand side. With Gmail, you can report an unlimited number of messages. You can also remove emails from the Spam folder, or delete them forever if you wish.

Archiving Your E-Mail

If you don't have the time (or the desire) to read an email right when it arrives, you can archive it for later, or apply a label (labels are displayed at the bottom of the toolbar on the left-hand side) and go to that label when you you're in the mood. Gmail will remind you which labels contain unread emails by emboldening the text with the number of unread messages noted in parentheses next to the label name.

Adjusting Your E-Mail Settings

Gmail enables you to personalize your inbox and tailor it to your own personal specifications. Just click on "Settings" in the upper right-hand corner of your Inbox, and you'll be taken to a screen offering a host of options and modifications for you to choose from. There are seven Settings categories to choose from, listed at the top of the interface.

- *General*—This setting lets you set up the basic elements of your Gmail account the way you want them. Here you are able to add a Signature to outgoing emails, turn on or off a Vacation Responder, which notifies senders if you are not available, among other things. This is also where you can navigate to or Gmail for mobile devices download so you can use Gmail on your Web-enabled cell phone or handheld device.

- *Accounts*—Here you can add another email address, get mail from other accounts, or change your security question and password.

- *Labels*—This setting allows you to rename or remove a label from among the labels you have applied to certain emails.

- *Filters*—This is where you edit pre-existing filters or create new ones.

- *Forwarding and POP*—Here you can choose your Forwarding and POP settings. If you want more information about how POP works, Gmail has links to help pages showing you how to configure POP and where to download it.

- *Chat*—This option lets you specify your Chat settings. You can choose whether or not to save your chat history, how many contacts will be shown on your page at once, turning sounds on and off, etc.

- *Web Clips*—If you decide you want clips of information from selected web sites to appear above your inbox, you can set it up right here. Gmail lets you choose which sites you want to receive clips from, or lets you browse sites by subject in case you see something of interest to you.

CHAPTER **10**

Google Talk

Instant communications is an integral part of business these days. Just think about how much time you spend on the phone with your boss, your coworkers, or other business partners. You need to be able to reach people at a moment's notice. That need stretches from the business area into your personal life, too. If you're going to be working late and can't pick your daughter up at karate class, you need to know where your child is and to give them a message that lets them know what's going on.

When a cell phone isn't suitable, for instance, because it's too expensive to make a long-distance call, or because you're in a place like the library and can't talk on the phone, and need to talk something over with one of your colleagues, you can type an instant message. Google is getting into the field of instant communications with Google Talk, an instant messaging service that you can use through Gmail, sign up for on a standalone basis, or obtain through the Google Apps package of business services. Chatting and instant messaging aren't always regarded as business tools. But in order to connect with colleagues in a timely way and in the way they like to communicate, you need to take advantage of all the options you have. Google Talk gives you another way to keep the lines of communications open.

How Can Google Talk Help Your Business?

Google Talk isn't just a supplement to phones and e-mail. It's also a way to save money. Like most of the other Google services described in this book, it's free. You can install it on each of your employees' computers and get them typing messages to one another quickly and without incurring any expense at all. And if you run up costly long-distance phone bills with international calling, you can opt to exchange chat messages with Google Talk instead. Since you're using the Internet to communicate, you don't pay anything more than you already do for Internet access. And you "converse" almost as fast as you would on the phone.

Not only that, but Google Talk can be used for an increasingly popular technology called Voice over IP, also known as Internet phone service. Programs like Skype and Vonage let you use your computer as a telephone; with a microphone and (optionally) a headset, you can literally speak (yes, I mean really speak with your actual voice, the old-fashioned way!) over your computer using Google Talk. Why use your computer as a phone when you already have lots of phones at hand? The answer is in your pocketbook. Programs like Google Talk enable you to talk to someone across the country or across the globe without spending a dime.

 There's one caveat to all the good news about Google Talk. You can only use it to type messages or carry on voice conversations with other individuals who use Google Talk. At the time this was written, you couldn't use the service to communicate with members of the other free Voice Over IP services, like Skype, for instance.

Getting Started with Google Talk

If you sign up for Google Apps as described in Chapter 6, you already have access to Google Talk. You go to your domain's start page and click Add Stuff on the right side of the page. When the list of utilities under the heading Add stuff to your homepage appears, click the Add it now button under Google talk. The Add it now button changes to Added. Click the Back to homepage link near the top of the page. The Google Talk gadget appears in the middle of the page. Click Sign in, and you can start sending and receiving messages.

When you go to Google Talk's home page on the Web (http://www.google.com/talk), you discover that Google Talk is available in two forms: either as a standalone application called the Google Talk Client, or as a Google Talk Gadget that you add to your personalized Google home page. The gadget is software that becomes part of your home page and that enables you to contact anyone who also uses Google Talk instantly.

The Google Talk Client is a standalone version of Talk that functions independently of your Web browser and that you can open at any time. It functions in much the same way as other IM clients, except that it also allows the archiving of chats into Gmail, organizes Gmail contacts as Talk contacts, offers PC-to-PC voice calls with the sending and receiving of voicemails as well as high-yield file or folder transfers. If you plan to use Google Talk frequently or at least on a regular basis, download the more robust client version instead of the gadget. The client is also useful if you use Google Talk for business purposes and you need to have a record of chat sessions that you can refer to later on.

Obtaining the Client

If you sign up for Google Talk all by itself, you need to download software that lets you type instant messages and make Internet phone calls on your computer; that's different than other Google services like Docs & Spreadsheets or Gmail, which are up and running on the Web as soon as you complete the signup process.

Once you are on the Google Talk page, click the Download Google Talk Client link to start the registration and download procedure. The process at that point is similar to one you've probably followed when you have installed other applications: You download the file, double-click the file once it's complete, and install it on your computer. But since Google Talk is also available as a "gadget" you can add to your Google home page or as a built-in part of the Gmail interface, you might want to explore one of those other options first before you go through the "old-fashioned" steps involved in downloading and installing software. And you can always use both the client and the gadget if you want to.

 Note: Google Talk works with most browsers and will work on Mac, Linux, and Windows systems. However, it does require that you have a plug-in application called Flash Player installed so your browser can process Flash animated content. If you don't have Flash installed, Google Talk will prompt you to download it; otherwise, you can find the free Flash player on the Adobe Systems Web site (http://www.adobe.com/ products/flashplayer).

Obtaining the Gadget

Having a Google Talk section added to your home page lets you know who's online in case you need to reach them quickly. And the Google Talk gadget, like Google's other services, has the advantage of being accessible from any computer that has access to the Internet. In contrast, the client has additional features but is only accessible on the computer on which it's been installed. The steps presented earlier in this chapter for adding the gadget to your start page are quick and easy. If you aren't on your start page and you want an alternate way to download and install the gadget version of Google Talk, you can also follow these steps:

1. Go to http://www.google.com/talk.

2. Click the "Launch Google Talk" button.

3. If you are already signed in, Google Talk launches immediately in a separate mini-browser window. If not, click Sign in. Enter your information, click Sign in, and the Google Talk gadget opens in its own window so you can start using it immediately. On the other hand, if you don't have a Google Talk account, click Create an account now and follow the steps below.

4. When the Welcome to Google Talk page shown in Figure 10-1 appears, enter your Google account information in the top half of the page. Then, in the bottom half, enter a username by which you want to be seen on the network. Click Check Availability to verify that the name you want isn't already being used by someone else. If it is, you'll need to obtain a new one.

Optionally, specify your first and last name, fill out the rest of the form, and click I accept. Create my account. The gadget is added to your home page.

It's nice to know, the moment you sit down at your computer, who's online and available to "talk" if you need to discuss business right away, and the Google Talk Gadget gives you a way to do so. You can type your message right in your home page (see Figure 10-2).

Figure 10-1. You need to choose a unique screen name for use with Google Talk.

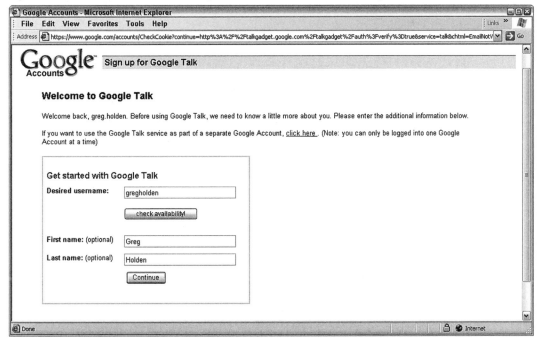

Figure 10-2. The Google Talk Gadget.

Each user who has an account in a Google Apps domain needs to add the gadget or the client separately in order to use it. If you log in as the administrator for your domain and you install the client, only you can use the client (unless you let someone else use your computer and you give them your login information, which isn't a good administrative practice). If you install the gadget for your home page, you'll have access to the gadget when you log in. But those who log in with a different account see a different start page and will have to install the gadget separately in order to use it.

 Tip: If you want to add some functionality to your Web site and give any visitors the chance to chat with you or other Google users directly from within one of your site's Web pages, you can add the Google Talk gadget to that page. You might want to add the chat gadget to a customer service page; that way if someone has a question and already has a Google Talk account, you give them the ability to type messages to you immediately. To add the gadget to an existing web page, you need to copy and paste a line of code into your site's HTML. You'll find a link to the code in the Google Talk page on the right side of the page just click on the "Get the code here" hyperlink.

Downloading the Google Talk Client

If you want to use the standalone version of Google Talk and you don't already have access to it, go to the Google Talk home page and click the link Download the Google Talk client. Then follow these steps:

1. When a dialog box appears, asking if you want to install a small setup file, click the Run button.

2. You may see a second dialog box entitled Security warning, which asks you to confirm that you want to download the software. Click Run.

3. When the license agreement dialog box appears, click I Agree to install the software.

4. When downloading is complete, click Finish. The Google Talk window opens, looking much like any other IM client (see Figure 10-3). When you are prompted to sign in with your username and password, type your Google Account e-mail address and password to start using the program.

Instant Messaging with Google Talk

The Google Talk interface is quite intuitive, and carrying out a typed conversation with someone else is a process you'll get used to right away. When you first open the client, you see two buttons at the bottom of the Google Talk window: Add and View. Click Add and type the e-mail address of someone you know who has Google Talk and who might want to exchange chat messages with you.

When someone you have added as a contact is online and you invite that person to chat, a new tab opens in the Google Talk window. Click the tab, and you're in the chat session with that person. Type your message in the box at the bottom of the

Figure 10-3. Google Talk looks and works like other well-known IM clients.

window and press Enter when you're done. The message appears in the main body of the Google Talk window so you can see what you've typed. In a few seconds, the other person's message will appear beneath yours. You can then type a new message and before you know it, you're carrying on an online conversation.

 Tip: Google Talk is a great alternative to e-mail or the phone. While I was working on this chapter, I ran into some problems talking to my assistant: I was unable to log on to Google because of a password problem (see Chapter 3). And when I talked on my cordless phone, it interfered with my laptop's wireless connection. Google Talk solved the problem: I was able to talk to the person I needed to connect with, without being knocked offline or having to overcome my e-mail problem.

Inviting Someone to Talk

If you see that one of your contacts is online, you can invite that person to chat by simply clicking the Add button. When the Invite someone to chat dialog box shown in Figure 10-4 appears, type the individual's e-mail address in the box shown and then click Next. When another dialog box appears informing you that the individual has been invited, click Finish. The e-mail address you just typed is added to the Google Talk window.

Before you can chat with someone, you have to invite them.

 Note: One thing you can't do with Google Talk that you can with other chat clients is adjust the font size and font choices. Changing the font size and type can make messages more readable, at least for those who are getting to be of "a certain age." At least, you couldn't do that kind of formatting at the time this was written.

Settling into the Rhythm of Chat

If you're using Google Talk for the first time and you don't have a lot of experience with chat, you quickly discover some things about carrying on a conversation with

Figure 10-4. Before you can chat with someone, you have to invite them.

Invite your friends to Google Talk

Google **talk** BETA   **Talk to more of your friends for free**

Send an invitation to the people you'd like to talk to for free. Once they accept and download Google Talk, you'll be able to talk to them immediately.

Pick from your list of contacts, or enter an email address directly. To add more than one person at a time, separate the addresses with a comma.

    user@gmail.com

[Choose from my contacts...]

[Next >>]   [Cancel]

someone else. If someone else is a lightning-fast typist (like me) and your chat "correspondent" is slower, you can easily flood the other person with words and make it that much more difficult for him or her to respond to what you're saying: you have already typed three separate comments, and the other person has yet to address the first topic you raised. It's important to wait and catch your breath. Google Talk gives you some help in this regard. When the other person is typing a message to you, the application will provide you with a message to that affect (see Figure 10-5).

If you see the "typing message" or "[username] has entered text," you might want to wait to see what the other person has to say. You don't have to do this, however. If you are in a hurry to get your thoughts out you can type them and press Enter. A second comment that is added to the chat session after the first is indented so everyone can see that it's separate from the preceding comment.

Another nice Google Talk feature is the ability to embed hyperlinks within a chat. You don't have to do anything to format a hyperlink; Google Talk recognizes the link based on the format of the text you have typed and turns it into a clickable link automatically (see Figure 10-6). When you click the link, a new default browser window opens and you go to the site referenced by that link.

Figure 10-5. Google Talk tells you when someone else is typing a message to you.

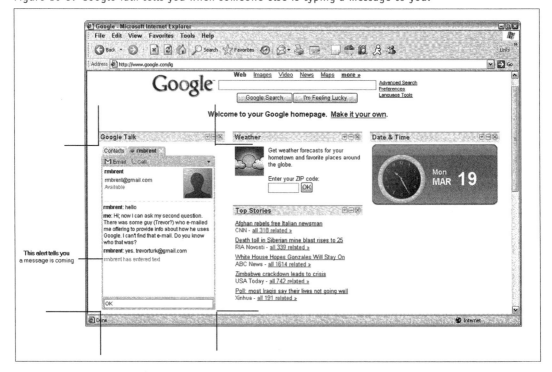

Figure 10-6. Google Talk automatically formats hypertext links so chat participants can follow them.

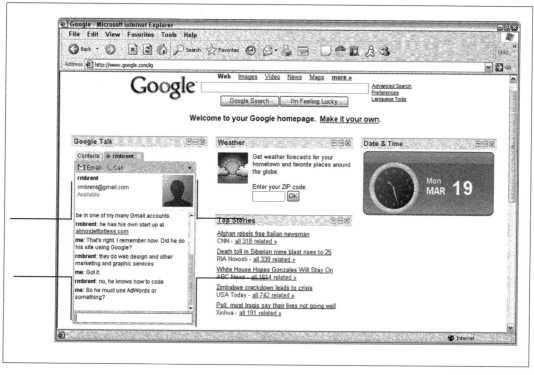

Letting Google Talk Alert You

One nice thing about Google Talk is that it gives you the chance to do "multitasking," to borrow a computer term. While you're chatting, and after you submit a comment, you can switch to another window to look at a Web page you're discussing. Or you can grab a cup of coffee, as long as you don't leave your fellow chat participant waiting for more than a minute or two.

Normally, when Google Talk is the application on top of the current page, you don't hear any sound to alert you when someone types you a message. But when you open another application or put a separate program window on top of the window that contains Google Talk, the program emits a chime to let you know a message has come in. Not only that, but a message appears in the title bar of the Google Talk window (see Figure 10-7).

 Note: In order to hear Google Talk chime, you need to have your computer's sound turned on (not on Mute) and you need to have the volume

Figure 10-7. If you're doing something else and you receive a message, you hear a sound, and see this alert.

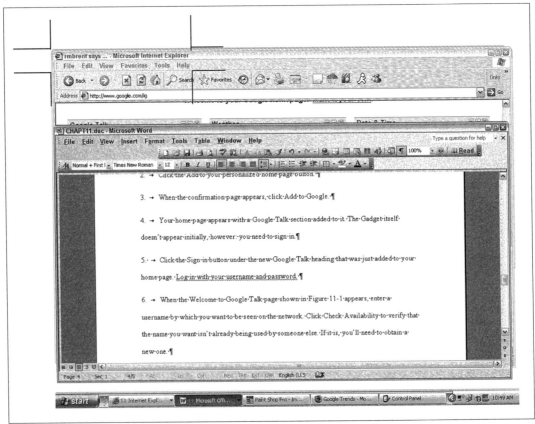

turned up. The sound might be different than a chime depending on your system's alert sounds configuration.

Signing Out

When you're done talking with someone and if you're going to be away from your computer for a while, it's a good idea to sign out from Google Talk. If you leave your office and are still signed in to Google Talk, someone could try to connect to you, only to discover that you're not really online when no one responds.

When you need to sign out, do one of the following:

- If you're using the Gadget form of Google Talk, select Sign out of chat from the drop-down menu next to "Available" under your name. After signing out, a gray ball will appear next to your name in your friends' Friends lists to let them know you aren't available to talk.

- If you're using the Client version of Google Talk, click the down arrow next to Available, which is just above the window where your contacts are listed and where messages appear. Choose Sign Out from the drop-down list.

Viewing Chat Logs

Most personal chat sessions are ultimately forgettable. You don't need a written record of what you and your friends said to one another (nor would you want one). But if you use Google Talk for any kind of business-related communication, chat logs become important. A log file is a record of what took place on a networked hardware or software device.

By default, Google Talk does keep a log file of your chat conversations. The file is recorded in your Gmail account and remains there as long as you have space to store the file. You actually see a message to this effect in the Quick Contacts box in your Gmail message window (see Figure 10-8).

Click the down arrow to the left of Quick Contacts and click on the *recent* conversations link to view past chats. You can also access your previous chats by clicking on the Chats link, which appears beneath the Inbox link on the left side of your Gmail page.

It can also be advantageous not to log your chat sessions, and if you specifically don't want Google Talk to log any chat sessions, you can do so by clicking Settings near the top of the chat window. When the Settings dialog box shown in Figure 10-9 appears, click Chat in the list of topics on the left. Click Don't save chat history in my Gmail account. Then click OK. You should save your chat files in accordance with your organization's e-mail retention policy; check with your network administrator to make sure you should be saving your log, and how long you should keep it.

Tip: If you are in the middle of a chat and you want to say something that is "off the record," you can temporarily suspend logging of your chat comments. This means your chat comments aren't recorded in a log file as you type them so there is no record of what you are saying. Just click the Options button at the bottom of the Google Talk window that you used to access your chat logs. Choose "Go off the record." When you do, the person you're talking to sees a message saying the chat has been taken "off the record." When you're done making your

Figure 10-8. By default, chats are logged as part of your Gmail account.

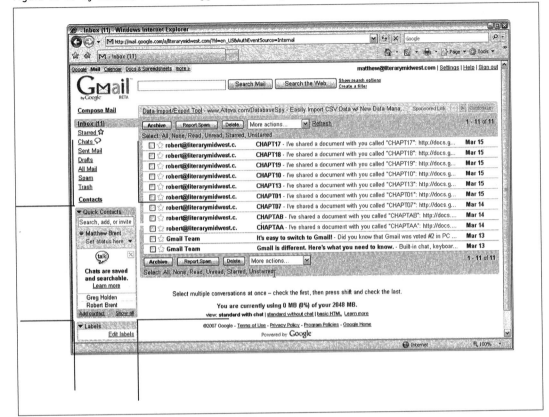

private remarks, click the down arrow again and choose "Stop chatting off the record."

Transferring Files with the Google Talk Client

When you are chatting with someone in a business context and you are collaborating on a project, you may want to send a file, you may want to share a photo or a text file. In either case, click the Send Files button in the Client. The Send Files button only appears in the separate window that opens when you initiate a conversation with someone else. It appears as a down arrow next to the Chat and Call buttons.

 Note: If you don't see a Send Files button when you're chatting with one of your friends, he or she isn't able to receive transferred files. The person

Figure 10-9. Google Talk will log all of your chats until you tell it not to do so.

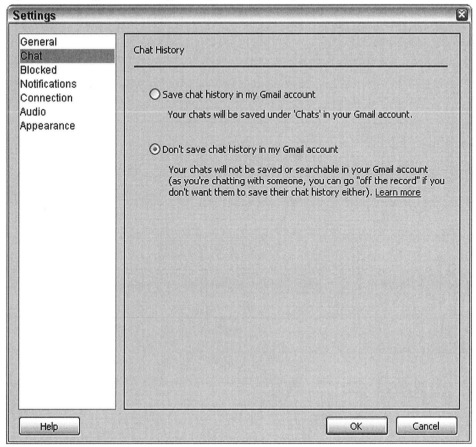

you are chatting with needs to be using the Google Talk client. If you are chatting with someone who is using another chat program or who is using the Google Talk feature available with the Gmail interface, you won't be able to exchange files with that person.

To send a file with Google Talk:

1. From an open Google Talk client chat window (the second window that appears next to the main Google Talk window when you are actually exchanging messages with someone), click the Send Files button.

2. When the standard dialog box for opening files appears, browse to the file or files you'd like to send (use CTRL-Shift to select more than one file at a time).

3. Select the file and click OK. Google Talk will insert your file into the chat session.

4. Once the file is added, you see a button labeled Cancel the transfer. Doing so will withdraw the offer. if you don't, the person with whom you are chatting can click Accept to download the file to their hard drive, or Decline to reject the transfer.

> **Tip:** If you have a list of files open on your computer, you can drag and drop the icon(s) for files and folders into the open chat window to initiate a transfer.

Voice Conversations with Google Talk

Voice over Internet Protocol (also known as Voice over IP) is an increasingly popular alternative to Plain Old Telephone Service (also known as POTS, and also known as traditional "land line" phone service). Instead of picking up the physical phone, dialing a number, and talking to someone, you sit down at your computer, dial a number, and talk using your computer speakers and microphone. Instead of a physical "hardware" phone, in other words, you use Google Talk as a sort of "softphone." Your computer also needs to be equipped with a sound card; if you can already listen to CDs and other audio files through your computer, you've got one.

> **Tip:** If you don't have your own computer headset (a combination microphone and set of earphones that you can use to talk through your computer) you can buy one in Google's online store (http://www.googlestore .com). At this writing the headset was available for $14.50.

The one restriction with Google Talk Voice over IP is that the person you talk to has to use Google Talk; you can't call someone's land line, and you can't call someone with Google Talk who is using another software program.

Once you have your computer set up, sign in to Google Talk. Then locate the person in your Friends list that you'd like to call: you invite them to talk just as you would with a chat session. If the person is online you'll be able to call him or her; pass your mouse pointer over his or her username, and a tab will open up if you're using the Gadget, and a separate window will pop up if you're using the Google Talk client (see Figure 10-10). Click the Call button to call your friend.

Once the person answers, you can start talking. When you're done, click End Call to hang up. If the person doesn't respond, you can leave a voice mail message, which goes into the individual's Gmail account.

This chapter introduced you to a program that gives immediacy to your online communications. if you don't want to talk, or if you want to have a conversation while you're transmitting files you're working on, try Google Talk. As long as the person you're connecting to also has Google Talk, you can chat or talk in real time. One of the most important ways to communicate these days is through the Web, and if you create your own Web page, you reach a potential audience of millions. The next chapter examines Google's service for those who want to create their own Web pages: Google Page Creator.

Figure 10-10. Click call to make a voice call with another Google Talk client.

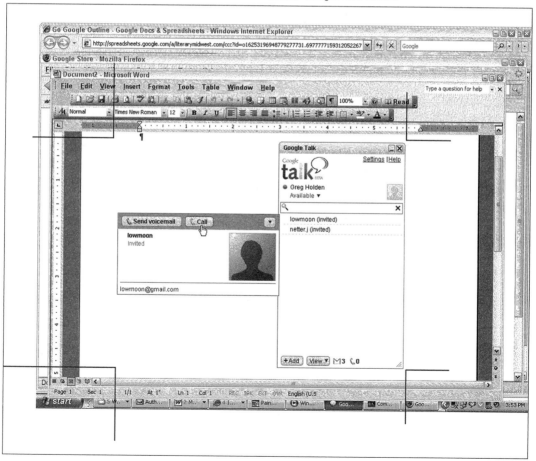

CHAPTER **11**

Publishing with Google Page Creator

When you sign up for a domain with Google Apps, you get your own start page. This page enables the workers in your organization to share files and communicate. But what about interested people who want to find out more about you on the Web? When you obtain a domain name, it makes sense to create a Web page or a full-fledged Web site to accompany it. Designing Web sites can be a technically demanding undertaking. But it doesn't need to be. Page Creator takes the hard steps out of creating a Web site and getting your words and images online. And not only that, it's free not only for Google Apps users but those who have only a Gmail account. The only price you pay for Page Creator is the agreement that you'll display small AdSense advertisements on your pages that have been created by Google. In return, you get a user-friendly interface that lets you assemble Web pages without having to know HTML or other code. You get up to 100MB of Web storage space for images and other files.

When you head to the mall or the department store, you need a list. When you start creating Web pages, a list comes in handy, too. Page Creator makes the mechanics of assembling Web pages so easy that you can focus on planning and architecting your site. In the first part of this chapter, you'll get an itemized list of everything you need to create a basic, professional-quality Web site using Google Page Creator, a service you access as part of Google Apps. Then you'll learn how to actually create the pages with this user-friendly, free tool.

 Note: In Chapter 12, you'll learn about Google's popular AdSense service, which allows you to display ads that are compatible with the content of your page. You have to apply to the AdSense program and be approved before you can start gaining revenue from such ads, however. But one of the big advantages of using Google Page Creator to assemble your site's content is the fact that you are able to display AdSense ads on your pages. The content of the ads is determined by the content of your Web pages. In order to display ads, you have to display "experimental content" on your site. (At the time this was written, AdSense for Page Creator was still considered an "experimental" feature.) Click the Site settings link in the right-hand column of Page Creator and then click the Enable experimental features button.

Mapping Out Your Web Site

Whether you create your site using Page Creator or another piece of Web editing software, it helps to know what your goals are and how your Web site will achieve them. You don't want to get halfway through the process and then have to redo a step or even the whole project Whether you are paying someone to help you create your Web site or pushing the buttons yourself, a checklist gets you to think before you act. The checklist presented in Table 11-1 lays out the steps in the process.

 Note: You've already completed the first couple of steps in the process of setting up a Web site, though you might not even realize it. When you register for Google Apps as described in Chapter 6, you select a domain name. You also obtain a Web hosting service, a company that will provide you with space where you can store your Web pages. That hosting service is Google itself.

Creating a Visual Site Map

When you start planning your site, you probably think first about what you have to talk about or what you want to say. It helps to flip your perspective around and think about your Web site from the end user's perspective. The more text a page contains, the more a reader has to navigate to find a particular bit of information. Each page should address one subject and make its point quickly. It might make sense to have different sections on different pages, like separating chapters in a book, or a list of current projects from a mission statement, for example.

One of the first Web page design issues you need to resolve is how to interlink the various pages in your Web site. Links are the Internet equivalent to roads, with

Table 11-1. Steps to Creating a Web Site

Step	What You Need to Do
Draw up your site's organization	Create a map or list of your home page and the pages within it, showing how they link to one another.
Create your main pages	Start small, with three or four pages that will function as your Web site's core pages.
Create a product catalog if you want to do e-commerce	Once you have your main pages, you can create individual pages to describe any goods or services you offer.
Provide contact information	Create a Google account that visitors can use to contact you, or a Web page with more specific contact information such as phone numbers.
Try out your Web site	Be the first visitor to your site. Test your pages to make sure they load quickly and everything works the way you want.
Spread the word	Use AdWords, the Directory, and search engine optimization to market your Web site.
Create a community	Your site will be really successful if you attract loyal customers, visitors, or clients. Provide them with newsletters or other information and give them a way to talk back through a blog.
Keep your site updated	You'll keep visitors coming back to your site by updating your content periodically.

the text representing the link serving as the road signs. They take the user from one place to another and guide a visitor not only around your Web site, but from your site to related sites, and back again. On the page at http://literarychicago.googlepages .com/, for example, it made sense to list links to the other pages at the bottom of the home page, because I want visitors to read through the content and get to the bottom. But I didn't feel it necessary to have the other pages link to each other because they are about very different subjects. You might prefer to have links at the top if your priority is to steer visitors to the page on your site that interests them the most and you don't mind them leaving your home page quickly.

 Note: By default, Google Page Creator uses not your custom domain name (for instance, mydomain.com) but its own Google-ized domain name (for instance, partnerpage.google.com/mydomain.com). You can access your home page by typing http://www.literarychicago.com in your browser's Address box and pressing Enter, but the URL is redirected to one of Google's URLs (in this case, http://partnerpage.google.com/literarymidwest.com). You can change this, however: open your Dashboard page, click Web Pages, and click the Change URL link next to Web address. On the next page, click the button next to your custom domain name, and then click Continue to return to the Dashboard.

Other issues to consider include the question of whether or not having a home page with virtually no text is appropriate, to the amount of text you choose to include on particular pages, to the font color, background color, and other issues that will affect the overall "feel" of your Web site. The amount of text depends on how important words are to the content you are presenting. If you are presenting a photo album, for instance, little or no words will do just fine. On the other hand, if you are reviewing a book and your audience consists of people who read, a substantial amount of textual content (say, five to ten paragraphs) is appropriate.

Font and background colors depend partly on how you want to portray yourself online, and partly on the age range and interests of your audience. A Web site that is simply intended to attract as wide a range of visitors as possible, from all walks of life, it makes sense to focus on your own favorite colors rather than trying to attract a particular type of person. On the other hand, if your Web site is about your candidacy for political office, patriotic colors like red, white, and blue are an obvious choice. A black background would work for a Gothic rock site or one that talks about ghosts or Halloween customs. High-contrast colors like yellow and green and sans-serif would attract a younger crowd. In other words, try to tailor your site's graphic identity to the kinds of visitors you want to attract, unless you don't have any group in mind, in which case you should choose colors that reflect your own identity or that of your company.

Dividing Your Content into Main Categories

You aren't *required* to divide your site into categories. In fact even if your Google Page Creator Web site only consists of a single page, it has value. You can use that single page to point to your blog, or to a Web site you have already created with another service.

The more links you make to your Web sites, the better your placement will be in Google's search results. My friend Jim Netter has a one-page site that he created with Google Apps (see Figure 11-1). He probably wasn't thinking about search placement

Figure 11-1. A single-page Google Web site has value too.

when he created his page. But he does use it to link to his blog, which is quite entertaining and content rich. The blog page also resembles the Google Apps page in content. It's a good illustration of a way to boost traffic to your home page or another page, like a blog.

Working with Google Page Creator

Google Page Creator is offered free-of-charge to individuals who have a Gmail account or to Google Apps users. What differentiates Google Page Creator from other page-building applications is that Page Creator requires no knowledge of html or other computer coding languages. In fact, Page Creator's interface resembles the layout of a word processor document, and requires no software to be downloaded. Your page will be hosted on Google's servers in the format, http://yourpage.google pages.com. Each Google Web page is allowed the usage of 100 MB for all files and attachments. This is a huge amount of Web server space, considering that the average Web page consumes much less than 1MB, depending on the number of images included with it.

Finding Your Way Around Page Creator

When you sign up for Google Apps, you automatically gain access to Page Creator from your start page. Follow these steps:

1. Log into your Google Apps site, go to your start page, and click Manage this domain. The dashboard page for your domain appears.
2. Click Web pages. The Web pages settings page appears (see Figure 11-2).
3. Click Edit your Web pages to access Page Creator.

You can also go to Page Creator by going to the following URL: http://www.[my domain]-a.googlepages.com

When you click the Edit your Web pages link, the Page Creator opening page shown in Figure 11-3 appears.

Google Page Creator has two main interfaces: the Site Manager interface, where you can view and choose between Google Pages you have created, and the Edit Page, where each page is edited individually. The first page you see after you click the "Edit your Web pages" link on your start page is Site Manager.

Site Manager

The Site Manager lets you manage your Web site as a whole. It allows you to select from among different Web sites you've created using Page Creator (or create a new

Figure 11-2. Use this page to either view your Web pages or edit them.

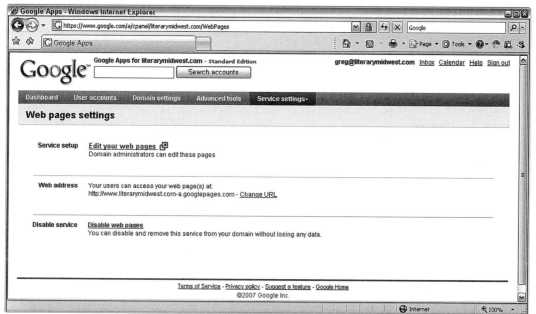

Figure 11-3. You see this simple page when you first access Page Creator.

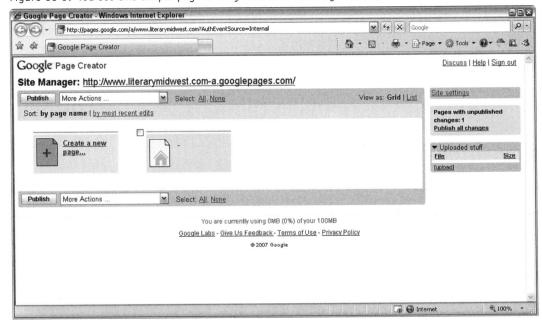

site if you only have one), and perform actions on the pages found within each site by means of easily-navigable drop-down menus. For example, the version of the page shown in Figure 11-4 shows two Web pages as well as the Create a New Page icon. You can either click an icon to edit an existing page or start a new one.

With a simple click, you can choose to publish a page—in other words, make it available for viewing on the Web—delete it, copy it, discard unpublished changes, or even send out an e-mail notifying people of its existence (Page Creator is linked directly to your Gmail account, after all). There is also a link to the Page Creator Help file, and a Discuss link, which directs you to forums created by users, including Google employees themselves, to address problems not covered by the Help file.

Edit Page

Edit Page is accessed from within the Site Manager page by clicking on the icon for the page you want to edit. When you click the icon labeled Create a new page, a box appears that prompts you to enter a title for the page (see Figure 11-5). Click Create and Edit, and you get a predesigned Web page you can edit as you wish.

This page you access resembles a word processor interface, with a column on the left-hand side containing buttons with familiar tools such as font size change, bullet points, or alignment change (see Figure 11-6). What makes Page Creator so user-

Figure 11-4. Site Manager lets you open existing pages or edit new ones.

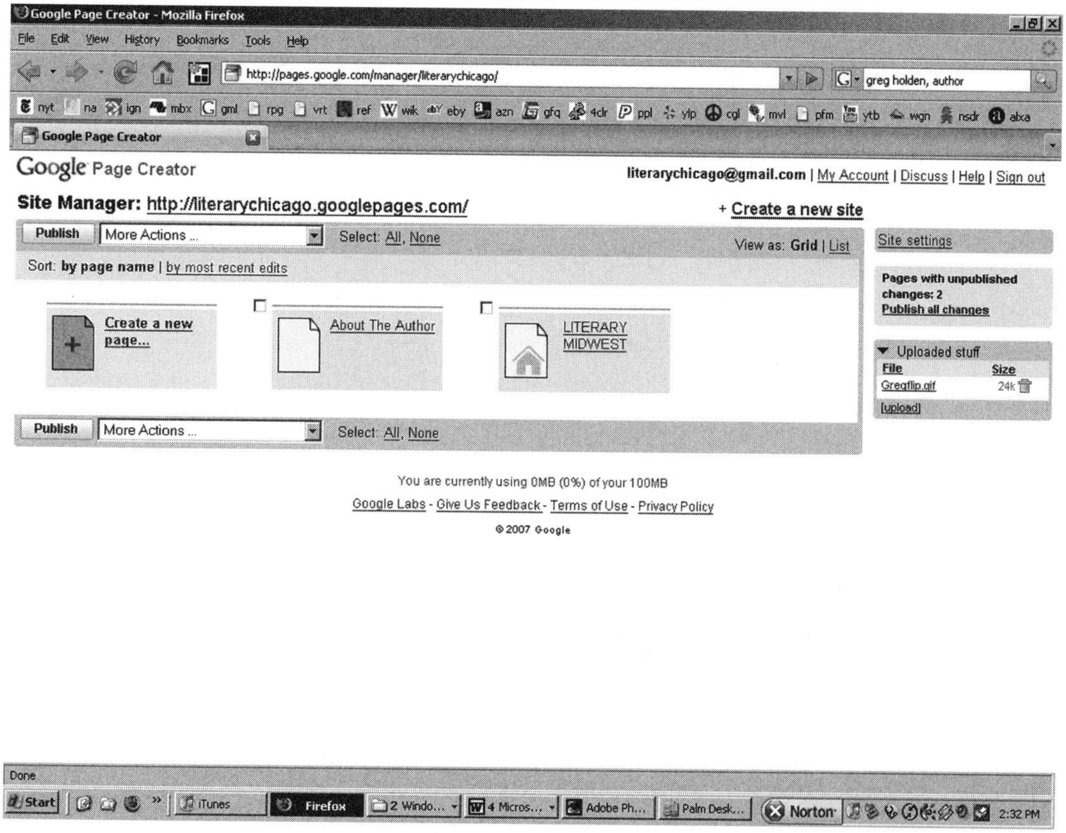

friendly is that you don't need to know any code to create your own Web page; the version you see in the Edit Page is essentially what your finished page will look like.

Choosing a Layout and Graphic Look

You don't have to use the default layout Google suggests for you. You can choose from a selection of preset page layouts. These page arrangements determine how text will be formatted in headers, columns, and main text area. You can always change the page layout by clicking on Change Layout in the upper right-hand side of the page once your page has been created. (You don't see the Change Layout link on the Site Manager page; it only appears when you click on an individual page's name to edit it.) When you do, the Choose Layout page shown in Figure 11-7 appears, with a set of common page arrangements. Double-click one of the arrangements to apply it to the current page. Keep in mind that even if you choose one of the layouts, you can edit it later on (change it to another preset layout or modify the current layout) if it doesn't fit your content needs.

Figure 11-5. Begin by entering a title for your page.

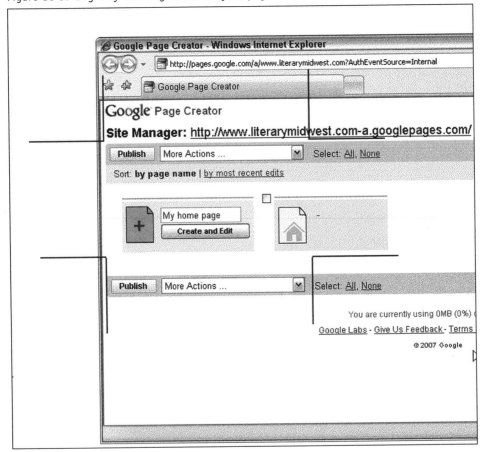

You can also change the graphic look and feel of a page design by clicking the Change Look link. This takes you to the Choose Look page, which is full of 41 different color and type designs for your site. If you want a better look at any of the designs shown in Figure 11-8, you can click the Preview link just beneath its thumbnail image.

Adding New Web Pages

When you are working in Page Editor, you can return to Site Manager at any time by clicking the *Back to Site Manager* link near the top of the page. When you click Back to Site Manager, a small box labeled Saving . . . appears to indicate that any changes you made are being saved. Once there, you can create a new page or a new site. New pages can be added in the Site Manager interface by clicking on the icon labeled

Figure 11-6. You edit your page using this user-friendly interface.

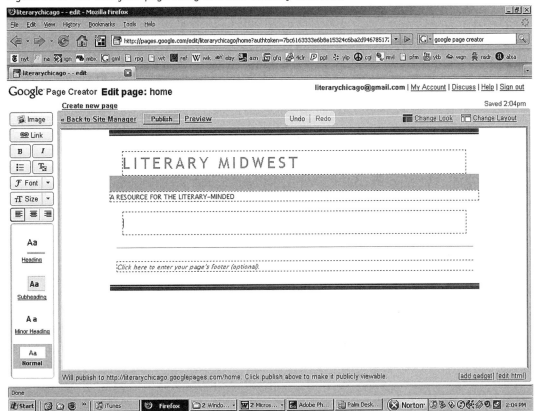

Create a new page. Once the new page is created, it will be displayed alongside the pages you already have.

The tricky thing is that, if you want to actually add the new page to the site, you have to create hyperlinks that join the pages to one another. Otherwise, the new page isn't automatically added to your site. Create a name for your new page, such as Contact Us. Then return to your home page and add the words Contact Us somewhere on the page (a logical location is the footer area near the bottom). Highlight the words by scrolling across them as shown in Figure 11-9.

Then click the Link button on the top left side of the Page Editor. When the Link box shown in Figure 11-10 appears, you can make a link back to the Contact Us page you just created. You have to select "Your page" and then select the Contact Us page from the list of your pages. You can also type in the words you want to appear in the hyperlink on which your users will click to get to the page in the *Text to Display* box.

Figure 11-7. Choose one of the predesigned layouts if you need to rearrange your page contents.

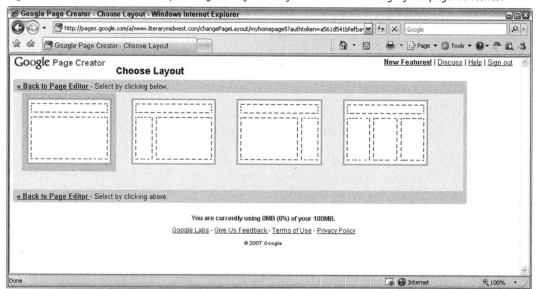

 Tip: If you know HTML and are comfortable with working with the code for Web pages, you can edit the HTML at any time by clicking inside any of the page containers (the headers, columns, or main content areas you choose when selecting your page layout) and choosing the Edit HTML link in the lower-right corner of the page. When the Edit HTML page appears, you can type or edit the existing HTML code for that page. By editing the code you can arrange the page layout using many more options than those provided by Google's templates.

Typing Text

Adding text is done in much the same way as in a word processing program: you click to position the text cursor in one of the containers on your page, and you start typing. The column to the left of your page's content area contains buttons with tools familiar to a word processor, such as changing font type and font size. However, you don't have control over the exact point size of the type that appears on your page: you are only given size options such as Normal, Large, or Extra Large. The type fonts you can choose are only the few that are supported by Web browsers, such as Arial, Verdana, Helvetica, Times, and Courier. You can't choose unusual fonts such as Pala-

Figure 11-8. Choose one of these designs to select a graphic look and feel for your page.

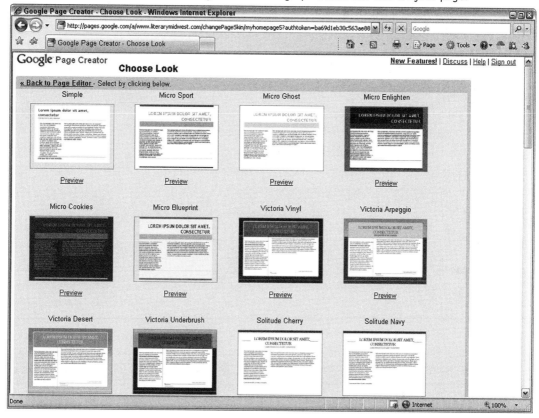

tino or Garamond because you don't know for sure if your viewer's system or browser will display them accurately. However, the Page Editor interface does support the standard keyboard shortcuts as word processing programs, such as Ctrl + B for bold, Ctrl + I for italic, and so on.

Adding Images

Images are added by clicking the *Image* button, also in the column on the left-hand side of the Page Editor. You have the option of browsing for an image on your hard drive or entering the URL of an image already online.

Once you are done adding images and typing text, you might think you need to save your page to preserve your changes. However, Page Creator, like Docs & Spreadsheets (see Chapter 7), has a useful feature for automatically saving your changes on a nearly constant basis. This makes it difficult to lose work if your browser or computer crashes. Page Creator will save your work for you when you move to a new page.

Figure 11-9. You have to create links to join your Web pages together.

Publishing Your Site

Once you have gotten your Web page to a point where you are comfortable with making it publicly available, click *Publish* above the site interface. Your site is now online on the Web server space Google has provided for you. Remember, it doesn't matter how much work you've put into building a page in the Edit Page interface. If you haven't published your site, you will not see it online. Publishing is not automatic the way saving is with regard to Google Page Creator. If you publish a file, and return to it later on and make changes, you need to click Publish again or your latest changes won't be visible online.

If you use Page Creator with a Google Apps domain, you can only publish a single Web site with that domain; you can add pages to that site, however. With a Gmail account, you have an additional option: Once you have published your first Web site, creating a new site is as easy as returning to Site Manager and clicking Create another site. (If you are logged in to your Gmail account and need to return to the Site Manager page within Page Creator, simply enter the URL http://pages. google.com in your browser's Address box and press Enter.) If you are working in

Figure 11-10. Use this dialog box to add new pages to your site and link to them.

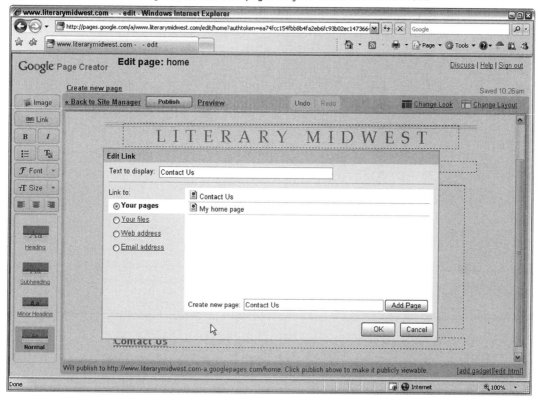

the Gmail version of Page Creator, click the drop-down menu beneath your Gmail address at the top of the page, and choose "Create another site." This will take you to a page where you choose a name for your site—you'll have to verify that your preferred site name is available and not being used as yet by any other person who has Web pages hosted with Google. You are allowed a total of five Google Web sites, as indicated in Figure 11-11.

Making Your Site Content-Rich

The content you add will play a major role in determining not only who will want to spend time on your site, but how people are attracted to it in the first place. Remember that most web search engines work by cross-referencing pages with other pages, so you'll want to touch on as many issues related to your Web site as possible. While the Literary Midwest Web site has information intended to pitch the Literary America project to potential publishers, it also has a page containing general informa-

Figure 11-11. Page creator gives you the ability to create five separate Web sites, each with its own URL.

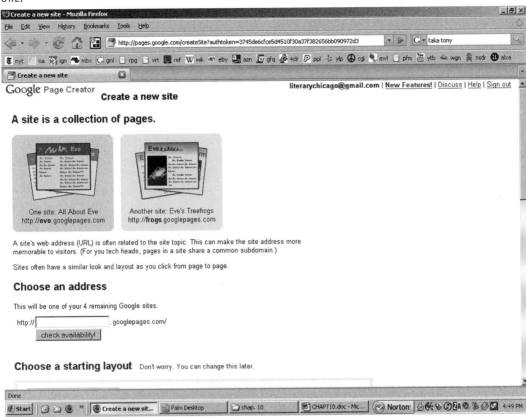

tion about sites of literary interest in the Midwest. This increases the chances that the page will be retrieved in responses to searches. The higher the number of headings, subjects, and keywords you have on your page, the greater the chances that it will be found and that people will want to visit it.

Adding Information About You

Your site can contain basic information about you and your company's origins. This type of knowledge can increase someone's interest in your business and create the possibility of networking with like-minded people with similar experiences to your own. The Internet is still relatively young, and people who visit your Web site probably don't know anything about you. You need to inspire trust in them. On the Internet, even though you don't see people face to face, you can still strike up one-to-one, personal relationships with them. Such relationships build trust and make it more likely that visitors will make purchases from you.

You'll get more benefits by putting this information on a separate page linked to your home page. An "About Me" or "About Us" page gets people clicking through your site and exploring other pages than the home page. Once visitors start exploring, you increase the chances that they'll stay on site and either contact you or make a purchase, which is probably just what you want.

Creating a Sales Catalog

Another page might contain a listing of products you sell or services that you offer. Try to be as specific as possible; a Web surfer's sense of your product will be wholly dependent upon what you communicate through your Web site. If two online bookstores are selling the same book at the same price, for example, one can make its product significantly more attractive by adding a photograph. This gives the Web surfer a sense of exactly what he's going to get in the mail after paying for an item online, and can make the difference in whether or not a sale is made. Page Creator does not yet have any means for conducting actual business transactions, but a page with such items as links to an email address, or PayPal account, or purchasing instructions should at least be linked to the catalog page, if not actually included in the page itself.

 Tip: By linking to an electronic payment service such as the popular PayPal (http://www.paypal.com), you make it that much easier for shoppers to follow through with purchases from you. If those shoppers already have a PayPal account they know that by clicking on the PayPal link they can log in with their PayPal username and password and transfer funds to you quickly.

Adding a Customer Service Area

Once again, while there is not a specific tool created to deal with customer service, a separate page, linked to any other pages concerning online sales, can be included. Information detailing shipping and handling fees, return policy, and a customer service contact email would belong here. Another way to save your visitors time and effort is to include a customer FAQ. You can even create one consisting of anticipated questions before hearing from any actual customers.

Creating a Contact Page

A contact page is one of the "must-haves" for any Web site. You need to give your visitors a way to e-mail, phone, or mail you, especially if they are encountering problems or questions with what they have purchased from you. While you may not want to list your home phone number on the Internet, it's important for someone who discovers you or your business via your Web site to be able to get in touch with you. Listing an email is an ideal solution.

Care and Feeding of Your Web Site

Think of your Web site as a plant that needs care and attention to grow and stay healthy. A Web site devoid of regular updates and monitoring becomes nothing more than a time-capsule. Updating an FAQ in response to actual customer questions is essential, for example. If you have a product listing, don't let an online catalogue stagnate with images of products you no longer have in stock or a lack of products you do have in stock. Many people devote their home page to a weekly update letting regular visitors hear about what's new with the site, products, etc. I cannot overemphasize how uninteresting it is to go back to a Web site over and over again over a long period of time only to find that nothing ever changes or evolves.

Testing Your Site

Before you publish your Google page, make sure to click *Preview*, which is listed right next to *Publish* above the text editing interface. This opens a new window displaying your site exactly as it will appear on the web. Previewing your Web page can really help to detect minor oversights in alignment, etc. I have also found that previewing can sometimes reveal minor discrepancies between what you see in the text editor and what the final page displays. Finally, go the Web page itself and test out all the links, etc. There's nothing more irritating or damaging to your credibility as an online businessperson than a broken link.

Marketing Your Site

Google explicitly states that sites created through Page Creator will not be given preferential treatment in its search engine result listings. The most effective way to advertise your site is to provide links to other, similarly-oriented Web pages. You look up such sites using Google's own search engine. If you sell flower arrangements, for instance, look up sites that sell plant food or flower pots. In addition to using Google's AdWords (see Chapter 5) program, you should look around for other places online to which you think linking would be appropriate. Don't hesitate to contact their webmasters and see if they'll link back to your site. The more connections you make, the better a chance you have of getting noticed.

Building Community

A Web site's life blood is the community that frequents it. Think about fast-rising and hugely successful sites like YouTube, Flickr, or MySpace. They all built their successes on creating an environment that kept users coming back for more. The best way to accomplish this is to create a Web page where people feel that they have stake in its existence: you want visitors to have a sense that they are, in some way visiting not just your site, but their site, too. Page Creator is primarily intended to make it quick and easy for you to publish content online. It's not intended to let your visitors add their content. But you can still add such features to a site you create with Page Creator by creating them with other programs and linking them to your site. And you can always create a blog with Google, which includes the ability to let visitors comment on your postings. The best approach for now would be to welcome user feedback and respond in a timely manner, plus regular updates.

Another way to make your Web site more interactive and your content more valuable is to click the link Add Gadget. This link appears on the bottom right of a page you are editing. When you click the link, a window pops up in the middle of your editing window. The popup window contains links to a variety of mini-programs called Gadgets that you can add to your page. The gadgets provide your page with additional content such as the current weather, the date or time, or a search box to another site such as YouTube. You need to use gadgets carefully and not add too many to your own page. A page full of gadgets not only looks cluttered but it draws content from another site and thus might slow down the operation of your own page. And unless the gadget has the name Google in it, you can't be sure who created it and whether or not it will actually work.

Keeping Your Content New and Fresh

Once again, it is hard to overemphasize the importance of updating your Web page. Respond expediently to emails and integrate customer questions into an FAQ. Be diligent about seeking out similar Web pages that you can link to. If one of your products has received a positive review, post all or part of it somewhere on your Web page. Try to be receptive to the comments of your visitors. Enlisting friends and acquaintances as your core user base is a good way to get started.

Web content that is frequently updated builds your credibility and gives visitors a reason to revisit your pages on a regular basis. Perhaps the most immediate way to publish content frequently on the Web is to create an online diary called a blog. A blog is a running commentary on your life or on your company's products and services. Google owns one of the most popular blogging tools around, and Blogger is described in Chapter 13.

C H A P T E R **12**

Boosting Your Bottom Line with AdSense

Advertising is one of the most popular ways for Web site owners to make a few extra dollars online. You agree to display someone else's ads on your pages, and in return, you receive a fee for this "rental space." The exact fee depends on how many browsers visit the site in a given period (a week or a month, for instance).

AdSense gives anyone with a Web site the ability to place ads there from Google. Google makes sure the ads relate in some way to the content on the Web page. You've probably seen AdSense ads before; they're the contextual ads that often appear in a block of two or three and are often lined up vertically on the page. A heading at the top reads "Ads by Goooooogle." The program works like this: you sign up and tell Google your site's URL and whether it is for a business or personal in nature. You choose how you want your ads to appear; Google scours through its database of millions of Web pages and returns ads that are related to your site's content.

AdSense also gives you the option to add a search box to your site. This enables your visitors to perform a search and turn up search results that complement your own content. In either case, if someone clicks on one of the ads you display, you earn a bit of revenue. You are paid either using the cost-per-click or CPC model or the cost-per-thousand-impressions or CPM model. In CPC, you are paid a small amount every time someone clicks on an ad. In CPM, you are paid when your ads are displayed 1000 times—in other words, when the page that displays an ad is viewed 1000 times. In either case, the earnings you make depend on how rich your site's content is and how many visitors your site attracts. Before you start working out the exact size and format of the ads you want to run, your first job is to create a Web site that has the content to make AdSense ads actually work.

Creating Web Content that Supports Advertising

One of the many nice features about AdSense is that, in a matter of a few minutes, it dynamically generates ads that relate in some way to the Web page content near it. For instance, if you create a Web page about science and astronomy, or if you simply make a passing mention of binoculars in your blog, you can place some advertising code provided by Google AdSense on the page and it will dynamically serve up a mixture of ads, all related to your site. In the case of the site shown in Figure 12-1, the ads are related to hockey because hockey clubs are the subject of the page.

The question every advertiser on the Internet faces is how to come up with content to support advertising. You have two general options:

- *Create a Landing Page.* Gather links and content from anywhere and every-where that are organized around a single theme. In this case, you don't actu-ally provide the content. You only create the page and "borrow" the names of Web sites or links to them. Such pages are only created to gain advertising revenue or to steer people to other Web sites, or both.

Figure 12-1. AdSense ads are gathered from AdWords text that is contextually related to your content.

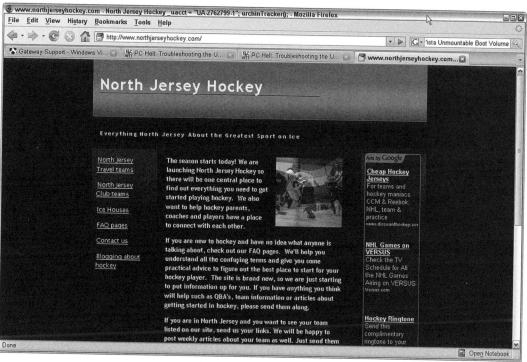

- *Create the Site First.* You devote your time and energy to a subject of interest; you build up the number of visitors gradually and by continually improving your products and services as well as the quality of their presentation. In this case the Web site is your primary interest; any advertising revenue you generate from it is "gravy."

Of course, every Web publisher wants advertising to be more than just "gravy." For a lucky few, it becomes a viable source of income. In either case, you need to turn your initial attention and energy not to creating the ads (that's done for you by Google) but instead to building a page that will attract viewers for the ads.

Sprinkling Keywords

Google indexes your page's content in order to determine which ads need to be placed there. It's to your advantage to attract AdSense ads that are directly relevant to your page topic. The more relevant your ads are, the more likely someone will click on one of them and earn you some money. The same search engine optimization techniques described in Chapter 4 apply with AdSense. One of the most important is making sure your contents contain lots of keywords—words or phrases that visitors will respond to. In this case, you aren't trying to sprinkle in words that will improve your placement on a search results page, but words that will attract ads that people will click on.

 Note: This book's editor passes along the following example showing how important keywords are to displaying relevant ads, especially in a page's title: She created a page listing local hockey clubs entitled North Jersey Clubs. Most of the rinks listed on the page have the words "house" in their name. As a result, the initial AdSense ads all had to do with moving. After she inserted the word "hockey" in the title they changed to be relevant to the content.

Layering Your Content

Web sites that are content rich—that have many "layers" of Web pages a visitor can click on to "burrow" into the site—will have more content that can be used to gather relevant AdSense ads. Try to create sites that divide contents into categories, and each category into individual products:

- *Layer 1*—Your home page
- *Layer 2*—Your site's main content divisions: Products, About Us, Contact, etc.
- *Layer 3*—Types of products: e.g., Clothing, Accessories, Hardware
- *Layer 4*—Divisions within Accessories: e.g., Belts, Hats, Ties, Socks

> **Tip:** Try to update one item on your site per day to keep visitors coming back. One of my favorite Internet radio stations, WFMU, includes a new humorous slogan and a "sound bite of the day" on the home page of its Web site (http://www.wfmu.org). Much of the rest of the site stays the same, although new radio shows are added frequently to the station's extensive archives. But regular visitors know there's a little surprise waiting for them each day.

Being Fruitful and Multiplying Your Content

It takes a lot of work to create content for Web sites, especially if you are continually expanding those sites and trying to run a business at the same time. But you need to make a commitment to add fresh and compelling content to your site, such as frequent promotions and new products. It's one of the keys to keeping customers satisfied and coming back for more.

Online shoppers are continually searching for sites with fresh and different content. The really obsessive Web surfers churn through one site after another, clicking, scanning, and moving from page to page. These are exactly the kinds of visitors you want to attract: the ones who will stay online for hours at a time, searching for a product, a service, or a bit of information that will satisfy their current needs and interests (or perhaps I should say obsessions).

> **Tip:** Consider inviting your customers to generate some of your Web site's new content. "My customers are often my greatest source of creative input," the owner of one online greeting card company told me. "They come up with great ideas and uses for my products." Invite your customers for suggestions and comments about your site, and ask for ideas about products and services they are looking for; they are likely to come up with plenty of suggestions that never occurred to you on your own.

Once you have an idea what the content of your site should be, you can sign up for the AdSense program and configure your ads in the process.

Getting Started with AdSense

It's easy to sign up for AdSense—as long as you have a Web page or Web site to advertise. When you go to the AdSense home page (http://www.google.com/adsense) and click the "Sign up now" button, you go to the application form shown in Figure 12-2, where the very first thing you have to fill out is the URL of your Web site's home page. You choose a language, and you provide your name and address as the "payee," which immediately gives you hope of receiving checks for your advertising efforts.

One of the most important sections of the application form is entitled Product Selection. Both of the AdSense options—AdSense for Search and AdSense for Content—are preselected for you. It's not an either-or decision. You can combine AdSense for Search boxes and AdSense for Content ad blocks on the same page if you wish, as well as referral ads.

Figure 12-2. You need a Web site up and running before you obtain an AdSense account.

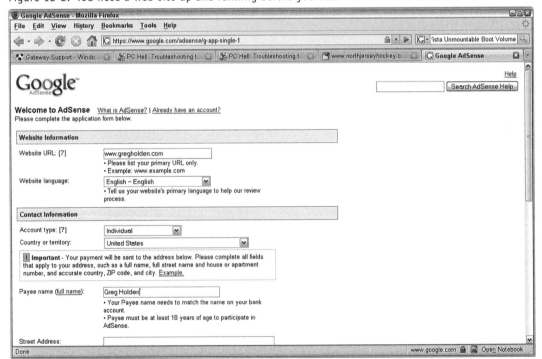

- AdSense for Search allows you to present a Google search box and search results on your Web page, and earn money if someone clicks on a search result ad. It's a good option if you don't have a lot of original content on your page.

- AdSense for Content is good for sites that have well-defined subject matter and a good deal of editorial content. A series of ads, images, or links that have relevance to your page's content matter are placed on the page by Google.

- AdSense Referrals are buttons that advertise particular software and services, mostly those offered by Google. If you are really happy with a piece of software, such as the free Web browser Mozilla Firefox or Google's Picasa photo management software, you can include a button on one or more of your Web pages. If someone clicks on your button and follows through by downloading software or signing up for a service, you earn a referral fee.

- AdSense for Mobile is only useful if you have optimized your Web pages so they display on the small screens used by Web-enabled cell phones or palm devices. This program allows you to display a single AdSense ad unit to the mobile version of your page.

Also pay attention to the five check boxes at the bottom, which you are required to check to guarantee that you will conform to Google's advertising guidelines. When you're done filling out the form, click Submit Information. On the next page, you can review and confirm your information; you are also given the option to use your existing Google account for AdSense—something I recommend, so you don't become overwhelmed with multiple usernames, e-mail addresses, and passwords for your Google services. After you apply, you can expect it to take two or three days before your application is approved.

Once you are registered, you need to decide what version of AdSense you're going to use. This isn't necessarily an either-or decision. But you at least need to know that four versions of AdSense are available—AdSense for Search, AdSense for Content, AdSense for Mobile, and AdSense Referrals—and how each one can help you earn money.

How Much Can You Earn? You'll Learn, Eventually

Signing up and becoming a member of AdSense is absolutely free. You can cancel at any time. The other financial part—being paid for what you earn—is something Google keeps a mystery. Google doesn't reveal exactly how much it receives from advertisers, and how much of that revenue is shared with you. It does say that if you use its AdSense for Search program, you are paid on a cost-per-click basis: when someone clicks on a search link, you earn a set amount for each one of those clicks. AdSense for Content pays either on a cost-per-click or cost-per-thousand-impressions basis; the payment system is determined by the advertiser (the company whose Web site or products and services are being advertised).

As Google says in its help files, "The best way to find out how much you'll earn is to sign up and start showing ads on your web pages."

Once you start showing ads on your Web pages, you can start determining how much you're actually earning by logging in to your Google account and clicking the Reports tab. You'll be able to see the total number of page impressions, ad clicks, page clickthrough rate (Page CTR, the number of times visitors click through one of the AdSense ad links to the advertisers page), Page eCPM (cost per 1000 impressions), and your total earnings so you can get an idea of how well the program is performing for you and how much you can expect to earn over time in the program. Once you earn $100, Google sends you a check at the end of each month.

Using AdSense for Content

Once you receive the e-mail from Google AdSense admitting you to the program, it's easy to get started. You fill out a series of forms, following the instructions that begin in the e-mail. Ultimately, to finally place the ads on your page, Adsense will supply you with a block of HTML to add to the underlying HTML code of the Web page where you want the ads to appear. Once you tackle that task, Google does the rest: it automatically indexes your page and sends you ads based on your content.

After you apply, it takes two or three days for Google to approve your application. When you receive an e-mail message notifying you that you've been added to the program, you can log into your account from the AdSense home page (http://www .google.com/adsense). Follow these steps to start placing ads on your site:

1. Click the AdSense Setup tab shown in Figure 12-3.

2. Click AdSense for Content.

3. Choose the type of ad you want to display. You have two options: a link unit (a list of topics with hyperlinks) or an ad unit (a series of ads that appear in block format. If you choose to display an ad unit, click the drop-down list and choose the type of ads you want: text only, image only, text and image. Text-only ads aren't as attention getting as image ads, but they don't take up much of your Web page space or distract from your content. Image only ads are eye-

Figure 12-3. Once you're approved, start with AdSense for Content.

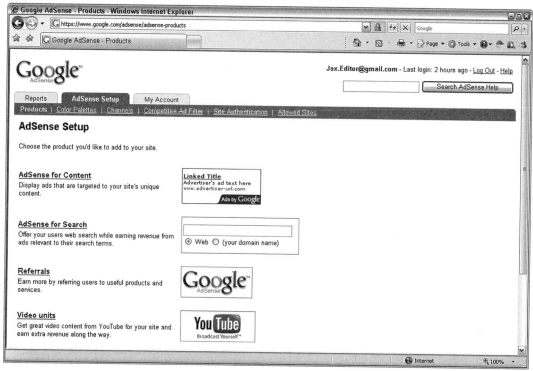

catching, but they don't tell the visitor what they'll find when they click through. Text and image ads are compelling visually and contain some textual content but take up the greatest amount of space of these three options.

4. When you're done, click Continue.

5. In the next AdSense for Content page, you choose the format and color scheme you want. You have the choice of three sizes of vertical ads, six different sizes for square ads, or three types of horizontal ad formats. The format you choose should complement your layout (a vertical columnar layout calls for vertical rather than horizontal ads, for instance).

Choosing an Ad Format

You have the ability to customize the appearance of ads, choosing colors and typefaces so they complement the existing design you have in place. Customization has its pros and cons, however. On the pro side, your page looks more coherent and unified; the ads seem to be coming from you rather than Google. On the other hand, you might not want your ads to look like your own content; you might prefer to have them appear like the standard Google AdSense ads that experienced Web surfers see all over the Internet. At any rate, you can choose to customize the look and feel of the content ads you display or the search results your visitors come up with if you use AdSense for Search.

 Tip: The size and format of the ad you pick should complement your page layout: if you have a single column of content, you might choose the horizontal option. If your page is divided into several narrow columns, the vertical format is probably preferable. If you want ads to appear on multiple pages, you need to add the HTML code to each page separately.

When you're done choosing the format of your ads, click Continue. The last page presents you with a block of HTML code that Google produces for you based on your ad specifications. Copy the code by clicking anywhere within it. You then need to paste it into the HTML for your Web page, using your Web editing program's HTML view option.

The exact content of the ads you place depends on the contents of the pages on which they appear. A page advertising baseball equipment will display baseball-related AdSense ads; a page describing home furnishings will get AdSense ads for things like couches, chairs, lamps, and so on.

Using AdSense for Search

In AdSense for search, you don't display ads as such. You place a search box on your Web page and allow people do conduct a search on Google without actually leaving your site. The search results appear in their own box (see Figure 12-4 for an example). If someone clicks on one of the links shown in the search results, they do leave your Web site to go to the advertiser's site. However, the good news is that you earn a cost-per-click fee when someone performs that clicking motion with their finger.

One advantage of using AdSense for search is that it keeps visitors on your site, at least for a while, because the search results initially show up on your page. With AdSense for Content or with other types of ads you display, visitors click on the ad and are taken to the advertiser's Web site. You earn a per-click fee for this action, but as a result, your visitors go elsewhere. With AdSense for Search your visitors are able to perform a Google search using a search box added to your Web page; when the

Figure 12-4. You can add a Google search box to your existing Web site to generate ad revenue.

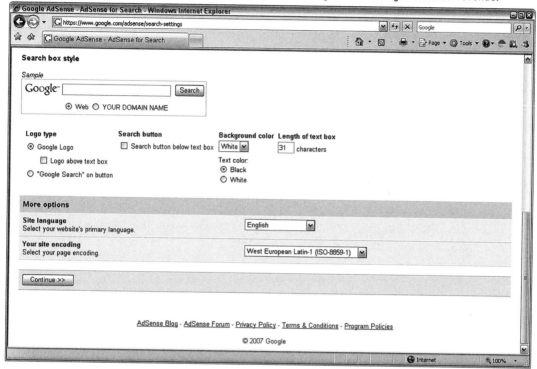

user enters a keyword or phrase into the box, the search results are added to a box within your page. You don't necessarily "lose" your visitor unless he or she clicks on one of the search results. (And if your content is valuable, the person will probably return at a later time anyway.)

Adding a Search Box to Your Site

The steps involved in setting up AdSense for Search on your site are similar to those for AdSense for Content:

1. Sign into AdSense, if necessary, and click the AdSense Setup tab.
2. Click AdSense for Search.
3. Click the Get Started Now! button.
4. On the first AdSense for Search page, you choose whether you want to have your Google search box search the Web only or the Web plus your own Web site. If you choose the second option, you'll need to submit up to three URLs for pages on your site. If you do include your site, the search will include only those URLs you supply.

5. Scroll down to the Search Box Style section and specify the type of logo you want to display. You can choose to display a Google logo along with your search box for some more graphic interest or (if your page has enough graphic interest already) the simple words "Google Search" on the Search button. You also need to decide whether the all-important search button appears beneath or to the side of the search box.

6. In the More Options section you choose:
   - whether you want search results to appear in a new browser window;
   - to make your search results tailored so they match the appearance of your Web site in the Site-flavored search section;
   - to prevent pornography or other mature sites from appearing in your search results by opting for Safe Search; or
   - custom channel. This channel is a content segment that you can use to track ad performance. Some channels, like URL channels, can be used to track clicks on all the ads presented on a Web page or part of a Web site. A custom channel is one that you set up with your own criteria, and probably most useful once you have been advertising for a while and have many kinds of ads on your site. You can track ads that have borders versus no borders, ads that use red as an accent color versus blue, and other qualities. Click Continue to move to the next page, Search Results Style, where you choose colors and a layout for the results your visitors see after they conduct a search using the search box you provide. You can choose from between several layouts, including horizontal and vertical arrangements. You can also add your own company logo if you have one; I highly recommend that you do so, because it looks more professional—it looks as though the results are coming from your own site rather than from Google. You can also choose colors that complement those used on your own Web site—again, it's a good idea to do so, because it looks more professional and reinforces your brand.

7. When you're done choosing layout options, click Continue.

8. When the next AdSense for Search page appears, you are told to specify the URL where a visitor's browser will go if he or she clicks on your logo. (You can never have too many links to your home page, remember.)

9. Click Continue.

When the final page appears, you again are presented with a block of HTML code. Click anywhere within the block of code to copy it; you then paste the code into the HTML for the Web page on which you want the search box to appear. If you're using

Google Page Creator, open the page in question and click the edit HTML link in the bottom right corner. When the Edit HTML window opens, paste the code for your ad into the code for your Web page.

Blocking Ads You Don't Want

Once you have gone through the time and effort of creating a Web site, you don't want to detract from your work by displaying too many ads or ads that are unsuitable for your audience. If you have created a site devoted to plush toys such as Beanie Babies, for instance, you don't want to end up advertising an X-rated movie called Love Babies. Google assures AdSense customers that its ads are "family-friendly" by filtering out any adult content. Just as important, it gives you a measure of control over the ads that appear on your page in response to search results. (That also applies to content-based ads, which are described in the following section.) You probably want to filter out ads for Web sites that function as your direct competitors, for instance. You can do that by actively blocking and filtering ads that fall into two categories:

1. Competitive Filters
2. Contextual Filters

Referring Visitors to Other Google Services

Google gives you another way to earn some extra money through advertising on your Web site through the AdSense Referrals program. You can refer your visitors directly to Google's products and services. For instance, if you extol the virtues of using Google's image editing program Picasa (software described in Chapter 19), and someone signs up after clicking a button on your page, you earn a $1 referral fee. You can advertise the following programs:

- Google AdWords
- Google AdSense
- Picasa
- Mozilla Firefox
- Google Pack

In this chapter, you were introduced to Google's AdSense for Search, AdSense for Content, and AdSense Referrals options. Like other Google programs, AdSense is free to use; once your Web site is approved, its contents are automatically indexed, and Google uses its search technology to retrieve ads from its AdWords database that will complement your own Web site contents. As long as you don't mind displaying some unobtrusive ads on your site, it's a great way to make some extra money. And you can stop the program at any time if you change your mind about advertising. Of course, you need to have a Web site in order to get AdSense up and running. Review Chapter 6 on Google Apps, which can supply you with a domain name, a Web site, and many other valuable business services.

PART **IV**

Communications and Sales Tools

CHAPTER **13**

Blogging to Improve Marketing and Customer Relations

As you probably already know, blogs are online diaries that have become wildly popular all over the Web in recent years. The term *blog* is an abbreviation for *Web log,* in fact. In Webspeak, a log file is a running record of the activity on a Web site that is updated every day. A Web log, then, is a running record of someone's own activities and thoughts, and while it can be updated every day, its content and timeliness are totally up to the author.

Some bloggers update once every few days or once a week, while others update several times a day. Google owns one of the most popular blogging tools on the Web, a service called Blogger. This chapter gives you an introduction to Blogger as a way to get the message out about you, your products, or your services, and to supplement the other services you already provide online with Google.

Setting Up a Business Blog

For many, a blog is a sort of online diary, a place where others can go to find out what someone is thinking about or doing. You're probably less familiar with blogs as business tools. The fact is that successful blogs are generating money for their owners. Many blogs have gained regular followings, and the number of users means that they also function as lucrative advertising tools. But money isn't the only business advantage to creating an online blog for your small- or medium-sized business. You can use blogs to help build your business in several different ways:

- *Placing ads—*Many bloggers are out to attract as many visitors as they can. Once they get a steady audience, they can use a service like Blogads (www

.blogads.com) or Google's AdSense (adsense.google.com) to generate advertising revenue.

- *Building community*—All blog tools, including Blogger, give readers a way to comment on what the authors say. Other readers can comment on previous comments; the author can comment on the comments in another blog post; and the resulting dialog bonds everyone and creates a lively site of devoted "followers."

- *Making announcements*—A blog gives you a way to get the news out about new product lines or promotions before ads hit the newspapers and long before the printed catalog arrives in a customer's mailbox.

- *Placing affiliate ads*—You sign up for well-known programs that steer potential buyers to Amazon.com or eBay.

- *Building interest in your Web site*—By talking about yourself, your knowledge, or your services, you encourage customers to commit to them.

- *Asking for donations*—If you need a few extra bucks, you make use of the PayPal Tip Jar, a feature that gives visitors a way to donate to your cause.

A blog is actually quite a sophisticated Web site in its own right. But Blogger takes away the technical hurdles of setting up archives and allowing comments to be posted, and lets you control the content. Starting out a blog is the easy part—so easy that you are able to concentrate on making your blog stand out from the crowd. How you do that is easy to say and far less easy to carry out: You come up with something compelling to say, and you keep adding fresh content on a regular basis. You can also customize your blog if you wish, adding images, unique typefaces and headings, and a look and feel that matches your Web site. The sections that follow describe both the technical aspects of getting started and the content behind your business blog.

 Note: Blogs can make money in certain circumstances, but a more practical benefit is that they save money. They are very cost-effective marketing tools: you can create and maintain a blog on Blogger for absolutely no money if you put in all the sweat equity yourself. In a corporate environment you might hire a designer to give your blog a distinctive look, and you might hire a writer to contribute copy once in a while. An article in *Entrepreneur* magazine on four blogs that were created by Denali Flavors to promote a new line of ice cream reported that the blogs only cost $700 to prepare and resulted in a 25.7 percent increase in visits to the company

Web site. Read more about it at www.entrepreneur.com/marketing/mar ketingideas/article80100-2.html.

Getting Started with Google Blogger

The mechanical part of creating a blog is straightforward: you start by going to http://www.blogger.com. Like other Google services, Blogger is free to set up and use as long as you wish.

1. Click the "Create Your Blog Now" arrow and sign in with your existing Google account.

2. The page "Create a Google Account" will appear. Click on the "sign in first" link as you already have a Google Account at this point. (If you don't have a Google Account for some reason, just complete the form according to the directions on the page.)

3. After you sign in, you will be prompted to "Sign up for Blogger." Fill in your "Display Name," check off that you accept the Terms of Service, and click the "Continue" arrow to continue.

4. Go to a page called Name Your Blog. You are prompted to enter a title and URL for your blog or to choose to host your blog some place else. At this point you realize: I've got to figure out what I want to do with this blog. Who do I want to reach? What am I going to say? And most important: Am I really prepared to write something in a blog every day, or am I going to get people to help me with this? Before you move forward, take a moment to do some thinking about your blog's goals and objectives.

Determining What You're Going to Say

A blog is a powerful tool for reaching new customers or holding on to existing ones and building loyalty—provided you actually have something to say, something that your audience will want to read and that will keep them coming back to you on a regular basis. Even if you never place an ad on your blog page, you can gain benefits from viral marketing: the word-of-mouth advertising that often comes from creating a blog that develops a "buzz." Suppose your company sells umbrellas. You can use your blog to share your knowledge and passion for umbrellas. Keep in mind that, with your blog, you're trying to connect with people who share the same passion—who love this particular type of product and want to hear more about it. Your first step in planning your blog might be compiling a list of possible topics:

- *News*—If you partner with a new fabric supplier or purchase a new line of exotic rosewood to use in creating your umbrellas, you should announce that in your blog.

- *Humor*—If you or someone in your company has a good sense of humor you can gather jokes or humorous anecdotes about umbrellas and how they have been used through the ages.

- *Instruction*—You know a lot about umbrellas, and you can convey your knowledge about materials, sizes, or rare brands to your customers in your blog posts.

- *Positive publicity*—Use your blog to spread positive information about your company; a blog is the perfect place to announce a charitable donation or a campaign to help a good cause, for instance.

- *Give out inside information*—You don't have to reveal trade secrets in your blog, but you can talk about individual employees, manufacturing techniques, or other "behind the scenes" glimpses into your company that will put a human face on your products.

The topics above could also be covered in a newsletter or a Letter from the CEO posted on your Web site. A blog is not the only place where you can communicate to your employees. Ideally, you'll use all of these communications tools to get the word out. But why is a blog better than these other, more traditional venues? For one thing, a blog has an air of timeliness—of being an up-to-the-minute record of events. These days, visitors to Web sites turn to blogs before they turn to newsletters or other pages because they are used to finding out what's new and getting the information in easily digestible bits. Your blog posts don't have to be lengthy or even overly substantive: just keep up with them and say something new on a regular basis, and people will keep coming back.

 Tip: When you're looking around for successful blogs to emulate, you should take a look at Google's own "official" blog (http://google blog.blogspot.com). You'll find announcements of new products and services at Google. You'll notice that many different authors contribute to the blog, which helps keep plenty of content flowing into it. You'll also notice that there are often two or three blog posts each day. It's a tough act to follow, but the blog gives you an insight into the company and how to run a simple blog.

Coming Up with a Title

A good blog title is like a good Web page title: it's short and easy to remember. Not all blog titles actually tell you something about the contents of the blog before you visit it. Some of the most famous ones, like Instapundit, indicate that you're going to be listening to someone spout off about all sorts of topics. But others are simply clever and easy to recall:

- *Blog Jam* (the blog of radio station WEMU).
- *Boing Boing.* A Directory of Wonderful Things, an award-winning blog ranked most popular by Technorati.
- *The Huffington Post.* This popular site contains a blog by Ariana Huffington but also includes blogs by many other contributors. The title promotes the author and builds her brand and credibility.
- *Gawker.* The title of this New York-based gossip site brings to mind passersby gawking at something strange or awful, which describes the contents pretty well.

If you want to scan some of the most successful blogs and view titles in a convenient list, go to the Popular Blogs page on the Technorati site (http://technorati.com/pop/blogs).

Identifying Who You Want to Reach

When you have a clear idea of the kinds of readers you want to attract to your blog, you'll have a better idea of what to say every time you sit down at your keyboard. Are you trying to attract new customers, or to give existing buyers a reason to visit your Web site to find out about new products or services? The people who tend to flock to blogs tend to be:

- Young
- In a hurry
- In need of quick information
- Looking for insights they can't get elsewhere

Once you decide who you want to reach you can tailor your content to fit the audience. But the hardest part of blogging isn't actually setting up the blog in the first place, but keeping it going. Consider building your blog activities into your regular daily schedule so it becomes a matter of routine and you can keep up with it. And remember to stay "on topic" so you don't drive away the audience you already have.

> *Tip:* If you're looking for suggestions of blogs that serve as good models to follow for your own blogs, as well as news about the "blogosphere" (the world of online blogs), visit Technorati, a blog tracking firm. Find out more at http://www.technorati.com.

Setting Up Your Blog

Once you have an idea what you want to say in your blog, you can continue the process of setting it up.

1. In the "Name your Blog page," enter the title in the "Blog title" box.
2. Enter the URL in the Blog address box. The URL you enter should be as short and easy to remember as possible: if you can, simply enter your blog's title.
3. Click the "Check Availability" link just beneath the Blog address box shown in Figure 13-1. You'll see a quick message "This blog address is available" or "This blog address is not available." If the address isn't available, keep entering words until you find one that hasn't been used yet.
4. When you see the "available" message, click Continue. This will create your blog in Blogger's domain, blogspot.com.

If you want to create your blog on another domain, such as your own business Web site, you can click Advanced Blog Setup. Usually, this is a good idea for businesses. But there's nothing wrong with being located on blogspot.com, either. Many of the most popular blogs are located there, and if you are included on blogspot.com, the site helps promote your blog as well. These instructions assume you'll be creating a blogspot.com blog. You can also start out on Blogspot and move your blog to your Web site later on. It can be a site hosted by Google or another hosting service. See the Blogger help article entitled "How do I create a CNAME record for my custom domain?" for more.

Figure 13-1. You need to come up with a short name for your blog; the name then becomes part of its URL.

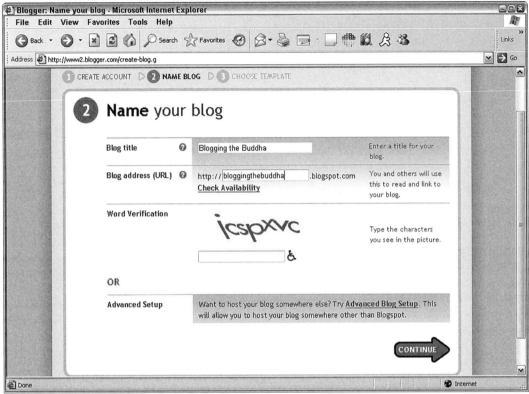

Choosing a Template

After you click Continue, you go to the "Choose a Template" page, where you choose a template that establishes the initial look and feel for your blog. While it's important to conform to your company's existing look and feel, and it's a good idea to customize your blog to look like the rest of your corporate materials (business cards, letterheads, and the like), customizing your blog can consume a lot of time and effort (I know this from experience). I advise you to choose a template you like just to get you up and running; once your blog is going, you'll be able to change the design later on. At this initial stage, you should focus on the content and getting in the routine of blogging; the care and feeding of your blog can happen later on.

In Figure 13-2, I've chosen a template called Thisaway Rose by simply clicking on the sample page thumbnail. When you've chosen your own template, click Continue.

You might be surprised to see the title of the next page: Your blog has been created! That's all there is to it. To be sure, there are more components to a blog. You'll need to identify where you want to archive posts that are out of date. You

Figure 13-2. Choose an initial design for your blog that you can customize later on.

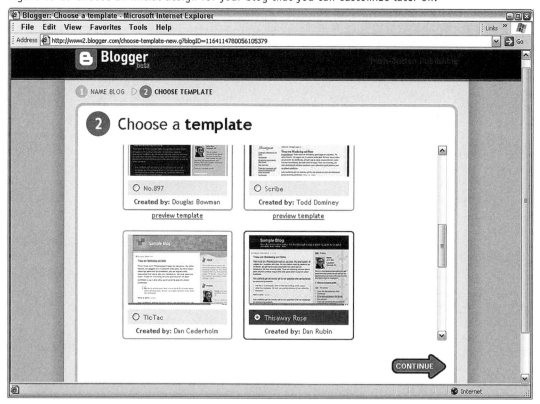

might want to set up a calendar so your readers can view your posts by date. But the name and URL and a design template are all you need to get started. Click Start Posting, and you go to the next step: creating your first post.

Posting, Editing, and Re-Posting

After you click the "Start Posting" arrow, you'll get to a page you'll see pretty often: the page for creating posts for your blog. The title of your blog appears at the top along with three tabs for Postings, Settings, and Template. The Posting tab offers you the options to Create, Edit posts, or Moderate Comments.

The Create Tab

1. Under the heading Create, you see a simple form with a box for a title and the text of your first blog post. The first message should be a welcome, or a brief summary of what your blog is about. My first post is shown in Figure 13-3.

Figure 13-3. Your first post should welcome visitors and explain what you want to talk about.

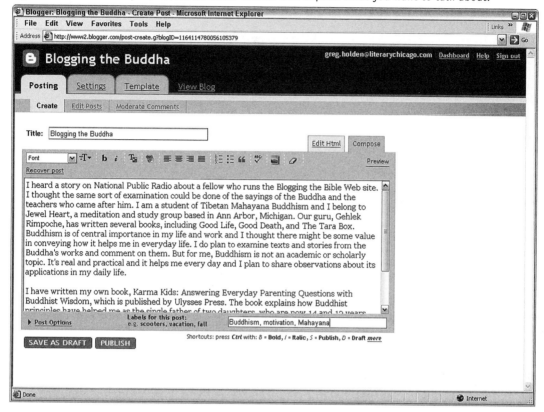

2. Fill in the "Labels for this Post" box below your entry. Select keywords that pertain to the post you have just created. By writing down a few labels, you make it easier for people to find your post based on your text or on the general subject of your blog.

3. Publish or Save. You see two buttons at the bottom of the page you're working on: "Publish" or "Saved." Google automatically saves your post as a draft as you are working, so you can't select the "Saved" button at the moment. If you want to save your post without posting, just navigate away from this page and your draft will be saved. Press the "Publish" button to place your first post online. If you go back and edit a post you've already made, the "Saved" button changes to "Save as a Draft."

Blogging is all about being spontaneous and getting your thoughts out in the world without too much fuss, so I suggest you simply click Publish to get your blog online. When you do so, a page appears that tells you your blog has been published. Congratulations: You're a blogger! Click View Blog to see the results instantly.

Usually, I tell people who want to publish on the Web to pay a lot of attention to design. But blogs aren't about design. They are about getting your thoughts and giving interested people a way to talk back to you, so I suggest that, in the beginning, you concentrate on what you want to say and posting to your blog at least once or twice a day. No matter what mood you're in, and no matter what you're doing, take a moment or two to write down some thoughts.

Editing Your Template

As I said earlier, once your blog goes online, you can edit its look and feel at any time. When I published my first post and looked at the result, I was less than happy with the colors I had chosen initially. Here's what I did to change them:

1. From the Blogger dashboard select the "Layout" link to customize your template. This takes you to the "Template" tab, which offers the options of "Page Elements," "Fonts and Colors," "Edit HTML," and "Pick New Template" at the top of the page.

2. The page elements page allows you to click and drag elements of your blog around the page and reposition them.

3. The "Fonts and Colors" page allows you to change the colors or fonts for everything on your page. The layout instantly refreshed so I could review my changes. I kept choosing colors until I found the ones I want. Once, when I choose link colors that were unreadable, I had to undo my changes by clicking the Clear Edits button.

Getting Others Involved

A blog that has a lot of posts in a short period of time tells people that the author is invested in the project and wants to contribute to it. A blog that hasn't been updated in weeks or months turns people off; this kind of blog actually makes you look bad, too. The first step in getting people to engage with you and your blog is to keep it up to date.

At the bottom of your post, you'll notice the "0 comments" link. Your blog, in other words, has a built-in mechanism for getting people to make comments. People only have to click on this link to access a form that lets them leave a quick comment about your post. It's a good idea to ask a friend or relative to leave a comment for you. Having some comments already made encourages strangers to leave their own remarks about what you've said.

You might also want to recruit your colleagues or coworkers to contribute their own posts. Setting up a "team blog" keeps your blog current, especially when you're out of town or unavailable (or just busy with other responsibilities). If you do allow others to post, you have the choice of giving them Administrator privileges or not. Administrators have the ability to change the blog's overall settings and delete posts. To begin with, you'll probably want to keep yourself as the sole administrator and let your contributors do just that: contribute their own posts. To invite someone to join, follow these steps:

1. Log into your blog, and click the Settings tab to bring it to the front.
2. Click the Permissions link at the far right of the Settings tab.
3. Click the Add Authors button.
4. In the "Invite more people to write to your blog," box type e-mail address(es) of the people you want to invite to contribute to your blog.
5. Click Invite. The recipient will receive an e-mail message inviting them to contribute, and providing them with instructions on how to do so.

Creating Your Profile

Along with your blog posts, visitors are naturally going to want to find out more about you. It's important to create a short profile at the outset so they can get some background and find out where you're coming from.

1. Log in and go to your Blogger Dashboard page. If you have more than one blog, you'll see them listed here. Once you have logged in to Blogger with your username and password, you'll always see the link Dashboard near the top of the page.
2. Click on the "Edit Profile" link in the sidebar column on the right-hand side of the page. A blog profile, like an About Me page on a Web site, builds trust in your viewers and gives them the feeling that they know you better. Anything you can say about your qualifications or background will lend credibility to your comments: Why did you start this blog? What are your qualifications and goals? These are the most important types of information you might want to add. A photo is optional: for privacy purposes, you may not want to include one, and you certainly shouldn't include your street address or phone number to keep out junk phone calls and mail.
3. You need to have a photo posted somewhere on the Web if you want to include it with your profile, because when the Edit Your Profile page and you scroll down to the Photograph section, you are prompted to enter the URL for your photo on the Web.

Tip: You can include one on one of your Google Web Page Creator pages; see Chapter 11 for more information.

4. Fill out the form on the Edit Profile page to fill out your profile. If you enter your birthdate, Blogger will automatically tell you and the world what sign of the Zodiac you are (see Figure 13-4).

Syndicating Your Google Blog

You may be familiar with the term syndication from the world of newspapers. When a column or cartoon is syndicated, it appears in many news outlets rather than one. Syndication does have an application when it comes to blogs. The XML markup formats RSS (Really Simple Syndication) and Atom are, in fact, used to create feeds

Figure 13-4. Create a profile to provide readers with background information about your blog.

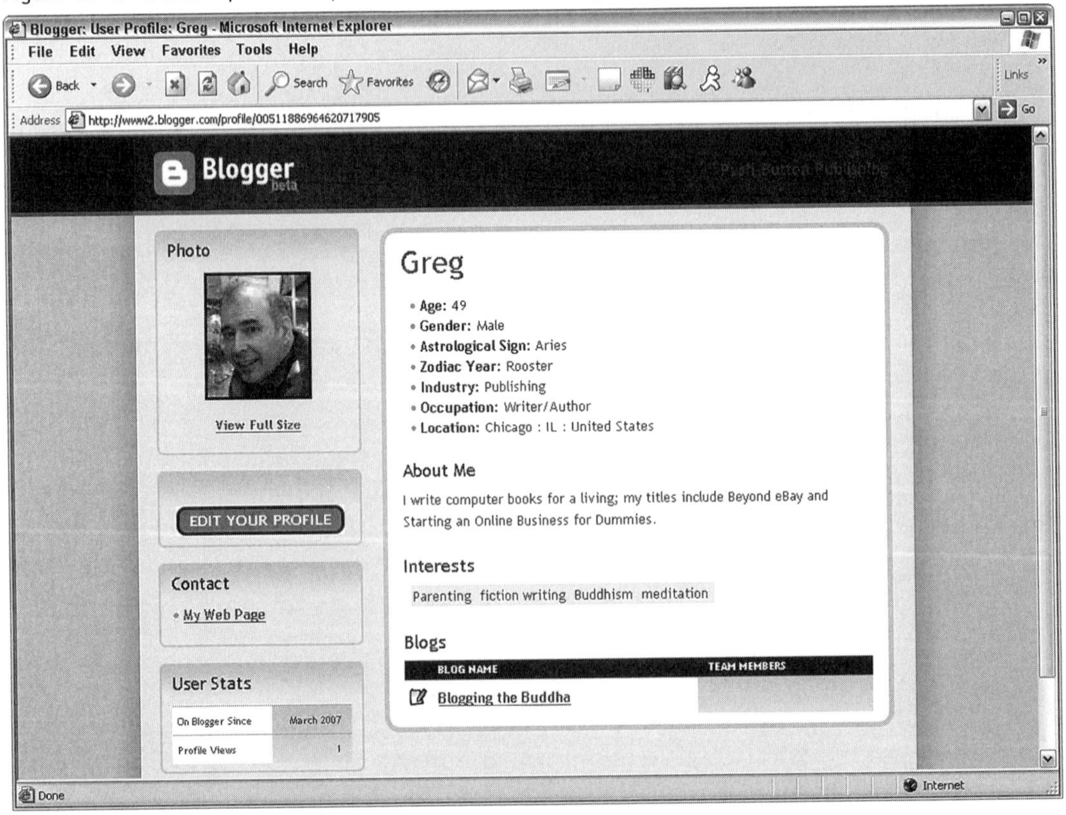

of a blog's contents. The feed can then be sent to software called a feed reader, which enables someone to read new blog postings as they appear without having to manually connect to the blog over and over. Someone who uses a feed reader to pick up the syndicated version of a blog is said to have subscribed to that blog.

Blogger has the ability to syndicate your blogs as well using the Atom format. If you activate Atom syndication for your blog, you tell Blogger to create a version of your publication that can be read by feed readers. Follow these steps:

1. Go to your Blogger Dashboard page and click the Settings link next to the name of your blog.
2. Click the Site Feed link.
3. Choose Full from the "Allow Blog Feeds" drop-down list.
4. If you want the full content of your posts to be published, or select Short if you want only the first paragraph or so to go to the feed. In general, it makes sense to include the full content unless your posts are lengthy and tend to be updated several times a day. If you flood your blog with lots of content, choose Short to give your subscribers a quick summary they'll find easy to digest.
5. Click Save Settings.

When you create a feed of your blog, you are assigned a URL for it. Chances are it takes the form of your blog's URL with /atom.xml attached to it. If you create a new blog with Blogger and you enable site feeds, you don't actually have to worry about adding such links; they appear in the blog automatically. If you created a blog a while ago before the automatic feed feature was added, you need to annually create a link to this feed in the body of your blog so interested readers can subscribe to it more easily. Adding such a link requires you to add a line of HTML code to your site's template. The following line adds a link to a feed of all of your blog's posts:

```
<p id="blogfeeds"><$BlogFeedsVertical$></p>
```

Be sure you type or copy the code exactly; if you type it, use straight rather than "curly" quotation marks.

Blogging is a user-friendly way to create content for a Web site on a daily basis and with a minimum of fuss. The problem is coming up with something to say on a regular basis and finding the time to enter new blog entries. Google can help here, too: it can't tell you what to think or say, exactly, but it can provide you with news items and ready-made bits of content that you can add to your Web site to enrich your existing content. You'll find out how to use these content-generating tools in Chapter 14.

CHAPTER **14**

Gathering Business Data: News, Gadgets, and More

Information is the coin of the realm when it comes to making a business run efficiently. The Internet is playing an increasingly important role in providing content that can lend substance to reports and make Web sites more credible and interesting. Google is one of the biggest sources of information on the Web, and it offers a range of specialized tools and resources for strengthening your business.

For instance, the more content rich your Web site, the longer your visitors will stay, and the better the chances that they'll make a purchase, register, or interact with you in some way. Creating content that will interest your customers and help sell your products and services is an art all its own. It will also improve your placement in Google's own search results; as you learned in Chapter 1, Google favors sites that contain a wide number of pages that are updated frequently over sites that only contain one or two interlinked pages. Google's Gadgets and news headlines will help with your Web presentation.

For internal reports and for simply being on top of current business trends, specialty search services like Google News, Blog Search, and Catalog Search will provide the background you need. Google Maps and Google Earth can tell visitors where to find you, while Google Notebook helps you take notes on any or all of these topics.

Working with Gadgets

The best Web content is not only current and frequently revised, but information that addresses the interests of the visitors you are trying to attract. Creating a Web site is one thing; updating it and making sure the content is useful can be really difficult, especially when you are trying to balance many different responsibilities. One of the best sources of business content is Google itself.

Google, as you learned in this book's early chapters, gathers information from all over the Web. It makes selected snippets of that information available in the form of small scale utilities called *gadgets*. You've probably seen gadgets, or tools much like them, in the course of surfing the Web. It's common to see stock quotes or the current weather, for instance. Google's gadgets draw such content from other Web sites, not your own; the creators of those sites make the content available online to people like you.

Choosing Gadgets

You can find Google's Web page gadgets in one of two ways. If you are working in Web Page Creator as described in Chapter 11, click the add gadget link near the bottom of the Page Creator window. The *Add a gadget to your page* opens in the middle of the Web Page Creator window (see Figure 14-1). The window gives you a selection of some of the more popular gadgets available. Some of the gadgets (particularly the ones that enable you to add Google services to your site, such as Google

Figure 14-1. This window lets you add gadgets to a Web page you're editing.

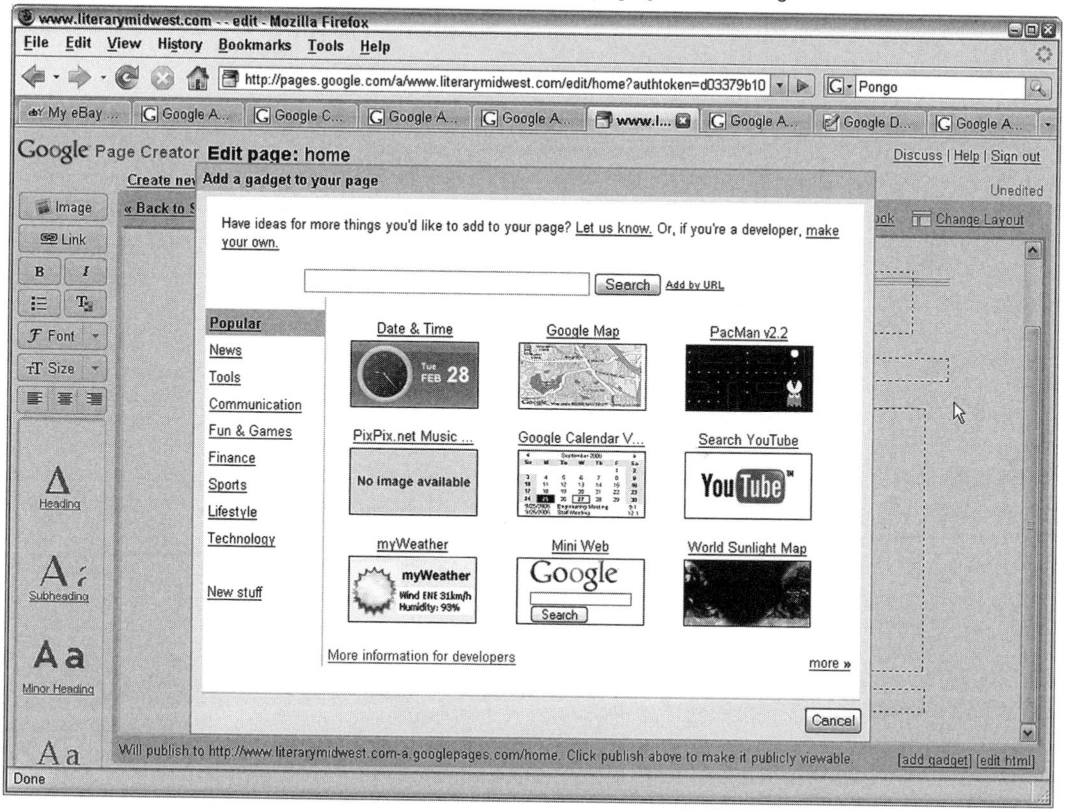

Talk) are created by Google. Others are created by software developers who go un-named. You don't know who has created most of the Gadgets distributed by Google. But the Terms and Conditions for creating Gadgets (http://www.google.com/apis/gadgets/terms.html) clearly state that developers must not use their Gadgets to distribute viruses or other malicious software. So you can consider them to be reliable. To add a Gadget, simply single-click it and you'll see a preview and have the chance to configure the Gadget if applicable. Click OK to install it.

On the other hand, if you don't use Web Page Creator, you have to access gadgets. Go directly to http://www.google.com/ig/directory?synd = open. The *Google Gadgets For Your Webpage* page will appear (see Figure 14-2) listing all the gadgets from which you can choose.

The interface here is the same as the Add a gadget window; you have the ability to search for gadgets by keywords or browse for them by category. The advantage of using the Google Gadgets For Your Webpage interface is that it enables you to add a

Figure 14-2. You can find gadgets at any time and add them to a Web page you own.

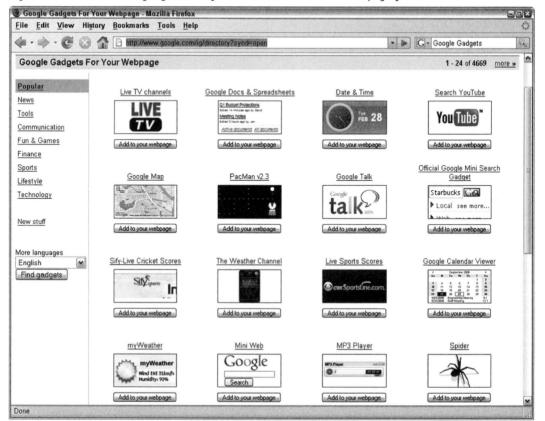

gadget to any Web page you own or have the ability to edit, whether it is hosted on Google or not.

Picking the Right Gadget for Your Pages

The Add a gadget to your page window gives you a variety of different ways to find gadgets. You can search for one based on a search term (sports, weather, and so on) at the top of the window. You can browse through the subject-oriented directory on the right side of the screen. Or you can browse page-by-page through the list of gadgets by clicking more at the bottom of the window.

The best gadgets, to my mind, are the ones that complement the mission and the subject of your Web site. If your site is all about tornadoes, for instance, it makes sense to include the weather—and not just the weather in your local area, but in the part of the Midwest known as "Tornado Alley." You would do this by including the Weather Channel Gadget in your page and customizing it so it covers a zip code in the area you want. You might include news headlines about violent storms that have broken out elsewhere in the world by including a Gadget such as the one for CNN Tabbed RSS News Feeds.

You should shop for the gadgets that will actually add useful content to your pages, such as:

- *Date and Time*—This adds the current date and time to your Web page. Click add gadget to display the available gadgets. Enter date and time in the search box at the top of the gadget page and click Search. Scan the list of time and date gadgets and click one you want. If you click World Clocks, for instance, a window opens with an extensive set of drop-down menus so you can set the clock format (digital or analog), choose one or two clocks, pick a time zone, and choose a time format. When you're done, click OK to add the gadget to your page.

- *Driving Directions*—Search for the Yahoo! Local Maps Gadget, click it, and enter your address as the default location. You don't need to enter a starting address. Click OK. The Gadget is added to your page, with boxes that the viewer can fill in to get driving directions from their own location to yours.

- *Mini Web*—This gadget adds a miniature search box to your Web page so your visitors can search Google right from it.

- *Search YouTube*—This gadget adds a different sort of search utility; you can search through video files on the popular site YouTube.

- *Google Calendar*—A calendar displayed on a page is a convenient way to let suppliers, employees, and others know about upcoming events affecting your company.

Note: If you have second thoughts about a gadget you've already placed in the page you're building right-click it and a button labeled Remove Gadget appears. Click Remove Gadget to take it away with a single mouse click.

Adding Gadgets

If you want to add a gadget to a Web page that isn't one you edit with Google Page creator, you can add it to your page as long as you have access to the HTML code for that page. You don't have to know HTML, either. In fact, one of the most useful gadgets was located right at the top of the list at the time this was written. Follow these steps to add a miniature version of Docs & Spreadsheets (the word processing and spreadsheet application described in Chapter 7) to your page:

1. Go to http://www.google.com/ig/directory?synd=open

2. Search for "Docs & Spreadsheets."

3. Click the "Add to your webpage" button beneath Docs & Spreadsheets.

4. When the preview page shown in Figure 14-3 appears, choose the options you want for your gadget. You don't have to choose any options if you want to stick with the default size, border, number of documents to preview, and default language. If you want to customize the box, change the border or another setting and click Preview. The miniature box shown at the top of the preview page changes in appearance to reflect your choices.

5. When you're done adjusting the gadget, click the "Get the Code" button. A new box opens in the bottom half of the page. The box contains the HTML code required to publish the gadget.

6. Click at the beginning of the code and highlight the entire code to select it all. (You can click anywhere in the code and press **Ctrl+A** to select all of it.) Make sure the opening HTML command <script src= is highlighted as well as the ending command </script>.

7. Press **Ctrl+C** to copy the code to your clipboard.

8. Open the HTML code for the Web page that you want to contain the gadget and press **Ctrl+V** to paste it into the page.

9. Save your changes and preview your page to see how your gadget works.

I found that the default size for the Docs & Spreadsheets gadget I added was far too small to make login easy; I changed the height to 500 pixels, re-inserted the gadget, and added it to a simple page shown in Figure 14-4.

Figure 14-3. You can customize your gadget's size and characteristics to fit your page.

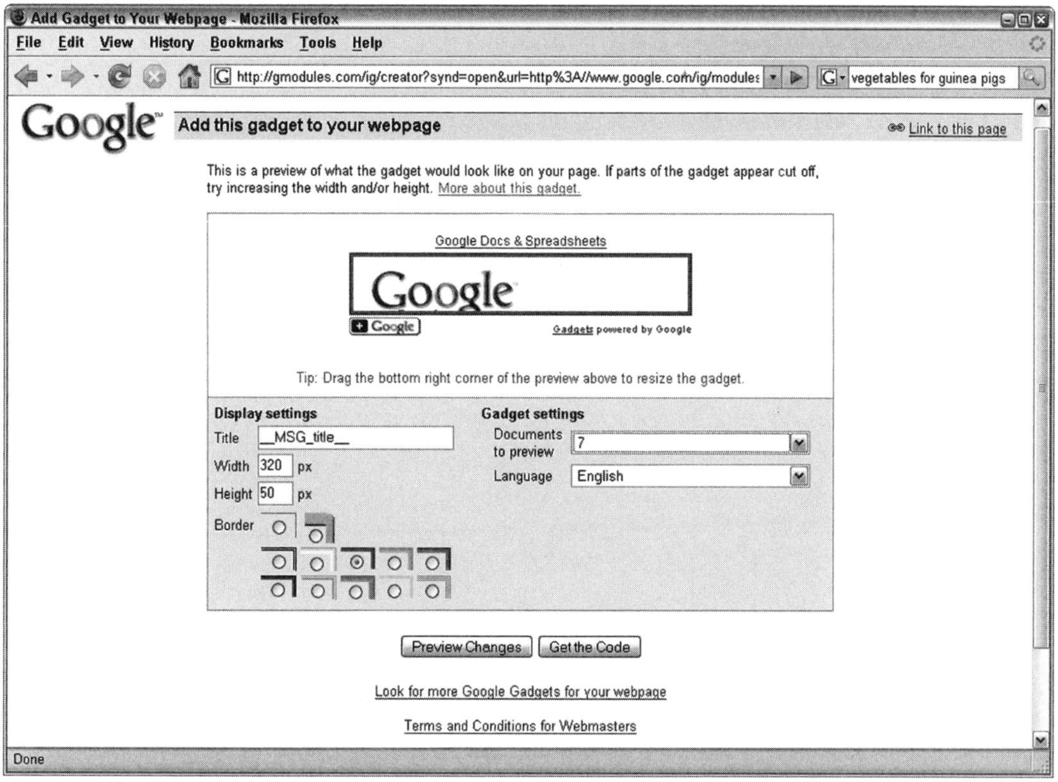

Adding a gadget to your page means that you create a link to Google's Web site. Whenever you use the gadget, you make a "call" to Google's Web servers. The servers need to respond in order for data—no matter what kind, whether it is the current temperature, stock quotes, or animations—to function. Because the gadget's contents are dependent on the remote Web server, you might find that your own site functions more slowly, or your page's total contents load more slowly due to the gadgets. This might happen if you have several different gadgets on a single Web page, each with a different connection to Google. If you see performance problems after adding a gadget, remove it; you don't want to sacrifice the quality of your site in an effort to improve it.

Even if you decide to include a gadget on one of your pages that's purely for fun, it can have benefits: anything that keeps your visitors on your site for an extended

Figure 14-4. Docs & Spreadsheets gadget lets you log in to your Docs & Spreadsheets utility.

period of time and that gives them a reason to return can end up generating revenue for you. Look at sites like Neopets.com, which keep young people on the site for hours at a time by giving them games to play. All that time leads to purchases of toys that are related to the creatures depicted on the site.

 Note: You can add a Gadget to your Google Page Creator page that enables you to add a new post to your blog, as long as that blog is hosted with Google. Click add gadget at the bottom of the page on which you want the gadget to appear. Do a search for Quick Blog. Click the Gadget and then click OK to add the gadget.

Adding News Headlines to Your Site

When it comes to creating content for your Web site, Google News (http://news .google.com) is literally "news you can use." Google's seemingly limitless directory of

Web contents can be mined for pages and resources that apply to your own area of business. Google News is, first and foremost, a search engine. When you need information about current events, Google News is a good place to start because you can do a keyword search as you would on the web, but this time, only from a collection of news reporting sources. Google News searches the web using computer algorithms, and is continuously updating from 4500 news sources. You can find yourself taken from the New York Post to Zee News, to Reuters, to newspapers you've never heard of before, but might find yourself reading in the future.

Why create a page full of "links to other Web sites of interest," when your Web site visitors can search Google themselves to find the same resources? One answer is time: while it's true anyone can search for information on Google, that doesn't mean that they should or that they want to. It can take 10, 15, or 20 minutes of valuable work time to gather headlines from your area of business, even on Google. Rather than doing the searching for all the news stories related to, say, breast cancer therapy, you can create a Web site that focuses on breast cancer therapies and that automatically searches Google for news headlines.

Personalizing Google News

Google News lets you rearrange its home page (http://news.google.com) at will, and by clicking the Personalize this page link you can either choose to add or remove standard sections or create a custom section to this Google Web page. You can also add Google News to your personal Google start page. But your personalized start page is not the same as the home page of your business's Web site. Your Web site is your public face to the world, while your personalized start page is something only you see. By adding Google News to your start page, you get your own news more quickly. Just follow these steps:

1. Go to your Google Apps Start Page by going to http://www.google.com/a, clicking Returning user, sign in here, entering your domain name, and clicking Go.
2. Click on the "Add Stuff" button in the top-right corner of your homepage. (This will open the Google homepage directory.)
3. Click on the "News" link on the left.
4. Click on the "Google News" gadget to add it to your page.

It would be nice if you could select a set of news headlines in a particular category, such as fashion or banking, and add the headlines to your own home page.

Most gadgets in the news category are current headlines from general news sites like CNN and MSNBC. But a few are specific to a certain area, such as high-tech or science news.

Perhaps the most practical way you can include "targeted" news headlines is to perform a search on Google News, copy the URL for the search results, and paste a link to that URL into your Web page. Suppose you are searching for headlines pertaining to mortgage interest rates in the state of Illinois:

1. Go to the Google News home page (http://news.google.com) and enter a phrase such as "mortgage interest rates Illinois" in the search box.
2. Click Search News.
3. When the news headlines appear, check to see if they pertain to the subject you are looking for. If they don't, refine your search terms.
4. Click anywhere in your browser's Address box to highlight the URL displayed, and press **Ctrl + C** to copy the URL to your browser's clipboard.
5. Open the page where you want the link to appear, and create some text that will serve as the highlighted hyperlink leading to the search results. For example: "Get news about current mortgage interest rates in Illinois."
6. Use your HTML editor to turn the highlighted phrase into a hyperlink, and paste the URL you copied earlier as the destination of the hyperlink.

Other Ways to Search with Google News

Sometimes, it can be helpful to look around online for other, more independent news sources for issues that are flying low on the radar of mainstream news. Places like http://politosphere.com/, http://www.thirdpartynews.net/, or http://www.politics1 .com/, to name a few, can lead you to stories you might not immediately find from searching Google News initially. Don't let that stop you, though, because you can often scan lower-profile stories for keywords that you might then enter into Google News to get even more coverage on the issues you are interested in.

Creating a Network of Business Links

The other way you can add current news headlines to your Web site is to create a page full of links to Web sites that contain content your visitors will be interested in or that pertains to your area of business. You can use Google's many other specialized search resources to locate current news headlines as well as opinions from the "blogosphere," the community of individuals who publish blogs in which they voice their thoughts and observations. Consider the following resources.

Google Blog Search

This Google service functions as a single directory of blogs all over the Web. It's practically impossible to provide a comprehensive and perfectly accurate picture of the blogosphere, because it's constantly changing. Google created a blog search index by aggregating all the RSS feeds produced by blogs into its index.

Go to the main Blog Search page (http://blogsearch.google.com), enter your terms in the search box, then click Search Blogs. As shown in Figure 14-5, a set of links near the top of the results presents blogs that are related to your search terms. If you click on one of these results, you go to the blog's home page, where you can navigate the entire blog. Other search results take you to individual postings that contain your search terms.

At the bottom of the blog search results page you see three links that allow you

Figure 14-5. Blog search gives you current opinions from the blogosphere.

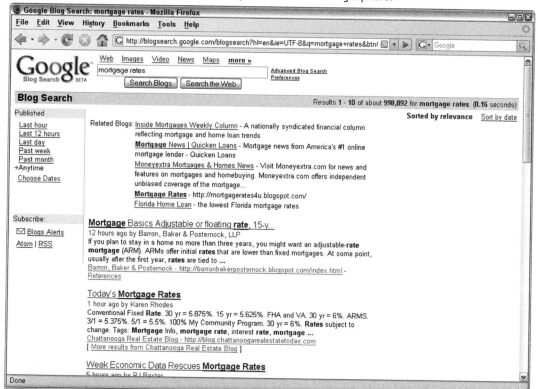

to be notified if someone writes a blog entry related to your search terms. For instance, if you do a blog search for Google Gadgets, the links will look like this:

- *Create an email alert for Google Gadgets.* Click this link, and you go to a Google Alerts page where you specify the criteria for e-mail messages that Google will send you periodically. The messages notify you if any blog search results for your chosen terms.

- *Add a blog search gadget for Google gadgets to your Google homepage.* Click this link, and you go to a page that lets you confirm that you want to add the search gadget. Click Add to Google, and the gadget appears on your personalized start page. Whenever you connect to your start page, you can view the top three blog search results.

- *Subscribe to a blog search feed for Google gadgets in Google Reader.* Click this link, and you connect to Google Reader, a service that gathers and organizes the "feeds" produced by some blogs. The Google Reader page presents the same blog search results you viewed earlier but gives you the additional option of subscribing to any of those feeds in case you want to receive updates from blogs you find particularly useful.

Google Finance

When it comes to business news and headlines, Google Finance is one of the most valuable resources you can choose on the site. It's the obvious place to turn if you want to check up on individual stock prices. But you can access other kinds of financial information as well. Go to http://finance.google.com to view general financial news headlines and market summaries.

Google Finance information is limited to U.S. companies, and it does not provide details on stock options or bonds. On the other hand, if you are researching a competitor or another company in your field, and that company offers publicly traded stock, you'll find extensive information about it. (You can test this out by doing a search for Google Inc.) You'll find a one-week stock chart, blog posts and discussions about the company, related companies, names and titles of senior management, and company summary, among other things.

In this chapter you learned about Google's many resources for business information. To be sure, Google provides you with information on virtually any subject. But when you're under pressure to produce reports that are complete and accurate, Google also provides you with specialized business content as well as information focused on particular topics. In the next chapter, you'll learn about another resource, one that can directly affect your bottom line: Google Base.

CHAPTER **15**

Buying and Selling on Google Base

The chapters to this point in Go Google have described ways for marketing your products and services—things that a small business or a lone entrepreneur can obviously market online. Even if all you have are your opinions about a subject, you can generate revenue through a blog, for instance. But after you list your product descriptions and create your blog listings, what do you have left? Just look through your filing cabinets, your notebooks, your sketchbooks, your photo albums, and your disk drives. Chances are there's a wealth of information you have created over the years that has never seen the light of day.

Google Base is an area where you can publish all the information that doesn't fit into your regular Web page or your blog, plus consumer goods that you want to sell in a format that resembles a classified ad. Google Base (http://base.google.com) is difficult to classify—and frankly, the name doesn't really describe it well. Google Information Base or Google Info Database might be clearer.

What Can You Do with Google Base?

You can use Google Base in two ways: as a consumer or as a producer of information or merchandise for sale. Most of this chapter focuses on Google as a business outlet: a place to make your content or products available to potential buyers. But it's also a specialty search engine that forms an interesting marketplace. It's far less well known than the main Google search service or Google Product Search. But it has the potential to be a viable place to buy and sell if it catches on. Simply knowing that Google Base is there and understanding what it does is the first step toward taking advantage of what Google is making available to you for free.

For the most part, people use Google Base to post merchandise for sale. Classified ads, job listings, and other "personals" make up the overwhelming bulk of the listings there. This isn't the only thing Google has in mind for the space, however. The company really intends for it to be a place where anyone can publish anything they have that they haven't yet published online because they don't have another place for it—poetry collections, recipes, letters, sketches, paintings, information booklets, and the like. Google Base can be a place to get your work before the public and get some feedback for it. If you offer items for sale, the Google Checkout system described in Chapter 16 can make that get paid quickly for them. Perhaps the best way to understand Google Base is to simply look around it. Go to the Google Base home page, http://base.google.com, and click on one of the item types listed on the home page. You'll find everything from Computers and Clothing to Recipes and Personals and immediately get some ideas. Go to the home page and click on one of the example categories. Here are a few examples of what you might put online:

- *Stock Photos*—I know some people who are terrific photographers. If you look through the Photographs category (you'll find a link on the Google Base home page; otherwise go to http://base.google.com/base/s2?a_n0 = photo graphs&a_y0 = 9&hl = en&gl = US) you'll see lots of photos of landscapes and other abstract scenes. The photos are offered for sale; one company offers up to 25 downloads per day for $199.

- *Recipes*—Did you ever want to write a cookbook? Do you simply want to share your favorite family recipes? You can post your recipes online and have them rated by visitors. In some cases, recipes are posted by individuals who simply want to share them. Others are published by businesses such as restaurants or cooking schools; clicking on the Google Base link takes you to the publisher's Web site. Google Base thus provides a way to steer more traffic to a business that wants to share information.

- *Vacation Rentals*—If you're looking for a place to stay during a vacation, or if you need to rent out a home in a desirable location, look to Google Base. It's already a popular venue with companies that specialize in providing short-term rentals.

If you have created an e-commerce-enabled Web site, you have a great way to present your goods or services to potential customers. But you may have also figured out that getting your offerings out in cyberspace is only half the battle. Being found is the other half. By listing on Google Base and applying descriptive terms called *attributes* to what you have to offer, you ensure that you'll be listed on Google's search engines. You also post links that can steer potential buyers and clients to your Web site: even if they don't purchase what you've listed on Google Base, they might contact you to find out more or purchase something else in your product line.

With each Google Base listing, you are able to include a hypertext link. The link can lead either to a more detailed description page posted on Google Base itself, or directly to your Web site, where someone can make a purchase or find out more about you or your products.

> **Note:** Simply posting a notice on Google Base doesn't mean your item is automatically indexed and listed prominently in Google Product Search or other parts of Google's search empire. The key with Google Base listings, as with listings in the "regular" Google Web search service, is in making your content relevant to whatever your intended customer is searching for. You need to include descriptive terms called attributes that will help your listings be found more easily. You also need to make your Google Base pages relevant by making links to your listings from your Web site. Your Google Base pages will also show up more prominently in search results if you make links to the Web pages that are linked to your Google Base product descriptions.

What *Can't* You Do with Google Base?

Although Google advertises Google Base as a place to "collect and organize information and to expose it to the world," not everything can be exposed. Google realizes that some of the content on the Internet can be described as immoral, improper, or basically illegal. It prohibits advertising many items, including:

- Pornography, especially materials including children
- Drugs and drug-related paraphernalia
- Illegal knives, guns, or other weapons
- Counterfeit identification cards and other ID materials
- Instructions on how to create explosive devices
- Prostitution services

It's a good idea to read through the Google Base–Program Policies page (http://base.google.com/base/base_policies.html) in detail. You may discover that some items can be marketed on Google Base under certain circumstances. For instance, you cannot sell drugs illegally. But registered pharmacies can market prescription drugs as long as they obtain a valid certification from the organization Square Trade (http://www.squaretrade.com). Some "adult" materials are allowed as long as you make it clear in the description that they are unsuitable for minors.

 Tip: If you want to get a look behind the scenes at how Google Base works and how real people use the service to upload their recipes and other information, checkout the Official Google Base Blog, http://googlebase.blogspot.com.

Shopping on Google Base as a Consumer

Google Base contains its own search interface—one that can be more extensive and sophisticated than the standard search form. Some types of information that are typically submitted to Google Base can be searched in complex and detailed ways. Suppose you are looking for a specific type of recipe to meet your dietary needs. You can go to the Google Base home page (http://base.google.com), click the Recipes link, and go to the home page for recipes. A detailed form at the top of the page (see Figure 15-1) lets you specify that you want recipes that have a certain amount of saturated fat, sodium, or specific ingredients.

When you click on the link for one of the recipes, you might be directed to a detailed description page on Google Base, or you might go to the Web site of the individual or business that posted the recipe. You never know exactly what you're going to find: you might go to a commercial site that collects thousands of recipes; you might be forced to view popup ads, and you might have to pay to view detailed content. On the other hand, you might go to a page posted by someone who lives in India and who is posting an authentic Indian family recipe simply to share it with others.

Searching for Merchandise

The Google Base home page can be accessed either at http://base.google.com, http://www.google.com/base, or http://base.google.com/base. In either case, you don't view a hierarchical directory of categories, as you might on eBay or on Google's own

Figure 15-1. Some items you submit to Google Base can be searched in a detailed way.

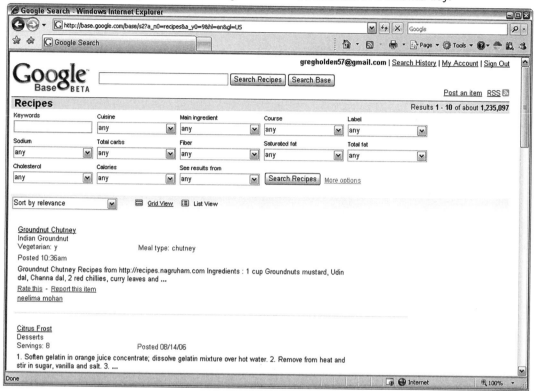

directory. Instead, you view a short list of "popular item types." The primary way to find listings on Google Base isn't by clicking hierarchically into categories and subcategories, but by entering a word or phrase in the search box shown in Figure 15-2 and seeing what turns up.

When you submit a search, you get many pages worth of results. You can sort the results by choosing an item from the "Sort by" drop-down list at the top of the first search page. You can also go to the category listing for the item near the top of the page (see Figure 15-3). Click on one of the individual product listings to find out more.

Searching for items isn't just a way to shop. It's a way to determine where to sell. You can search to locate merchandise that's similar to what you have to offer so you can find the best location for it. If you have an item to sell, you can click the "Post an item" link near the upper right-hand corner of the page, too.

You can also refine your search by adding attributes to the search terms you submit to Google Base. For instance, if you submit the following, you'll only turn up items that are in new condition and not new or refurbished:

Figure 15-2. Not surprisingly, a search box is the primary way to find items on Google Base.>>

Flat-screen TV Condition: new

If you search for the following you'll only search for items that are new and that are by the manufacturer Toshiba:

Flat-screen TV Condition: new Brand: Toshiba

Descriptive terms such as "Condition" and "Manufacturer" are known as attributes. Other common attributes you can add include:

- Location
- Payment
- Brand
- Manufacturer
- UPC

Your item will only turn up in response to searches if the seller has added such attributes. When you post your own items for sale, you need to be sure to add such

Figure 15-3. You can sort Google Base search results to find what you want.

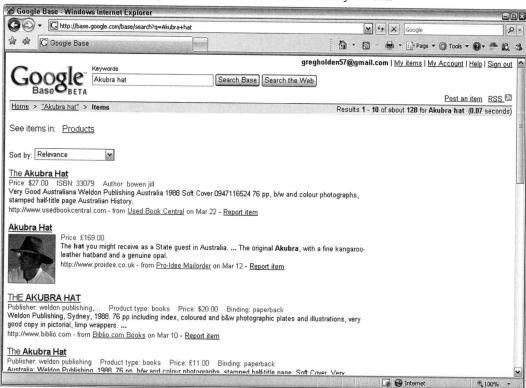

attributes so your items will be found more easily. The attributes differ depending on the type of item you are looking for. It's best to browse or search through the category in which you are interested and scan other item listings to see what attributes sellers have entered; then you can enter such attributes yourself if you want to help buyers find your items. For instance, if you go to the Google Base home page and click Housing, the drop-down menus at the top of the search indicate the attributes you should use for any listing in the Housing area: Listing type (for rent, for sale, sublet, and so on), Price, Property type (condo, coop, farm, land), Bedrooms, Bathrooms, and location (a main city within 30 miles of the location). This particular category also gives people who are looking for housing a map they can click on to find housing options in a particular area of the U.S. (see Figure 15-4).

Paying for What You've Purchased

In many cases, when you click on a link for a Google Base listing, you are taken to a commercial Web site. Once there, you use the checkout procedure that the e-commerce merchant already has in place. Usually, you'll be able to pay with a credit card, either directly or through an electronic payment service such as PayPal. (Pay-

Figure 15-4. Some Google Base categories contain maps and other attributes specific to what's being offered.

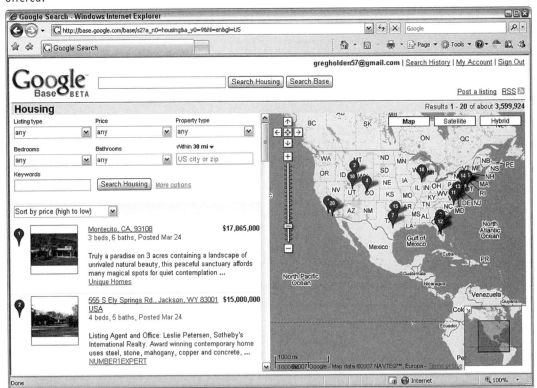

Pal, in fact, is owned by eBay and is used by a large number of eBay buyers and sellers to complete transactions.)

There is another option, however. It's called Google Checkout, and it's Google's own transaction system. Checkout lets members purchase products by clicking the *Buy* button on a product listing page and having the amount deducted from the checking account or credit card account that is associated with their Google Account. Google Checkout facilitates the entire credit card transaction. In order for the system to work, of course, both buyer and seller have to have Google accounts. Buyers can enter credit card information so the purchase price can be deducted from the account. Sellers need to have a checking account connected to the Google Account so the amount can be transferred into it. You'll find out more about Checkout and other options for merchants in Chapter 16.

You can find Google Checkout items by doing a search and then checking the Google Checkout Stores only check box. When the Products home page appears (see Figure 15-5), click the Search Products button to view results from merchants who accept this payment service.

Figure 15-5. You can find Google Checkout merchants by checking this box on the search form.

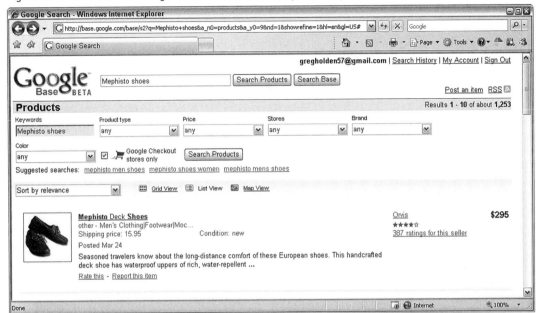

Typically, you then click a Buy or Add to Cart button to access the shopping cart page the merchant has established. On the shopping cart page, click the Google Checkout button. You then go to Google's Secure Checkout page, shown in Figure 15-6.

Selling on Google Base as a Provider

As a businessperson, you can take advantage of Google Base to purchase copiers, computer equipment, and other supplies. But the service is even more important for entrepreneurs who want to have another place to advertise their sales listings. If you already sell through an eBay Store or Yahoo! Store, you can automatically publish links to your descriptions on Google Base to drive more traffic there. If you only have a few items to sell, you can upload them to Google Base either on an individual basis or in bulk. All of these options are described in the sections that follow.

Listing Items for Sale

It's easy to create a new sales listing on Google Base. The first step is to click the Post an Item link that appears on virtually every Google Base page. If you are on the Google Base home page—

Figure 15-6. Google Checkout is a popular option with Google Base sellers.

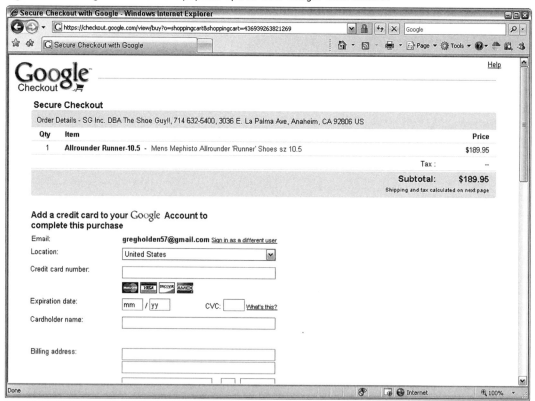

1. Click the One at a time link in the blue box that provides sellers with links where they can get started. The Post an Item page appears.

2. Choose a category or item type where the item should be listed. Choose an option from the Choose an existing item type drop-down list (see Figure 15-7) to see if your item fits into one of Google Base's existing categories. If it does not, click the button next to Create your own item type and type a name there. (When in doubt, the catch-all Products will probably suffice.) It's better to pick an existing category because shoppers are more likely to find your items there when they browse Google Base. Well-known, long-established categories will attract more traffic than new ones.

3. Click the Next button and the Edit Item Screen will appear.

4. Enter details about your product for sale as well as photos. If you have sold on eBay or other marketplaces before, this sort of form will be familiar to you. But if you're selling for the first time, you want to take your time and come up with a title and description that are detailed, that play up your item's desirable features, and that contain important keywords shoppers might enter if they're looking for what you have to sell. Among the important features of the form are:

Figure 15-7. You begin by identifying a Google Base category where your item will be listed.

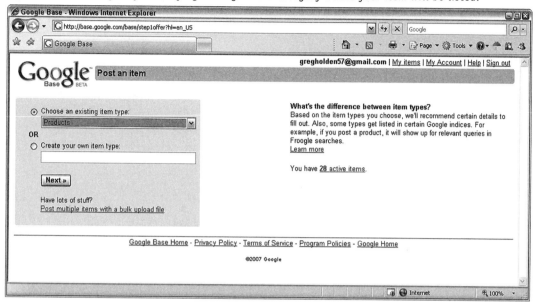

- *Title*—This should be short but be sure to include brand names and model numbers as well as sizes and colors if these apply.

- *Price and price type*—Price lets you specify a price for each tem you are offering. However, Price type lets you specify whether the price is fixed (in other words, non-negotiable) or negotiable (choose Negotiable or Minimum price).

- *Product type*—Enter some descriptive keywords that describe the type of item for sale.

- *Condition*—Used, New, Like New, or Refurbished are typical options.

- *Location*—Be sure to include a location to attract buyers who are interested in picking up locally.

- *Pictures*—Google Base is exceptional among e-commerce Web sites in the range of file types you can attach to a listing. Most sites only accept JPEG or GIF images. Google Base will let you save files in JPEG, PNG (Portable Network Graphics, GIF, TIFF (Tagged Image File Format), and BMP (Windows Bitmap) format and upload them to its Web site. In addition, you can upload as many as 15 separate files.

Each of the aforementioned fields will potentially serve as an attribute that a shopper can enter in order to locate what you are selling. So don't skip any parts of the form. Items with images are sure to attract more attention than those that don't. Try to crop your images close to the object you are trying to depict. Use bright lights rather than the flash from your digital camera, which might create flares or distracting "hot spots" in your object. Also consider photographing in bright light outdoors. Try to keep your image file size at 50K or less so your images will appear quickly in your viewer's browser window. Since Google Base gives you the ability to include as many as 15 images, you don't have to be stingy with photos; include as many as you can.

If you are selling something that is used, be upfront about photographing any cracks, scratches, or flaws that buyers need to know about. It's far better to be upfront about flaws than to "surprise" the buyer who only sees them upon receipt. You might end up with an unhappy buyer who only wants to return what was purchased.

Tip: To keep image sizes small, I personally photograph merchandise in the coarsest TIFF resolution available, 640 × 480. I then open the images in a graphics program and save them in JPEG format at 72 dpi resolution. Computer monitors can only display 72 or 96 dpi (dots per inch/pixels per inch), so it doesn't make sense to take photos for the Web that are high resolution and that end up being 1MB or more in size. They'll take too long to appear in someone's browser window, and the viewer will become frustrated and fail to follow through with a purchase.

When you have captured your images, save them on your computer with a short name that will help you find them easily. I decided to sell a signed copy of one of my books on Google Base, so I named my two image files book1.jpg and book2.jpg. Figure 15-8 shows how I filled out the Edit item form.

Whatever you sell on Google Base, speak as positively as you can about it. Play up what makes your item unique. My book isn't particularly unique—you can find it more cheaply on Amazon.com, I'm sure—but I thought offering to sign it for someone would make it more desirable. My description, accordingly, began as follows:

Selling Beyond eBay
A new book autographed for you personally
By author Greg Holden

Selling Beyond eBay, published by AMACOM in 2006, takes a detailed look at how to extend your sales reach beyond eBay to many other kinds of e-commerce venues—including Google. You learn how to sell on marketplaces including:

Figure 15-8. Be sure to fill out as much of the Edit Item form as possible.

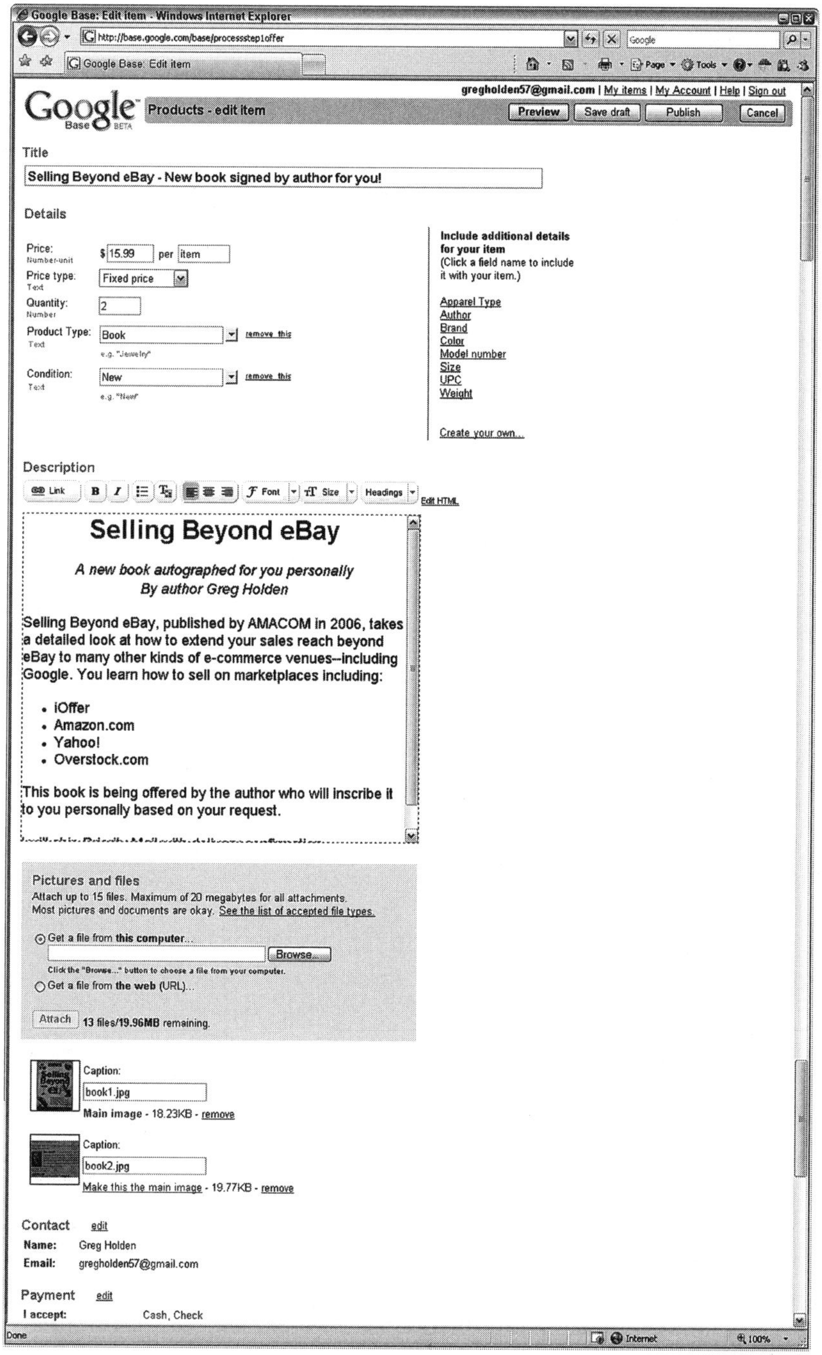

- iOffer
- Amazon.com
- Yahoo!
- Overstock.com

This book is being offered by the author who will inscribe it to you personally based on your request.

I also took advantage of the Edit Item form's toolbar, found just above the Description box, which enabled me to format my listing's heading and subheading and to center them as well. I also included a bulleted list to make the text more readable and add visual interest. Nothing adds interest like images, however. I checked Get a File from This Computer and clicked the Browse button to upload the two images I had previously saved on my file system.

5. Click the Preview button at the bottom of the Edit Item form. This gives you a chance to view your listing so you can correct typos or other errors before it goes online. My own listing is shown in Figure 15-9.

6. When you're ready, click the Publish button, and your item will go online.

If you selected Google Checkout as one of your payment options, and if you have not yet set up a Google Checkout account, a Web page will appear that lets you sign up for an account (see Chapter 16 for more). Listing on Google is similar to preparing a file for listing on Google's consumer search service Google Product Search (which is also described in Chapter 16).

Listing in Bulk

If you operate an e-commerce Web site or if you depend on online sales for all or part of your income, you're looking for shortcuts to beat the one-at-a-time listing procedure listed above. Luckily for you, Google Base will accept a file that contains your item descriptions and is saved in one of several common formats:

- TSV (tab-delimited)
- RSS 1.0 or 2.0
- Atom 0.3 or 1.0

Once you have a file prepared—

1. Go to the Google Base home page and click the Bulk Upload link.
2. When the Bulk Upload file page appears, click the Register a new bulk upload file link.

Figure 15-9. Be sure to preview and proofread your listing before it goes online.

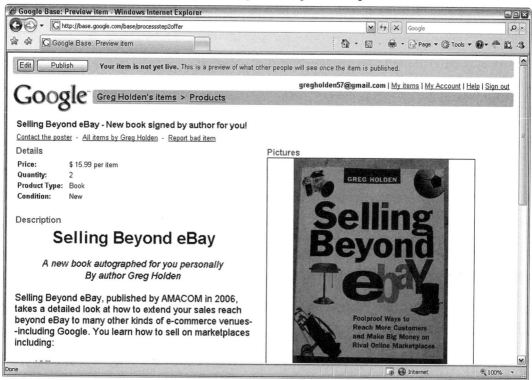

3. When the Settings page appears, review any information that Google Base already has about you based on previous sales, make any additions or changes, and click Next.

4. In the next page, entitled Specify a Bulk Upload, you name your upload file and choose an option from the Type drop-down list that describes the type of items you want to list.

   Although the Products choice is pretty inclusive, you can only choose one option at a time, so your bulk upload file can only contain one type of item. If you want to sell a completely different group of items, you'll need to create a separate upload file.

5. Click Register bulk upload file and continue to formatting instructions.

6. In the next page you describe the attributes of your bulk upload items. You need to include at least eight attributes: title, description, brand, product type, condition, link, location, and price. You can also make choices from 58 other possible attributes; see the Formatting Instructions page for a complete list. When you're done, click the I'm done formatting my file. Continue to the

upload button at the bottom of the page, and follow the instructions on subsequent pages to complete your file upload.

Connecting Your Online Store to Google Base

If you already sell online through an eBay Store, a Yahoo! Store, or another outlet, you can advertise your sales items on Google Base through a tool called the Google Base Store Connector. Google Base isn't setting itself as a direct competitor to these popular sales outlets. It's a venue where you can link to your sales descriptions on your conventional sales outlets, however. Like other Google tools, the Store connector is free and easy to use. Even if your eBay or Yahoo! store listings already appear in Google search results, the Store Connector gives you another place for your sales to appear online.

 Note: The Store connector only works with eBay Stores located in the U.S. It requires you to have Windows Vista or Windows XP or 2000 with Service Pack 3 installed.

To get started with the Store Connector—

1. Go to the Store Connector page (http://base.goodle.com/base/storeconnector) and click the blue Download the Google Base Store Connector button. You immediately download the setup file for the program.

2. Click Run to download and then automatically run the application.

3. Follow the steps shown in succeeding screens to complete the setup. When you finish, the Store Connector window shown in Figure 15-10 appears.

4. Type your eBay or Yahoo! Store login information in the boxes provided and click Copy items for my store. In just a few seconds, the main categories contained in your store are copied. If you click the plus sign (+) next to each one of the categories as shown in Figure 15-11, the current listings within those categories are presented.

5. Click the Publish items to Google Base link at the bottom of the window, to copy your sales listings to Google Base. You may be prompted to sign in with your Google Account. A progress bar appears at the bottom of the Store

Figure 15-10. Store Connector is configured to copy your eBay or Yahoo! Store listings to Google Base.

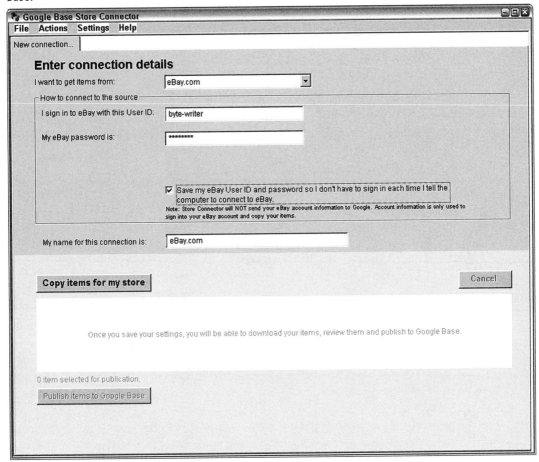

Connector window to indicate the progress of the data transfer. A window appears notifying you when your listings expire and you'll need to republish them on Google Base.

6. When the information has been copied, you can click View my items on Google Base to actually view your sales listings.

7. When you click this link, a new browser window opens, displaying your active items for sale (see Figure 15-12). If you ever want to return to this Dashboard window in the future, you can log in to Google Base with your Google Account and click the My Items link. As you can see, the page not only shows you what's currently listed for sale, but also shows you how many page impres-

Figure 15-11. You can uncheck any categories or individual items you don't want to publish.

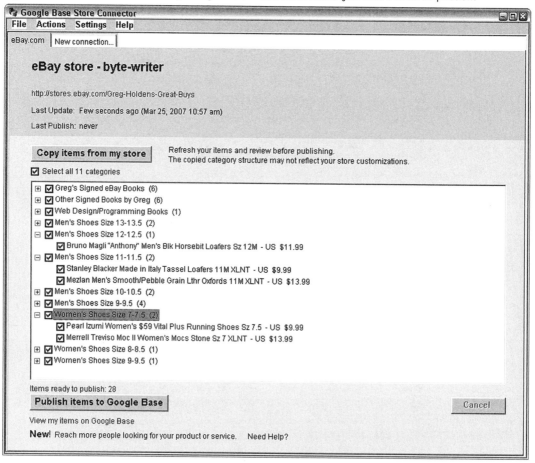

sions the listing has received on Google Base and how many times visitors have clicked on the Google Base link to actually view your sales item on eBay or Yahoo!.

Note: If you run an eBay Store, your store listings are automatically listed on the main Google search service. You can also export your store listings to Google Product Search, and I explain how to do this in my previous book for AMACOM: *Selling Beyond eBay*. Still, it can't hurt to list your store descriptions on Google Base as well: you can never have too many links pointing to your online merchandise for sale. And if you send a feed

Figure 15-12. Google Base gives you a Dashboard page where you can track your items for sale.

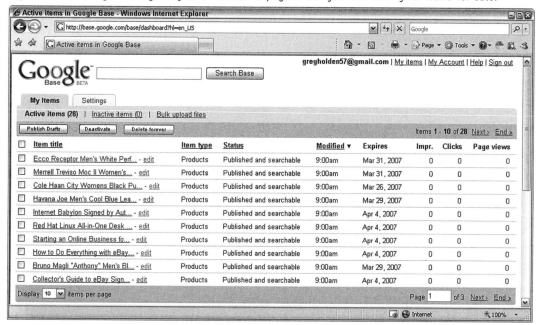

of your listings to Google Base every few days, your listings will appear on the main Google search engine as well.

Should You Sell on Google Base or on eBay?

While you're filling out the Google Base form and uploading photos to list your item there, you might wonder if you're really making your item visible to the widest possible audience. The Sell Your Item form on eBay's site is similar; isn't it a better choice to list on eBay?

For items where you aren't sure of the value and you don't know how much someone will be willing to pay, it's a good idea to list on eBay. eBay's auction formats let you throw your item open to the whims of its bidders, and you might find that they are willing to pay more than you ever imagined for your object. If you want to sell something especially valuable, choose eBay. eBay, after all, is a more well-established marketplace that has more than 40 million registered users. Google Base has been around only a short time, and it has far fewer users.

On the other hand, eBay charges fees not only when you sell an item but simply when you put it up for sale. For everyday household goods that aren't going to attract lots of bids, it might not be worth the trouble to sell on eBay. Google Base, on the other hand, is free; you only pay if you receive a payment with Google Check-out, and even then the fee is relatively low: you pay 2.5 percent of the final sales price plus 25 cents per transaction. If you're looking to save money and want to sell items at a fixed price for up to 30 days (far longer than eBay's maximum 10-day period for an auction), Google Base is a good choice.

In this chapter you learned about a cost-effective and easy-to-use place to sell items at a fixed or negotiable price: Google Base. Google Base has lots of advantages: it can give you a way to publicize merchandise you already have up for sale on another site, such as eBay. You can also list merchandise for sale for the first time on Google Base. But Google Base isn't the only option for e-commerce entrepreneurs. If you want to sell other merchandise online or gain more attention for your sales items by adding them to Google's database, you should investigate the services described in Chapter 16.

CHAPTER **16**

Improving Catalog Sales

Google isn't primarily an e-commerce hosting service—a business that gives Web server space, a sales catalog and shopping cart software, and a checkout service for small business owners who want to sell their goods and services on the Web. Nevertheless, enterprising online entrepreneurs can put together several of Google's sales-oriented tools to make some extra money. You can create a Web-based catalog with Web Page Creator, post catalog listings and descriptions online, and send shoppers to a checkout area called (appropriately enough) Google Checkout.

Google's online tools are especially good for individuals who already operate as online merchants. If you already have merchandise to sell, and if you already have an online sales catalog, Google gives you several ways to expand your online sales. One of those options, Google Base, is described in Chapter 15. In this chapter, you'll explore options that can, together, help you increase your sales performance and make your transactions go more smoothly.

Listing Your Sales Merchandise on Google Product Search

Google Product Search, or GPS (http://www.google.com/products), is a search service within a search service. It's Google's search engine that's targeted at shoppers who need to find consumer goods. GPS is an aggregator, a site that gathers the contents of many different Web sites and puts them in one convenient location. It also filters out articles about a product and returns only listings for items for sale. Instead of having to search through five, six, or more separate online retailers to find the one with the best price for a Prada purse, for example, you can do a search for "Prada purse" on Google and get page after page of results from many different retailers. You can quickly compare prices and pick the best deal.

GPS also enables you to list the contents of an existing online store—such as an eBay Store, a Yahoo!Store, or a Microsoft Small Business—in its search database.

Even if you have a brick-and-mortar business you can have your store listed on this popular search tool. Product Search, like the regular Google search engine, uses computer programs called spiders to assemble content. The spider scours the contents of millions of Web pages, indexing their contents and storing them in a huge database. Web pages that offer products for sale are automatically indexed in GPS; eBay Stores pages are indexed as well. And as you can see from Figure 16-1, GPS's user-friendly search interface looks just like Google's.

Transmitting a Feed to GPS

Simply having a presence on the Web isn't enough to ensure that your items' brand names, model numbers, prices, and descriptions are going to be included in GPS. You'll greatly improve your chances of being included by Google or GPS if you take the effort to make GPS aware that you exist—and not only that, but transfer your sales catalog listings to GPS in the form of a *feed*.

Like Google, GPS uses automated indexing programs to scour pages from merchant Web sites and compile it in an index. Small-scale e-commerce sites might not

Figure 16-1. Google Product Search is Google's specialty search service for consumer merchandise.

get indexed automatically by GPS. But merchants can improve their chances of being included by transferring catalog listings to the search service. There are two options:

- Transfer your sales to a part of Google called Google Base, a storage area for files of all sorts. Everything on Google Base ends up being listed on GPS.
- Keep your sales listed only on your own Web site but use Google Checkout to conduct electronic transactions with your buyers.

Before you try either of these options, it's a good idea to check the Google Product Search (GPS) Web site to see if other merchants selling your products are listed there by other sellers. The site's search interface is as simple and easy to use as Google itself. PS database is already crammed with listings from prominent online retailers, and it's hard to compete with them if there's nothing unique or exceptional about what you have to offer. For instance, listings for brand-name items that are well known, like a Sony Playstation or a Gucci handbag, will find lots of competition. On the other hand, if you want to compete with the "big guys" and you have something unique to offer, follow the steps shown below:

1. Go to the Information for Sellers page (http://www.google.com/base/help/sellongoogle.html).
2. Click the Log In to Google Base button and log in with your Google Account information.
3. Read the Terms of Service, if necessary, and click the button saying that you accept the terms.
4. When the Sell with Google page (direct URL: http://www.google.com/base/help/sellongoogle.html) shown in Figure 16-2 appears, read the instructions. (Notice that you've jumped to Google Base, Google's marketplace for sellers, described in Chapter 13.)
5. If you want to list your existing sales items in Google's database so they can also be indexed more readily with Google Product Search choose Products from the Choose an existing item type drop-down list.
6. Next, you need to decide whether you are going to list your products one at a time or all at once. If you want to choose the one at a time option, click Next to move to the next page. If you have a group of products you want to list all at once, click the bulk upload link.

The instructions differ depending on which option you choose (one at a time or all at once). More detailed instructions for each link are listed below. The one at a time option is discussed first.

Figure 16-2. You list items on Google Base, where they will automatically be indexed on GPS.

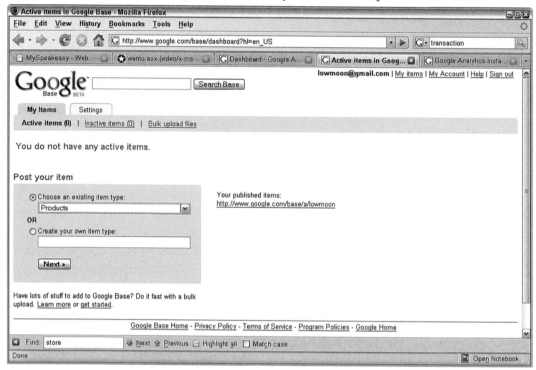

Posting One Item at a Time

If you only have individual items to post rather than a whole catalog's worth, or if you only have one item in a particular category, follow the directions below for posting the item to GPS.

1. Click Next to choose the one at a time listing option.
2. When the Edit Item page appears, fill out the information for your single item. If you want more details about this process refer to the Google Base instructions in Chapter 15. The point is that, in order to list a single item on Google Product Search, you list it on Google Base; once you do, it will automatically be listed—and, at the same time, it will be listed in Google Base's own searchable directory.

Uploading in Bulk: Creating the File

If you have lots of sales items to list, the one at a time option will prove too time-consuming. Instead, list your items all at once. You do this by creating a bulk upload file and then registering it. First, you create the bulk upload file. If you have a sales

Figure 16-3. Fill out the Edit Item form to list a single item in Google Base and on Google Product Search.

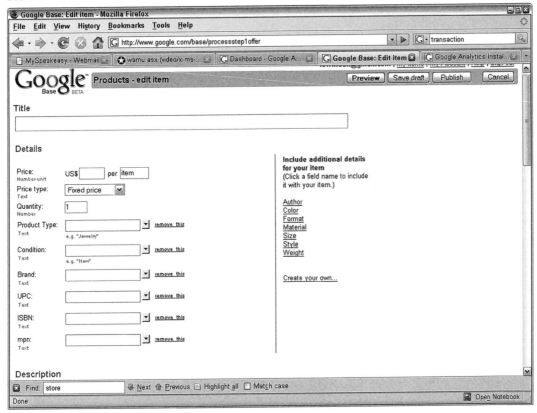

catalog, the process of creating a feed is a matter of exporting the information to a tab-delimited text file or an XML file. Exactly how you create the file depends on the kind of online store you have. If your inventory is maintained in the form of an Excel spreadsheet, the .xls spreadsheet format is supported. You can also create a tab-delimited text file (.txt). If your catalog already exists on the Web, you have to depend on your catalog host to help you create a file in one of the four formats that use eXtensible Markup Language (XML) instructions:

- Really Simple Syndication (RSS) version 1.0 or 2.0
- Atom version 0.3 or 1.0

If you create a tab-delimited file, the fields required vary depending on the type of item you are listing. If you list a product, your file must include the ten field attributes shown below:

- *Brand*–This is the brand name of the product.
- *Condition*–You describe the condition: new, used, refurbished, and so on.
- *Description*–This is your product description.
- *Expirationdate*–If the item expires on a certain date, list the date here.
- *ID*–This is your internal product ID number.
- *Imagelink*–This is the URL of the image that illustrates the product.
- *ISBN*–If you are selling a book, list its ISBN number here.
- *Link*–If the product appears on a Web page, list the URL here.
- *MPN*–If a Manufacturer's Part Number is listed for the item, list it here.
- *Price*–This is the price of your product.
- *Product_Type*–You need to list the category or subcategory that describes your product here.
- *Title*–Enter the title for your sale here.
- *UPC*–Enter the UPC for your product here.

You'll find detailed instructions for exporting data from an Excel spreadsheet to a tab-delimited file at http://base.google.com/support/bin/answer.py?answer = 58083& hl = en. You'll also find instructions on this page for creating an XML file.

Make sure the data fields are separated by tabs. Save the file with a file name that ends in .txt (if you are creating a tab-delimited file) or .xml (if you are creating an XML file as described in the following section). Then, you can upload the file as described in the section "Upload Your Feed" below.

Creating an XML Feed from eBay Store Listings

I have an eBay Store, and eBay makes it easy to convert any store's contents to RSS format. The steps should be somewhat similar for other hosting services. Do the following:

1. Go to My eBay (http://my.ebay.com), log in with your eBay User ID and password, and click Sign In Securely to view your My eBay page.
2. Click the Manage My Store link.
3. When the Manage My Store page appears, click Listing Feeds.
4. On the Listing Feeds page, you learn that you have two options for creating a feed of your store. eBay will automatically make your store listings available in the popular RSS feed format. But under the heading Search engine and comparison sites, you learn that eBay will make a file of your eBay Store listings available to third-party search engines such as Google Base, which, in turn, makes your catalog available to GPS.

5. Make a note of the URL where your data feed will be listed. The URL will be in this format:
http://esssl.ebay.com/GetListings/Seller'sStoreName
For instance, if your site's name is Greg's Great Buys, you would go to the URL:
http://esssl.ebay.com/GetListings/GregsGreatBuys

6. The punctuation and blank spaces are removed from your store's name when eBay posts them to the URL. When the file is ready, click the button next to Make a file of my Store Inventory listings available, and click Apply. eBay will create a file of your sales listings that presents each item with the following fields:
- Item title
- Item description
- The URL of the item's individual description in the eBay Store
- Whether the item can be ordered
- Current price
- Availability
- Item number (this is a numeric code eBay assigns to each item
- Shipping cost (if you specified it in the Shipping & Handling field)
- Gallery picture (if you included this thumbnail image with your description)
- Quantity: the number you have for sale (eBay Stores frequently offer multiple instances of an item for sale)
- Price currency: Dollars, Euros, Yen, and so on

7. As eBay explains, you might have to wait up to 12 hours for your file to become available. Go to the URL to view your file, and when it is ready, click Save As, and save the file on your computer. You'll see two links at the URL. The first link is an XML file in the eBay Store listing export format; the second is a Google Base file in RSS format. Click the link for the Google Base file, and you see a simple list as well as a Subscribe now button (see Figure 16-4).

Registering Your Feed

Now that you have your RSS or tab-delimited text file, you need to register it with Google Base.

1. If you're not already signed in, when you go to the Google Product Search home page at http:/www.google.com/products, enter your Google Account username and password and click on Sign in button. After you sign in, you might need to redirect yourself back to www.google.com/products. You don't

Figure 16-4. You or others can view your XML feed and subscribe to it.

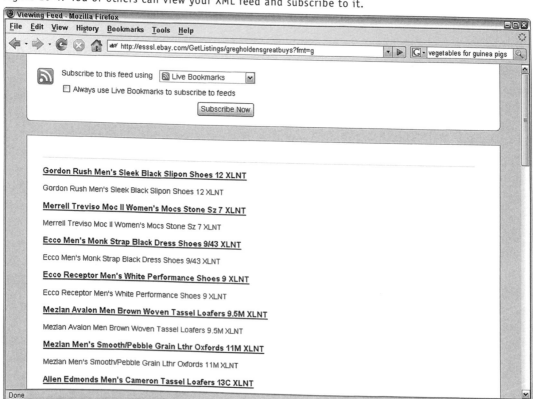

need an account that is special to Google Base; you can sign in with the
Google Account you use for other Google-related services.

1. Click on the Information for Sellers link.

2. Click the Log in to Google Base button.

3. Click the Bulk upload files hyperlink.

4. Click Register a new bulk upload file link.

5. Complete the About Me page. Take the time to add a description of your
store or your company as well as the URL to your Web site if you have one.
If you are running a business online, any chance you get to advertise your
store's name and URL is worth taking.

6. Click the *Next* button.

7. Enter the name of the bulk upload file in the File Name box.

8. Select an item type from the Item Type drop down box or create a new type.

9. Click the Register bulk upload file and continue to formatting instructions
button.

10. On the Bulk Upload Files tab, any files you have registered will appear on this page. Press the Browse button to direct Google to the location of your file.

11. Press the Upload and process the file button. You will get a message that Google Base is uploading and processing your file.

Adding Your Catalog Contents to Google Catalogs

The most common way to advertise goods or services to purchase online is through a catalog—a set of Web pages that contains descriptions and prices of various items. Those of us who spend several hours a day online begin to think that every kind of content is now available on the Internet, but it's not necessarily true. There's still a wealth of information that's only available in printed form, and that includes the many mail-order catalogs that are sent out to shoppers. As I write this, the popular

Figure 16-5. Use this form to upload your XML file.

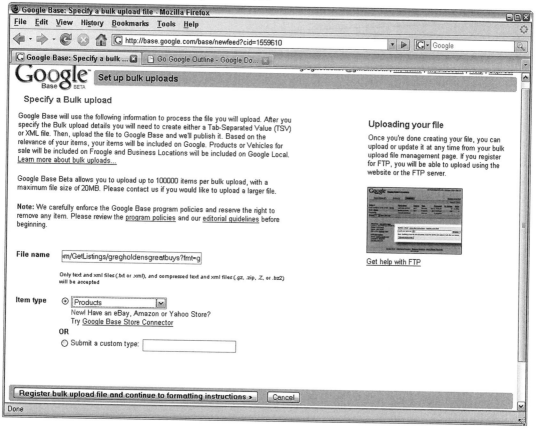

furniture store IKEA sends me a regular sales catalog by snail mail. But the company's options for shopping online are woefully limited. If you do have a catalog, whether it's online or in printed booklet form, you can take advantage of Google Catalogs to help you sell your merchandise and receive payment as well.

Google Catalogs does for sales catalogs what Google Product Search does for individual items listed in online stores. It helps shoppers search through actual sales catalogs that merchants post online. Rather than a series of hyperlinks, these catalogs are reproduced in Adobe's Portable Document format (PDF): you flip through them one page at a time as though you're flipping through a book. PDF files can be slow to load, but if you can't get your catalog online any other way, Google Catalogs gives you a good option.

Google Catalogs gives shoppers several advantages over actual printed catalogs: Customers don't have to order and wait for them to arrive in the mail, and you can search through them by keyword, too. Shoppers do have to call you using the phone number you provide with your catalog. But many shoppers prefer this low-tech way of making purchases because it allows them to speak to a store employee in person and convey their credit card information verbally rather than transmitting it via the Internet. And it saves a lot of money in printing, paper, and mailing costs.

 Tip: As an alternative to telephone sales, you can also publish the URL of your Web site along with your catalog. That gives shoppers who are comfortable with buying online the option of accessing your online catalog so they can purchase there.

Publishing your catalog with Google Catalogs gives you a way to include high-quality photos and formatting with your sales descriptions. You also don't go through much effort: you can mail your actual printed catalog to Google, and they scan the printed pages. Rather than producing static photographic-style images of your catalog pages, Google uses optical character recognition to turn the text into searchable body text on Web pages. It's also up to you, the individual merchant, to make sure the most current version of your catalog is posted online; you need to re-post your catalogs as they are produced.

 As Google admits in its Help files, its character recognition technology is not perfect and may produce occasional errors. (If you see an error, you are encouraged to report it by sending a message to catalogs-help

@google.com.) If it's important to you to get all your listings just right, you might want to scan them yourself and put them on your own Web site.

If you want to add your printed catalog to Google Catalogs, go to the information page for catalog vendors at http://catalogs.google.com/googlecatalogs/help_merchants .html. Make sure your catalog fits into the requirements; at this writing, only U.S.-based mail-order product catalogs are allowed; information sheets and other printed brochures cannot be included.

You then have to sign up for a Google Catalogs account (click the sign up link on the information page or go to http://catalogs.google.com/catalogs/application).

Fill out the application form on the Welcome to Google Catalogs page to join Google Catalogs. After you fill out the application, you obtain a personalized code that you can e-mail out to your customers to steer them to your Google Catalogs page. It's free to sign up for Google Catalogs, however. When you obtain an account, you get a mailing address you can use to send Google a copy of your printed catalog; you can also mail them a CD containing a PDF version of your catalog if you prefer. Once Google is on your usual catalog mailing list, it will receive new copies of your catalog as they are produced and the latest, updated version will then be posted online.

Facilitating Purchases with Google Checkout

Google Checkout is an online payment service, which lets individuals pay for items with a credit card and then transfers payment to the seller (after subtracting a fee for handling the money). It's a competitor to the popular payment service PayPal, which is owned by eBay and is used by many eBay members to complete auction transactions. Google Checkout accepts payments from buyers who use Visa, American Express, MasterCard, or Discover.

 Note: If you sign up for a merchant account with PayPal your customers don't have to pay anything to send you a payment. But you are charged a fee for receiving the money. PayPal subtracts between 1.9 and 2.9 percent, plus a 30-cent flat fee, for each transaction. Google Checkout is free until the end of 2007; on January 1, 2008, a 2 percent plus $.20 transaction fee went into place. However, if you purchase ads through AdWords, you get up to 10 times your AdWords purchases for free. In other words, if you spend $50 on AdWords in January, you get up to $500 in transaction fees on Google Checkout for free. Any transactions beyond that are charged the 2% plus $.20 transaction fee.

Google Checkout has the advantage of being integrated with Google's AdWords paid search marketing service (see Chapter 5 for more on AdWords). If you advertise your business by placing AdWords ads along with Google search results, and if you use Google Checkout, you get a Google Checkout "badge" added to your AdWords ads. The badge is supposed to tell shoppers that they can pay you using Google Checkout; it also has the advantage of making your ad stand out from others that are usually crowded around a typical page of search results. Instead of having to bid a slightly higher cost per click fee to give your ads a better placement in search results, you can get a badge, which will instantly give your AdWords ads more visual interest.

 Note: Google says its Checkout service is intended for merchants who are offering tangible goods (objects that can be packed up in boxes and shipped to buyers). But if you belong to a nonprofit organization that has 501c3 tax-exempt status, you are allowed to process transactions for intangible goods, such as digital or downloadable products, services, subscriptions, and even donations. Google Checkout is free for nonprofits.

Signing Up for Google Checkout

If you put an item up for sale through Google Base's Edit Item form (a process described in Chapter 15), and if you haven't yet signed up for Google Checkout, you'll automatically be sent to the registration form for the Checkout service just after your item is listed. Otherwise, you can sign up for Google Checkout at any time by going to the service's home page (https://checkout.google.com).

1. Click the Sign up now button.

2. The next page asks you if you already have a Google Account. By now hopefully you will click Yes.

3. Then you will be asked if you would like to use a single account for all Google Services. If you select yes, you will then be prompted to Sign in to Google Checkout with the existing e-mail and password that you use to access other Google services.

4. Click on the Sign in and Continue button.

5. In the first page, entitled Setup Your Account, you enter information about yourself and your business (see Figure 16-6). You fill out the form with your contact information, check the box at the bottom of the form that says you agree to the Terms of Service, and click Complete Sign-Up.

6. Click the Complete Sign Up button and you are registered for Google Checkout.

Google may not overtly portray itself as an e-commerce Web site, the fact is that that it provides potential customers with a way to list items for sale (including photos that Google hosts). It gives merchants a way to market its items in Google's own

Figure 16-6. Use this form to become a Google Checkout merchant.

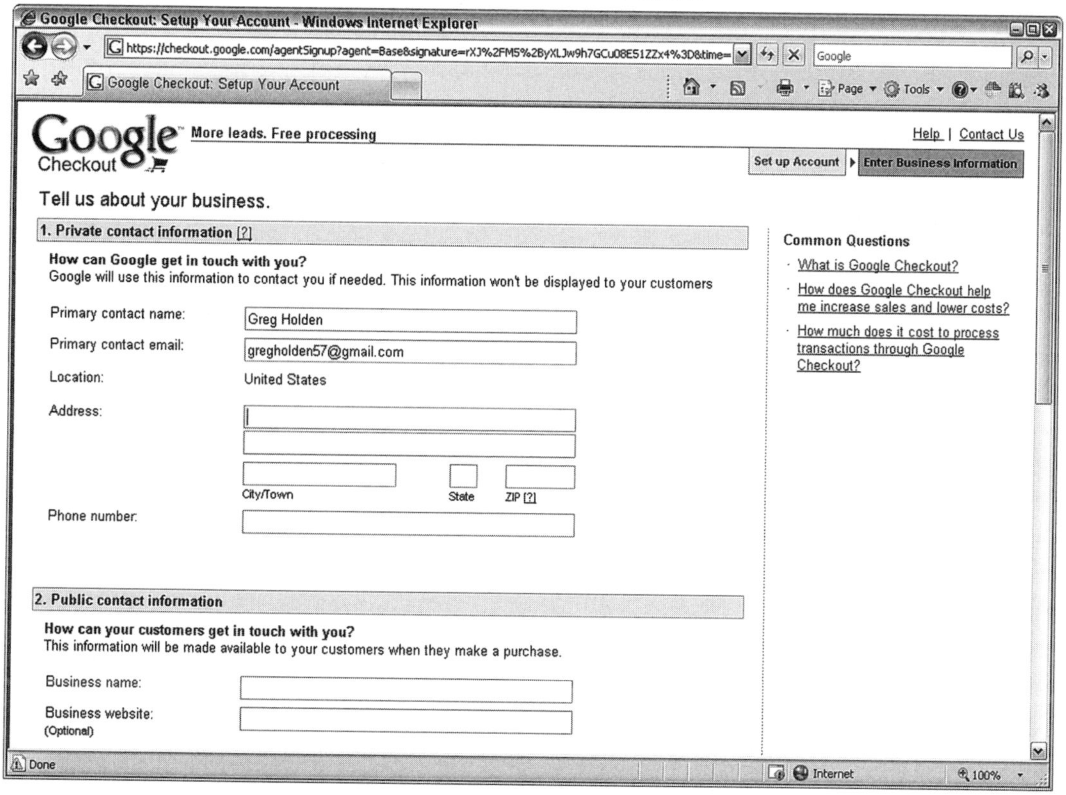

search results. And it gives buyers and sellers alike a way to complete transactions through Google Checkout. For a business that sells through an e-commerce Web site, it's a great way to increase sales. Another way is to track the visitors to your own Web site. Google can help you with that, too, through its Google Analytics service, which you learn about in the next chapter.

CHAPTER **17**

Improving Web Site Performance with Google Analytics

Many of Google's services are focused on gaining more attention for your Web site, whether you have created it to promote yourself personally or to attract more potential clients and customers to your business. Once you have created a site with Page Creator and begun to promote it with search optimization and an AdWords ad, you can't rest on your laurels. Simply sitting back and watching the customers knock on your front door or visit your Web site's home page isn't enough. A successful e-commerce business takes a proactive and ongoing approach to gathering data about its shoppers to get to know them better. It's important to track who simply browses through your Web site and who goes on to make a purchase from you. This sort of analysis and research can turn a stagnant e-commerce site into a productive one.

Google Analytics is an advanced and sophisticated tool that, on the surface, provides you with extensive data about who visits your Web site. But Analytics is much more than that. It enables you to put the pieces together and improve your overall business presence. You can decide whether to improve your home page design, your blog, or your AdWords ad performance. You can then decide whether or not to improve your local reach using the Google Maps search service, which is also described in this chapter. Analytics is an amazing tool considering that it's free, and that Google isn't primarily a Web hosting service: it gives you as many as 80 separate reports that can be customized to your needs and that give you an up-to-date profile of your site with data that is typically updated in less than an hour.

Using Google Analytics to Boost Your Business

Google Analytics is a Web traffic monitoring and analysis program that can provide detailed reports showing you how many people visit your site from day to day, where your visitors are located, which visitors are coming for the first time and which ones are returning, and what your top referral sources are, thus making it a powerful marketing tool.

But this brief explanation only scratches the surface of what Google Analytics can do. For the novice of data monitoring, understanding Google Analytics and fully using its capabilities will require that you also gain an understanding of certain fundamental concepts of data analysis. In fact, there is so much to learn about Google Analytics, and so much indispensable information already available online, that this section of the book is intended more as a roadmap that will point you in the right direction and get you started. Once you know where to look online, you will be able to find the resources you need to use the many tools at your disposal to tailor Google Analytics to your company's particular needs.

Understanding Web Traffic Analysis

When you create a Web site, your hosting service should provide you with a way to track the number of visits each page receives as well as some indication of where they are coming from. This isn't information for its own sake: you want to be able to analyze and act on the data. By learning about who visits your Web site, how your visitors find you, and what they do while they are browsing through your online presentation, you can tailor your product selection and presentation to better meet their needs.

Traditionally, the practice of Web site traffic analysis is referred to as reviewing the "log files," the information-packed and techie-looking files that contain computer addresses and Web page URLs. Such information needs to be displayed in the form of a graph or chart to understand it better, and that's exactly what Analytics does. Typically, you want to look at information over a particular period of time, whether it is a month, day, or week. You need to pay attention to facts such as:

- *Domain Reports*—This kind of report tells you which domains your visitors come from.

- *Referrer Reports*—A "referrer" is the site that referred someone to you—in other words, it's the site a visitor was visiting just before it came to your site. By tracking referrals you can see which links steer you the most visitors.

- *File Type Reports*—These sorts of reports tell you what type of files are being accessed by your visitors—they might be images, presentations, PDFs, and so on.

- *Browser Reports*—These tell you what kinds of browsers your viewers are using so you can tailor your content to particular versions or types if needed.

Often, log file reports present you with a "Top Ten" list of pages visited, files accessed, domains that visit you, countries of origin, and so on. When you're trying to choose from Analytics' rich set of reports, you might keep such options in mind so you can present your coworkers and managers with the information they need to make informed decisions about your Web site and what sort of content is contained on it.

Tip: Internet World's article "Evaluating Web Traffic" tackles much the same topic at http://www.internetworld.com/magazine.php? inc=031501/03.15.01webtraffic.html.

Setting up Your Google Analytics Service

To get started with Google Analytics, go to the service's home page http://www .google.com/analytics/ and enter you Gmail username and password in the fields shown in Figure 17-1.

1. In the following screen, click on the Sign Up button to continue to the *New Account Signup* screen shown in Figure 17-2, where you enter the full URL, account name, country of origin, and time zone of the Web site you would like to track.
2. When you're done, click the Continue button.
3. Next, you enter your personal contact information and press the Continue button.
4. You are then taken to the Terms of Service. Check off that you agree with the Terms and Conditions and click the Create New Account button.
5. Finally, you are required to embed an HTML code block into each page of your Web site. Google recommends that you paste the code just before the closing tag of each page, unless your page uses frames or custom JavaScript functions. (See the Google Analytics Help Center's "Installing the tracking code" section for more information.) As you can see from the diagram, we used the site created in Chapter 11 with Google Page Creator as an example (see Figure 17-3). Enter the code block underneath the header of your Web site's html code, and specifically, just above the tag.

Note: The word urchin appears in the HTML block you copy because Google Analytics was modeled on Urchin Software Corp.'s analytics sys-

Figure 17-1. Google Analytics is accessible to you with your Google Account.

tem called Urchin on Demand. Google acquired Urchin Software in April 2005.

In the case of a Page Creator page, simply navigate to your page in Google Page Creator site manager and click on "edit html" in the lower left-hand corner of the Edit Page, and copy the code block directly below the existing text or before the command (see Figure 17-4).

If you do not carry out this final code embedding, you will still be able to view your Google Analytics page, but no data will be gathered for your Web site. Furthermore, it takes a few days before you start to see any interesting activity, and the longer you watch the data, the more interesting and informative it becomes. The page being tracked is shown in Figure 17-5.

Getting to Know Google Analytics

Once a few days have passed and Google Analytics has had time to gather information about the site you want to track, you can return to the Analytics home page and

Figure 17-2. You need to have a Web site to track in order to set up Google Analytics.

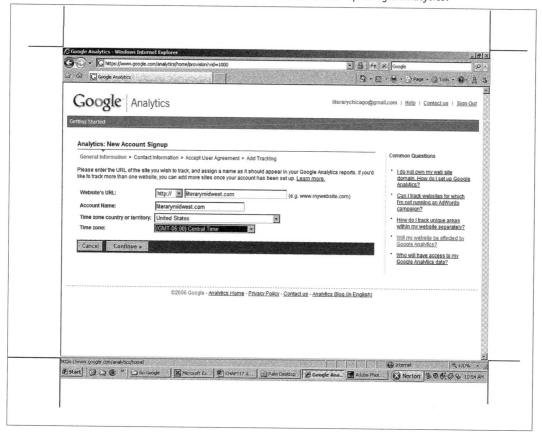

sign in to your home page. As you can see from Figure 17-6, you can track more than one Web site if necessary.

Your Google Analytics home page has two primary views: Analytics Settings, where you can see the existing Web sites that you have signed up, and their general statuses; and View Reports, where various data analysis items are displayed. You should take some to time to familiarize yourself with these pages, because many of the questions you may have can be answered therein.

On the Analytics Settings page, in the upper right-hand corner, you can click on "Contact Us" to either ask a question or suggest a feature, and if you click on "Help" you are presented with an exhaustive help page with topics listed under five categories: Getting Started; Account Administration; Tracking Central; Reports Central; and Common Tasks. If that isn't enough, the sidebar on the left has a search engine built right into the Help Center, plus Troubleshooting Tools, the Top 25 Articles related to help files, and a Terminology section. Click View Reports to view details about the Web site you are tracking.

Figure 17-3. You insert a block of HTML into your Web page so Google Analytics can track it.

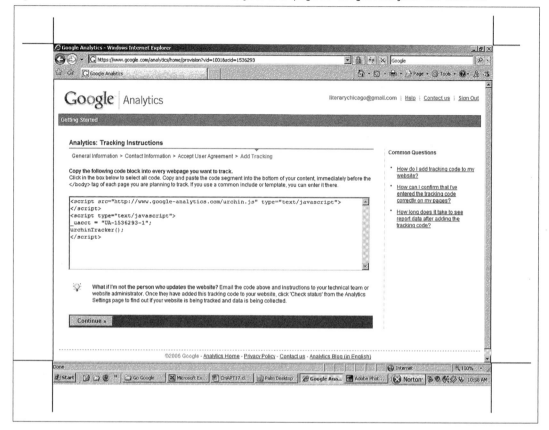

The View Reports page, shown in Figure 17-7, is where the Google Analytics data is accessed. A sidebar on the left serves as the "Dashboard," or the controls that you can use to generate a wide range of reports from Visitor Loyalty to Referring Sites to Top Landing Pages. Another "Dashboard" that can be displayed is the Conversion Rate, which touches upon Conversion, a key issue in Google Analytics. In a nutshell, Conversion is the process of "converting" a site visitor to a site customer.

Exploring Google Analytics' Powerful Toolbox

Another recurring concept in Google Analytics is ROI—not Return on Investment, but in this case, Region of Interest—the geographic location where your visitors are coming from. Your business's ROI is a location that displays a statistically significant increase in visitor origin (where your visitors live, geographically), or it may be a

Figure 17-4. If you use Page Creator to create your page, you can copy and add the Google Analytics code using this window.

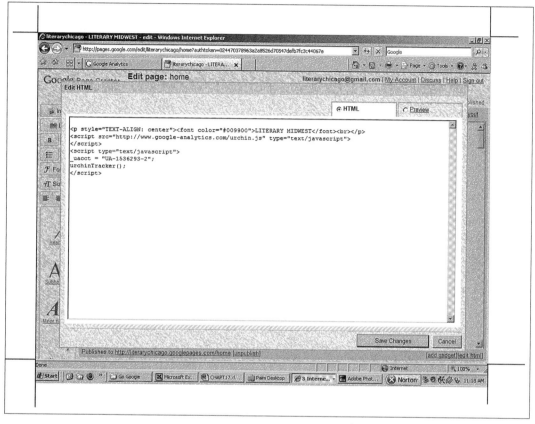

location where you would like to cultivate a stronger customer base. Many of the Google Analytics tools can help you monitor your ROI as a way to achieve your conversion goals.

One way Google Analytics does this is through keyword campaign comparison. Keyword tracking is the process of evaluating keywords you use to advertise your site in order to see which keywords drive traffic to your site. Using Google Analytics, you are able to track all keywords you have purchased on Google AdWords, as well as keywords you have purchased on non-Google search engines such as Yahoo! Search Marketing or MSN Search, plus ads, paid links, etc. General statistical tracking is quickly generated as Executive Summaries through the each of the three standard Dashboards that come with every Google Analytics account: Executive, Marketer, and Webmaster. Web traffic and e-commerce are cleanly displayed through charts and graphs that would have taken hours to compile and produce otherwise.

The popular Google AdWords paid search advertising service is connected to

Figure 17-5. A page being tracked with Google Analytics.

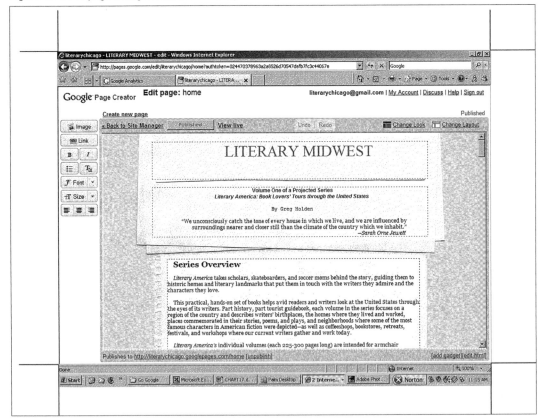

Google Analytics. In fact you can access Analytics directly from your AdWords page, and keyword data is automatically imported and analyzed. This gives you a quick and easy way to check your ROI plus other statistics for each keyword you have purchased.

If you have a seasonal sale, exhibit, or other time-sensitive event that is being advertised on your site, you can also do interactive trend reporting, by checking the progress of your Web site over the course of a designated period of time. If you conduct e-commerce sales through your site, your transactions can also be traced through keywords and keyword campaigns, giving you valuable insight into the nature of your business if you happen to be running an e-commerce Web site. You can trace sold products through their ID or SKU number. You can also track the sales amount, the sale price, the quantity ordered, and the shipping destination. Once you have a picture of the traffic on your Web site, the Funnel Visualization tool helps you visualize how your visitors navigate your site so you can understand their experience and identify and deal with any obstacles they encounter.

Figure 17-6. You can track multiple Web sites through Google Analytics.

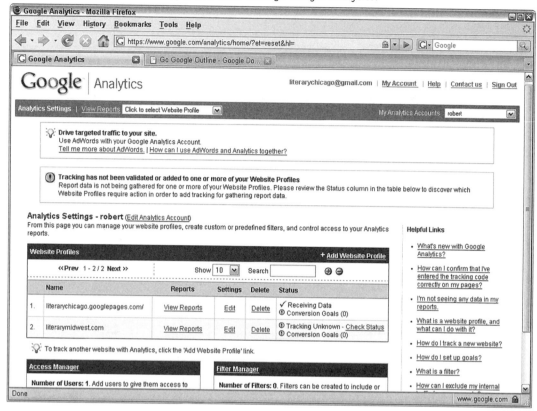

If you want to go through your Web site's links yourself, use the Site Overlay tool to navigate your Web site yourself, and see firsthand what the visitor's experience is like. You can deepen your analysis of visitor and customer traffic using the Advanced Visitor Segmentation tool, which lets you compare data across different criteria. For example, you might compare returning visitors versus geographic location to see what countries attract most of your recurring visitors. Use the GeoTargeting report to pinpoint this geographic location and use the information to streamline your marketing campaign. Finally, Google Analytics makes it easy to compare and contrast any of the data, whether it's organized by date, by type, or a combination, to create segments for optimal business analysis.

Find Out More about Google Analytics

Since this section is really only meant to get you started, the previous section may seem like a whirlwind of information. Worry not! Google Analytics provides many

Figure 17-7. The View Reports page provides you with data about your Web site.

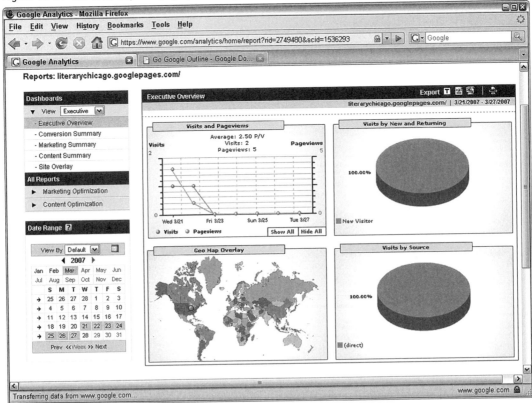

resources that will have you keeping up with the jargon, and using these tools like a pro in no time. The Official Google Analytics Blog, which you can access by clicking "Blog" on the toolbar at the upper right-hand side of the Analytics home page (www .google.com/analytics) or by going directly to http://analytics.blogspot.com, offers not only assistance and troubleshooting, but numerous other resources that are regularly updated. The right-hand sidebar of the blog has a "Useful Links" area, containing links to the Help Center and to a User Forum, among others.

In the blog itself, you'll find analytics-related posts that include everything from job solicitations, to other web traffic monitoring sites, to coupon giveaways, and many other interesting items.

Exploring Conversion University

Aside from the Help Files and User Forums, Google's Conversion University (http:// www.google.com/analytics/conversionuniversity.html) is also offered free of charge, and contains a wealth of knowledge at your disposal. Once again, "conversion" in this context means the conversion of visitors to customers, and Conversion University proposes a handful of articles organized by subject, with new articles being regularly posted.

Driving Traffic

The articles in the Driving Traffic Section of Conversion University deal with marketing your site, teaching you strategies for using the means available to you, such as SEO (search engine optimization), newsletter e-mails, and the like to increase the volume of traffic to your site. Your ultimate goal is getting the most for your money by learning to target your marketing more effectively.

Converting Visitors

This section of Conversion University is focused on teaching you to convert visitors into customers. Here, you can read about ways to modify your site copy, creating attractive pages, and tailor your site to the people who visit the most frequently, in the hopes that they'll become more than just visitors. You will learn about the importance of factors such as an easy checkout, for example. If a potential customer decides it's more trouble than it's worth to buy something from you, his business could be lost forever.

Tracking and Testing

This section teaches how to interpret the data you're gathering. What should you look for? How many people clicked on your Web site because of AdWords, and then left? How many pages did the average visitor view? Knowing how to interpret this type of information will help you to test online initiatives, and generally maximize the tools you are presented with through Google Analytics.

Analytics in Context

The articles in this section discuss the importance of strategy when using web analytics in general. Such strategies include the importance of setting goals before you start measuring, reacting to what your data is telling you, and trying to maximize the positive trends, instead of getting bogged down in trying to produce the exact hard numbers you desire.

Technical Consulting and Support

If you are using Google Analytics to track traffic to and from a sophisticated commercial Web site, you might well want to hire a professional to do the work for you. You can find a list of partners who can provide professional services especially for Google Analytics. Go to the Partner Provided Support page (http://www.google.com/analytics/support_partner_provided.html), which directs you to a list of Google's partners, located in 27 countries around the world. These business partners can help you to implement data analysis and marketing using Google Analytics, and tailor their services to your business needs with such services as phone and Internet-chat support, installation and configuration, personalized training, data analysis, and more.

Getting Local Attention with Google Maps

Once you have a set of tracking data from Google Analytics, you can get a clear picture of just how many visitors come to your Web site from your own country, and even your own state. For many brick-and-mortar businesses, the bulk of regular customers come from the immediate city or neighborhood in which they are located. Along with trying to get placement in the regular Google search database, you also need to make sure your site is well-placed in Google Maps. Maps gives business search results for a specific local area: Go to the Maps home page (http://maps.google.com/maps) and enter information that describes your location in the search box on this page: you can enter a zip code, an address, or a city and state. For example, I enter Chicago, IL and I click the Make this my default location link. (If you already have a default location the link reads Change default location.)

Once I have a location specified, I can search for businesses in that area. A couple of years ago, I was asked to improve the search placement results of a restaurant in my area called Kaze Sushi. When I do a search for the term "sushi" with the default location I have specified, the Maps results show all the sushi restaurants in the city of Chicago ranked by their Google search engine placement. The results, shown in Figure 17-8, show me the names of the other restaurants with which Kaze Sushi is competing.

Armed with these local search results, I can study the Web sites of the competing restaurants to see how the higher-ranked local sushi restaurants use keywords on their Web sites to get good placement on Google. I can also analyze how many links are made to the higher-ranked sites, and where the links come from. (Go to the Google Advanced Search page, http://www.google.com/advanced_search?hl=en, enter the URL for the site you want to track in the "Find pages that link to the page" box, and click Search.) I can then refer to Google Analytics and see where my own Web site referrals come from, to see if my site's referrers are the same as those of the higher ranked sites. If they are not, and if I don't get many visits from my local area, I know

Figure 17-8. Google Maps can help you analyze your competition in your area of business.

that I need to cultivate links with local businesses to drive more traffic to my Web site, and ultimately, to my brick-and-mortar facility.

In this chapter, you got a brief introduction to Google's Web site analysis service, Google Analytics. In the chapter that follows, you'll learn about two more Google services that are remarkably sophisticated. Both help you organize the contents of your computer and your local file system in the same way that Google helps organize the Web and your own Web site. Google Desktop helps you get a grip on your own files, and Picasa gathers and orders image files so you can work with them more easily.

CHAPTER **18**

Organizing Your Business Files

The services described to this point have focused primarily on organizing the contents of the Internet, and on improving your business presence and workflow. Workflow has a great deal to do with the files contained on your local computer and your network. At times, it seems like Google has the Web totally organized—now, if you could just do the same with your local file system, you'd be able to find that file on your hard disk as easily as that bit of information you needed to find online for that business presentation you were preparing.

Google to the rescue! This chapter focuses on several services that use Google's search capabilities to help you find files on your desktop. You'll learn about Google Desktop, a file system organizer that provides an alternative to Windows Explorer, and Picasa, an exciting new way to view and work with graphic images to create winning business presentations as well as personal photo albums.

Getting Started with Google Desktop

Google Desktop differs from other Google services in two significant ways. For one thing, the program is software that you download and install on your computer. It's not like Google Apps, an online service you use with your Web browser. Desktop installs as a sort of Web browser interface for your local file system. The other difference is that the program is big and its operation is slow. My assistant and I both found the program slowed down the operation of our computers' file systems significantly. There is, apparently, a price to be paid for getting your desktop organized.

Installing Google Desktop is as easy as it is to install other Google applications, however.

1. Go to http://desktop.google.com/.
2. Click the Install Google Desktop button. An application called GoogleDesktopSetup.exe is downloaded to your computer. Double-click the file to open it.

3. A screen appears stating that you need to close open applications. Click Yes to close them.

4. A dialog box appears informing you of the progress of the installation. When the process is complete, a Welcome to Google Desktop! dialog box appears. Read the terms of service and click I agree.

A dialog box appears (see Figure 18-1) asking you to choose your desktop features. You can select Google Enhanced search, Sidebars and Gadgets, to make Google your homepage and default browser, and the Improve Google Desktop by sending crash reports and anonymous usage data.

- *Google Enhanced Search.* By default, Google Desktop lets you search files on your computer and network by filename or to launch applications. The Enhanced Search option lets you perform more detailed searches, including file contents, e-mail messages, and Web history.

Figure 18-1. You specify your initial settings when you sign in to Google Desktop.

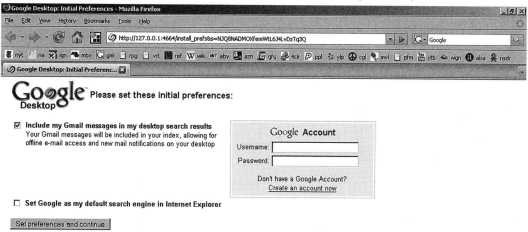

- *Sidebar with Gadgets.* Check this option if you want to include Gadgets that display the news, weather, and other bits of information in your Desktop.

- *Set Google as your homepage and default browser.* Launch Google as your home page (the first page you see when you open your browser) and make Google the default search service for your browser, as opposed to another service such as MSN Search.

- *Send crash reports and anonymous usage data.* If you select this option certain aspects of your usage data will necessarily be sent to Google to improve performance or allow some of the Sidebar items to function properly. For the most part, however, your personal files will remain safe and sound on your own hard disk, untouched by Google's servers. On the other hand, if you choose to enable certain features, such as "Improve Google by sending crash reports and anonymous usage data," your shared information will be cached in Google's servers. It can be likened to the cleaning lady who can't organize your sock drawer without seeing your socks. Google has posted quite a bit of information about how the process works, in addition to being receptive to questions and concerns, but it's worth at least skimming through Google's Privacy Policy at http://desktop.google.com/privacypolicy.html to more fully understand what it means to download and use this type of software (see Figure 18-2).

When you have chosen options, click Done. The sidebar installs itself in the form of a "Deskbar" in the Windows toolbar. Click the down arrow in the Deskbar and choose Sidebar to install the Sidebar on the right side of your desktop. A window appears just to the left of the Sidebar that gives you some options for how to use the Desktop. (Press Ctrl twice to show the Quick Search Box, for instance.) Click the Got it! button to close this window.

 Tip: You may want to proceed with installation in the evening or during a period when you don't need to use your computer heavily; the installation process can be lengthy, depending on the size of your hard disk. It's also a good idea to run the Disk Cleanup utility to clear out temporary files and free up as much space as possible.

Once installed, Google Desktop will automatically begin the process of indexing your e-mail, Web history, documents, program files, and everything else on your file system—a process that can be quite lengthy, indeed. Specifically, it indexes the following types of files:

Figure 18-2. Pay close attention to Google's privacy policy to make sure you want Desktop to search your files.

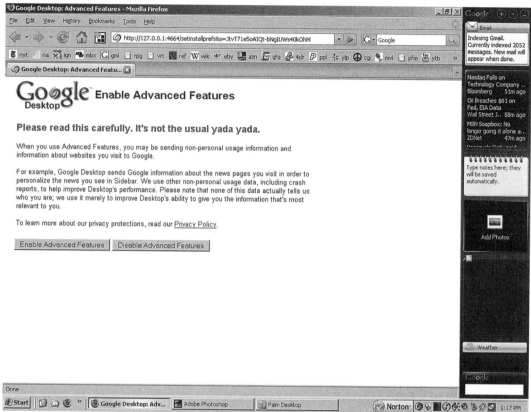

- Email Messages
- Word, Excel, and Other Microsoft Office Files
- Adobe Acrobat PDFs
- Chats Conducted with GoogleTalk, MSN Messenger, AOL Messenger, and Other Tools
- Web History Files
- Text Files
- Audio and Video Files
- Compressed Archives Such as .ZIP Files

As I indicated, it took many hours for my computer to be indexed (this is done while your computer idles). This is a one-time process, however. After installation, Desktop will continuously update its index.

System Requirements

Unlike other services or applications described in this book, Google Desktop is big. You will need at least 1 gigabyte free on your hard disk to accommodate the application alone. Not only that, but it can take up an additional 4 gigabytes to fit the file index, depending on how many files you have on your computer. You may also want to defragment your hard drive before downloading Google Desktop. My assistant Robert experienced significant system slowdown after his first download, and it took him a few tries before Desktop started working correctly on his computer. The Desktop Help pages did directly address the issue, but defragmenting and clearing his browser's temporary files seemed to work.

Searching Your File System

Once the application is configured, you can go to your Google Desktop homepage, and start searching. Google Desktop contains two separate interfaces: the search utility and the sidebar. The search interface will be quite familiar to anyone with some experience using the Internet-based Google search engine. In fact, it's pretty much identical except for one small, but vital detail: In addition to the usual categories, such as Web, Images, Groups, etc., you will see Desktop. Now, the files on your own personal hard disk will be displayed in sequential order just the same way you are used to seeing results online. It's really kind of a thrill seeing it for the first time.

Personalizing Information with the Sidebar & Gadgets

In some ways, the installation and indexing process is the slow, difficult part of working with Desktop. Once the program is up and running, you'll probably get used to exploring your desktop and find this new tool a quick and enjoyable experience.

The Desktop screen doesn't take up your whole desktop. The search utility appears in its own window at the bottom of the Desktop. The sidebar itself sits on the side of your desktop. (Both interfaces are shown in Figure 18-3.) The sidebar column can be dragged and dropped either on the right-hand or left-hand side of your screen, and contains any of the Gadgets (miniature programs that provide information or perform functions; see Chapter 14 for more) you choose to place within it.

The sidebar automatically appears when you install Google Desktop, but you can minimize it or even close it in much the same way you would any window on your computer. The sidebar gives you a convenient way to organize your Gadgets and keep track of them. Some of the Gadgets get pretty creative, and new ones are being made available all the time. In the preceding figure, you see a news headlines gadget, a

Figure 18-3. Google Desktop takes the form of a sidebar column.

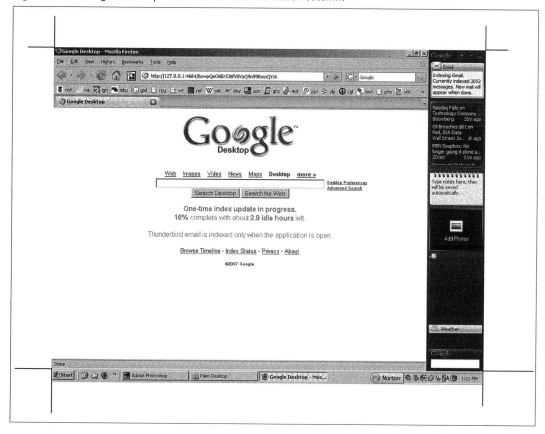

note-taking tool, and a photo utility crammed into the narrow sidebar, for instance. You can also obtain utilities such as an Audio Sampler, Cupid's Gadget (which allows you to "like mark" people so they know you might be romantically interested in them), and on and on. Go to http://desktop.google.com/plugins/ to see the continually updating selection.

That's not to say that there isn't a wide array of more "serious" Gadgets, too. You can use the Google Sidebar to organize your workspace for you and bring you items of interest or work-related importance without you having to go retrieve them yourself. There is a clock, a post-it notepad, streaming updates from your Gmail inbox, and news updates (which you can click on to be taken to the full story online). These more basic functions are available from the moment your Sidebar is available. How you choose to configure everything afterward will depend on your personal preferences or business needs.

At the top of the Desktop you see three buttons: the plus sign (+) adds Gadgets to the Sidebar; the down arrow opens a drop-down menu; the minus sign minimizes the Sidebar. When you choose Options from the drop-down menu, your browser displays a set of Google Desktop Preferences. The browser window contains four tabs that control how the Desktop performs searches, how its display looks, and many more basic settings.

Keeping Track of Business E-Mails

Google Desktop makes searching your business e-mail messages easy. When you enter a keyword on the Desktop search interface your displayed results will be identified by their file type. All you have to do is click on the link indicating the number of e-mails containing the information you want, and only e-mails will be displayed. You'll never waste time scrolling needlessly through your inbox again. Searching e-mail can be a little tricky depending on what operating system you have or e-mail service you use. Google is compatible with Microsoft Outlook 2000 and above, Outlook Express 5 and above, Mozilla Thunderbird 1.0 and above, Mozilla Mail 1.4 and above, and/ or Netscape Mail 7.1 and above. Searching Hotmail or Yahoo! can be done, but since they are Web-based, you will essentially be searching them via the Web pages that you've visited.

Finally, searching Gmail using Google Desktop requires that you allow Desktop access to your Gmail. To do this:

1. Select options from the drop down menu in the sidebar.
2. Click on the Google Account Features tab.
3. Click the check box to enable Index and search e-mail in my Gmail account.

Locating Files with the Quick Search Box and Advanced Search Form

In addition to being able to search from the Google Desktop page, you can also use the Quick Search Box. You toggle between displaying and hiding the search box by pressing the Ctrl key twice. Results start popping up before you have even completed typing in a word. The Quick Search box operates the same as the smaller search box that is built into the Sidebar. As you type in a file name or keyword, the search function searches your desktop first. Then it searches the Web. You can also start Gadgets via the Quick Search Box by entering all or part of their filenames and then selecting them from the drop-down list that appears.

If you want to do a fine-tuned search, you can always go to the Google Desktop homepage and click on "Advanced Search." The Advanced Search link for Google Desktop is hard to find. It's not at http://desktop.google.com. Rather, you need to go to the Google home page, http://www.google.com, click the link "more" at the top of the page, and choose Desktop from the drop-down list. Then you can click Advanced Search. This feature lets you place restrictions on your search, such as limiting the file type, or the time period during which the sought-after file was created. Together, the Quick Search and Advanced Search features give a roadmap that will take you to wherever you want to go on your computer, allowing you to devote your valuable time to your business. You gain the ability to gather Web pages you've recently visited along with documents you've created. The results come up in the same place, which allows you to quickly answer a question when you need to remember the last time you worked on a particular topic or project.

Searching Microsoft Office Files

You can use Google Desktop to add a search toolbar directly into Microsoft Outlook. This saves you the need to switch to the sidebar if you want to save desktop space. Searches produce results containing a brief selection of the email found, and you can streamline your search by selecting from columns such as "Subject," "Date," and other attributes.

You can also limit a search to other types of Microsoft Office applications, such as Word, Excel, and PowerPoint files. You can do so by clicking the link in the blue header that appears above your initial search results. Alternatively, you can also restrain a search by adding an operator to your search terms. The filetype: operator tells Google Desktop to only find files of a specified type. For instance, to find only Excel spreadsheet files, search for filetype:xls. In the same way that you refine your search to include only emails, you can confine a search to only certain data types, including:

- Outlook/Outlook Express
- Excel
- Internet Explorer
- AOL Instant Messenger
- MSN Messenger
- Google Talk
- Netscape Mail/Thunderbird
- Netscape/Firefox/Mozilla
- Images (GIF, JPEG, BMP, and so on)

Each type is identified by an icon that should be quickly recognizable (i.e., Word is identified by the "Word" icon), and are displayed based on how recently they were viewed.

Note: To find a list of operators you can use with Google Desktop searches, go to the Desktop for Windows Help Center (http://desktop .google.com/support) and search for "Refining a Search."

Google Desktop as Security Guard

Google Desktop also has built-in encryption software that is designed not only to help protect you against phishing or mailware, but also to display a warning if you are accessing a Web site that may not be secure. This "security guard" function is in effect for links from documents, e-mails, or simply browsing the Internet itself. You also have the power to prevent other users from searching your computer by clicking on the Desktop icon in your taskbar and choosing to "Lock Search." This option means that you will only be able to perform a Desktop Search if you enter your current Google account password on the Desktop home page. Personally, I suggest you only do this if you are in a business environment or if you are very security conscious. If you have virus protection and firewall software in place that is regularly updated that should be enough to prevent unauthorized use of your computer.

Google Desktop Enterprise Edition

Desktop Enterprise Edition offers all the same functions of Google Desktop, but adds the ability to search an office intranet system, and allows administrators to set up security features, configure the office system, or deploy features throughout your office's network. Google Desktop Enterprise Edition is also free, but there are services and products associated with it that can be purchased. Such services include tech support, or the Google Mini, a hardware device that enhances your business's internal search capabilities. Learn more by visiting http://www.google.com/enter prise/index.html.

CHAPTER **19**

Organizing Your Images with Picasa

Picasa is a free, downloadable software package offered by Google. While still in its developmental phase, Picasa nonetheless offers many powerful tools allowing you to organize, manipulate, and modify the images stored on your computer's hard drive. Because Picasa organizes your images chronologically regardless of their location, it becomes not only easier to compare the volume of images created from one month/ year to the next, which can be useful if you are in a business environment and need to inventory your images, but also to simply find files that you may not have remembered were there. Essentially, instead of having to go through your hard drive searching for stray images, you have only to install Picasa, and the work will be done for you.

Picasa combines tools previously found in separate programs, such as the slide show creation of PowerPoint, for example, and the photo manipulation of Photoshop. You won't get anywhere near the quantity and sophistication of specialized tools found in the aforementioned programs, but Picasa's interface is both intuitive and easy to use, and allows you to perform surprisingly powerful actions without any prerequisite knowledge. Also, don't overlook the fact that Picasa is free, thus potentially saving you hundreds if not thousands of dollars.

Finally one big plus to keep in mind is that Picasa is, after all, a Google product. So it has many built-in methods for getting your photos online. Tasks such as creating a Web album, emailing images, or even adding them to a blog can be performed at the click of a button.

Downloading Picasa

Picasa, like Google Desktop, is software you download and install on your computer. Downloading Picasa is easily done by navigating to http://picasa.google.com, and clicking the *Try Picasa now* button in the right-hand side of the home page. This will take you to a software download screen where you will download Picasa as an executable file to your hard drive.

 Note: Picasa requires that your PC have at least a 300MHz Pentium processor and MMX technology, and at least 64MB of RAM, although 128MB is recommended. You must have at least 50MB free on your hard disk, although 100MB is recommended. Picasa is not yet available for Mac OS, although there is a Macintosh uploader that can be used for Picasa Web Albums, and an introductory Linux version of Picasa can be found on Google Labs.

Getting Your Photos in Focus with Picasa

Once installed, Picasa will ask you whether you want it to scan your hard disk for photos and organize them. If you choose not to let it do this, you will have the option of importing any photos left out at a later time. Picasa's ability to scan your hard disk for photos and organize them for you is one of its most powerful applications. The process can take a few minutes, depending on how many photos you have stored, but once it has completed its task, you will find yourself staring at an attractive interface with your photos and other digital image files displayed next to a sidebar on the left indicating the location of the photos you are currently viewing (see Figure 19-1). You can even click on the folder name above the photos to open a new window to the actual files on your computer.

 I should add here that when I downloaded Picasa for the first time, I tried to move some files around in the actual folders where they were located on my hard disk, and it caused Picasa to start freezing up. As with all introductory versions of programs, you may run into a bug or two, but I have yet to find anything catastrophic.

Uploading New Images with Picasa

To add new photos to your file system from a digital camera, CD, or other device, you don't need to open a graphics program. First, connect the device to your com-

Figure 19-1. Picasa organizes and presents you with folders containing image files on your file system.

puter. Then, choose an album you have created and set aside to receive the image files. (An album is a virtual collection of images that only exists on Picasa and not on your file system.) If you need to create a new album, choose File > New Album. Then click "Import," this will take you to the "Import Tray," where you can browse for photos either from your hard disk or from attached devices, such as a scanner, flash drive, digital camera, etc. Picasa also lets you easily back up pictures to a DVD or CD going to the "Tools" dropdown menu, and selecting "Backup Pictures." This makes it extremely convenient to archive images to be used online, such as catalogue items, for example.

Alternatively, you can choose Copy pictures to computer and view them using Picasa2, which appears in the standard dialog box that Windows XP displays when you attach a device to your computer using a USB cable or other connector (see Figure 19-2). Once you have Picasa installed, the Picasa2 option appears along with other standard options.

Figure 19-2. You can use Picasa to import and preview photos from digital cameras or other devices.

When you click OK, Picasa opens and displays the images in the device in an Import Tray on the left side of the window. Click an image to display it in larger format on the right. Click one of the two Rotate buttons to rotate the images if they aren't oriented correctly (see Figure 19-3).

Organizing Your Photos with Picasa

Photos can easily be dragged and dropped from one folder to another, and Picasa will double-check with you before making the change permanent. You can also re-name files or organize them into albums using the Albums grouping, which is located directly above the grouping that shows the folders where files are located. Picasa creates an "instance" of each photo you put into an album so you can have a photo in several albums without it taking up extra space on your hard disk.

Viewing and Editing Images

Picasa isn't just a tool for organizing and viewing photos. It's also an image editor. Picasa presents you with an impressive array of tools with which to modify or fine-

Figure 19-3. Choose the image files you want to import with Picasa.

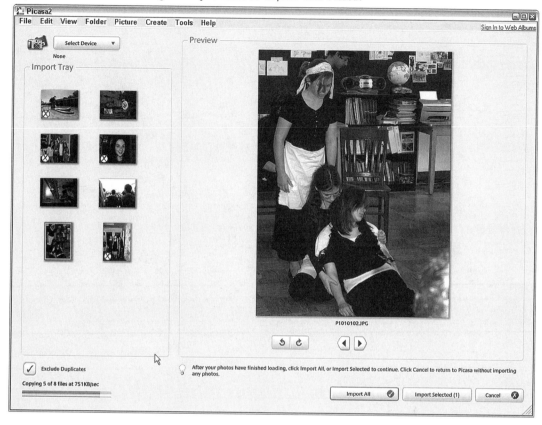

tune your photos. Simply click on the photo that you would like to modify, and you are taken to an interface with a toolbar on the left-hand side and the photo displayed in the center.

Picasa's 12 visual effects allow you to do everything from eliminating red eye to adding glow or a sepia filter, to enhancing shadows, to rotating and cropping with the click of a mouse. To crop an image, select it, then click the Crop button. You can automatically crop the image to a standard size (such at 5 × 7). Or click Manual to click and drag across the image. The area you want to preserve "lights up" while the area to be cropped is faded in the background (see Figure 19-4).

The ease with which you are able to use these tools stands in stark contrast to the learning curve I remember from my first experiences with Adobe Photoshop—a program that is far more powerful, but correspondingly more expensive as well as difficult to use. Picasa is actually closer to Adobe Photoshop Elements, software designed specifically for editing digital images. Many effects and tools will seem familiar to

Figure 19-4. Picasa acts as an image editing tool.

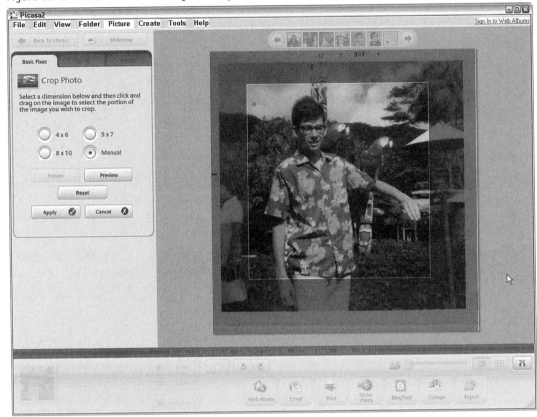

anyone who has done photo editing before, but all is done with a mere click of a button.

Slideshows and Presentations

As I worked on this book, Google released Google Presentations, an online application that performs some of the basic functions covered by Microsoft PowerPoint (see Chapter 6). Until then, you can use Picasa for creating presentations with your image files. Making slideshows is particularly easy with Picasa—something I found out first-hand when I wanted to create a slide show for a birthday party. I grouped all the images in a single folder labeled Birthday. Then, all I had to do was click the folder to select it, and then click the Slideshow button above the album of choice. The slideshow began.

A set of buttons at the bottom of the photos (see Figure 19-5) enables you to change the time interval between images or to exit the slideshow. You can also create

Figure 19-5. Picasa allows you to change the time interval between images or to exit the slideshow.

movies from a selection of photos, accomplishing an impressive presentation, indeed. Select the images you want, go to the Tools dropdown menu, and select Movie. You are then able to choose delay times, dimensions, and video compression settings. Picasa will render your images into an AVI file and save it to your hard disk. Since you are also able to add IPTC standard captions, which are fully editable and searchable, Picasa becomes a powerful business presentation tool, as well.

Picasa Online

Picasa allows you to email pictures directly from the viewing interface, as long as you are currently connected to the Internet. You can use your Gmail account, your default email provider through MS Outlook, or directly through Hello (see below for details about Hello software download). You can also create an online photo album quickly and easily that will resemble a Google image search. Once in Picasa Web Albums, you can search photo tags and see not only the album you posted, but other people's albums as well.

If you have created a blog using Blogger (see Chapter 13), Picasa will allow you to upload pictures to it directly. Just select the picture you would like to upload, click the "BlogThis!" button, and enter the username and password for your Blogger blog. You are then taken to a screen where you can then sign in to your blog using the "Sign In" button, or create a new blog if you do not already have one. These buttons can be found in the toolbar directly below the displayed image.

Using Hello to Conduct a Collaborative Meeting

Hello is a downloadable software package provided by Google and designed specifically to work with Picasa. Hello allows you to conduct online image-sharing through an instant messaging interface. Download Hello from http://hello.com. Aside from the obvious applications of Hello as a way to share pictures with friends and family, Hello can also serve as a way to transfer image files from your computer to a Web server for business purposes. Images are viewable almost instantaneously after being sent. You can download the ones you want at full resolution and print quality, making it faster even than email.

This chapter introduced you to two sophisticated pieces of software that have profound implications for businesses that need to make their workstations easier to navigate. If your company has images or other shared files scattered across several networked workstations, or buried deep within folders and subfolders on an individual computer, Google Desktop and Picasa can help you find those files so you can work with them and share them more easily. These two programs, which are downloaded to your computer rather than being accessed on the Web, are powerful and all the more remarkable for being made available free of charge. In the chapter that follows, you'll learn about other software you can download and install on your computer that can improve your workflow even further.

CHAPTER **20**

Moving Forward: Google Apps Premium, Pack, and More

The tools described in preceding chapters of Go Google enable your business to work more efficiently and streamline workflow by using Google's online services. Once you begin to communicate, market yourself, and share documents online, you can take some additional steps forward. These tools enable you to work more reliably and securely. Google has many more services than the ones described in the preceding chapters. New ones are always under development in an area called Google Labs (http://labs.google.com). This chapter examines some business-oriented tools that will help you function even more efficiently as you perform more of your everyday office tasks online.

Moving Up to Google Apps Premium

In Chapter 6, you learned about Google Apps—a set of shared business tools that, combined with a domain name, e-mail, and user accounts, provides small businesses with a complete working environment that challenges the normal "purchase-install-upgrade" way of obtaining and using business software. The standard version of Google Apps is free, as is an Education version designed for university environments. Larger enterprises that are receptive to Google Apps can move up to Google Apps Premium, a service that costs $50 per user per year. This might seem expensive, but it's still far less costly than software like Microsoft Exchange, which is similar to Docs & Spreadsheet, but is hosted on a server on your local network rather than on Google.

If you have a larger business with many branch offices or if your workers are highly mobile and need to share information with the home office while they are on the road, it's worth considering Premier Edition. The features offered are basically the same as with Google Apps. There are a few additional features provided with Premier; and the additional $50 per person also buys you a higher level of reliability and customer service:

- You are guaranteed that your e-mail will be accessible 99.9 percent of the time.

- You have the option not to display textual advertisements alongside your Gmail messages; with Standard Edition you are required to view such ads. (Normally, these "Sponsored Links" appear in a column just to the right of the e-mail message you are reading.)

- Your shared applications include places where you can reserve office re-sources, such as conference rooms and equipment.

- You are able to make use of Application Programming Interfaces (APIs) so you can automate signing on and other functions.

- You are able to call Google directly for technical support on a 24/7 basis.

- You gain access to third-party applications that complement Google Apps and that aren't available to Standard Edition customers.

There are lots of advanced tasks you can perform when you know your service is guaranteed to be online all of the time (or at least 99.9 percent of the time). Some examples of opportunities or considerations businesses need to keep in mind when they share information online using Google Apps Premier are listed in the sections that follow.

Exchanging Information with Business Partners

The term *extranet* might sound intimidating, but it's essentially what you're setting up when you use Google Apps for your business data and you create a business account so someone outside your company can gain access to it. You might think of an extranet as being like an apartment or condo building with a doorman: only resi-dents can get past the doorman, but they, in turn, can allow in other visitors to whom they give access.

An extranet works on the same principle: it can be viewed as part of a company's internal network that is extended to users outside the company, whether they are mobile employees or suppliers. Participants keep their data safely behind a firewall, but authorized partners can access the information they need over the Internet. You can think of your extranet as a set of private Web pages that you only let a special group of individuals access. Under normal circumstances, setting up an extranet would mean hiring IT consultants and using a mixture of leased lines, frame relay connections, and Web server security to admit outsiders to parts of your internal network. But for small- to mid-size companies looking to provide extranet access to perhaps ten to twenty employees, a Google Apps site will work just fine. Here are a few examples of what you can do on an extranet. You can:

- Securely place proposals or requests quotes online.
- Publish training information that applies to specific employees.
- Your employees can use the extranet to securely access parts of your database so they can personalize customer or vendor information.

Putting Visitors in Control

When you give a business partner an account so they can use Google Apps, you give them the opportunity to create their own content. One of the more advanced technical functions of an extranet involves the creation of customized content in response to users' needs. You might post an order form on Docs & Spreadsheets that you share with your partners; they can fill the form out to order products from you and without having to phone or e-mail you. You can also post documents online that provide a "paper trail" so customers can check the status of their orders, or make note of delivery schedules on a Google Calendar you create just for them. This kind of personalization makes individuals feel in control and improves their level of satisfaction.

Demonstrate Your Stuff Online

Tired of running out to different businesses with all kinds of slide projectors and copies of presentations all for time-consuming meetings? Are you too busy handling day-to-day business activities to keep doing proposals and presentations that are required to increase your business?

If the answer to either of these questions is *Yes*, then you have the option of presenting your work in formats that Google Apps or your Web site can present online. Docs & Spreadsheets will handle HTML, Word, Excel, or other formats; Page Creator can be used to publish HTML files as well as JPEG or GIF images or PDF files. If you use a Web page to show a layout, a sketch, or other proposal, you don't have to make the presentation visible to the wider public—either give out a "secret" URL (a URL that leads to a page to which there are no hypertext links, and that visitors learn about by getting the address from the company) or set up password authentication for the directory on your Web server that holds the presentation. Then issue a password to the company that needs to see your stuff. You'll save yourself—and your clients—the time and trouble involved in setting up meetings. As questions occur, they can send you e-mail or speak on the phone—or even hold "virtual meetings" using Gmail or Google Talk.

Security Considerations

It's natural to approach the prospect of putting financial or personnel information online with caution. Such data needs to be protected, and simply putting out a "private" URL won't do it. In that case you need to rely on the sorts of Internet-based security schemes—authentication and encryption—that are already making e-commerce and information exchange viable in cyberspace.

Authentication is the process of requiring someone to verify that they are an approved user by providing a username and password. In technical terms, this means that the directory on the Web server that holds the sensitive Web page, graphics, or other files is set up so that, whenever a visitor connects to that directory, a standard password-protection box is presented. In the case of Google Apps, an approved user needs to enter a Google Account username/password pair that matches one of a set that your site's administrator enters.

The big question mark with regard to Google Apps in the corporate world is security. Suppose you open your Google Apps domain to selected customers and others outside the company. The question to ask is: once your passwords start getting "out there" in the world, how do you protect your company's information from hackers, thieves, and other unauthorized intruders?

Google Apps, at both the standard and Premium level, uses a simple password system to limit access to the site as a whole. You can't password-protect areas within the site—though when a user logs in with his or her password, he or she can only view Docs & Spreadsheets files that he or she has created or that other users have specifically allowed that user to view. But passwords aren't the only key to keeping business information secure. The first, and in many ways the most effective, step in ensuring the security of your Internet-based network is to assemble the key players on your staff and initiate communication about security. Get together the managers, computer managers, and legal staff. Discuss possible solutions, such as keeping sensitive information off the network altogether.

Improving Your Browsing Experience with Google Pack

The Internet has been known since its earliest days as a resource for free software. Along with its storehouse of information and the many different ways it provides of accessing specific types of information, Google also makes itself a software resource through Google Pack. The Pack is a free set of software programs, some of which are provided by Google and some created by other organizations. All are designed to give you what you need to surf the Internet quickly and safely and organize your computer as well.

When you go to the Google Pack home page (http://pack.google.com) and review the software offered, you discover that it is divided into two groups: a core group of applications that come with the Pack, and a set of optional add-ons. At this writing, the core group includes the following:

- Google Earth, Google's software for viewing street scenes or parts of the world in 3-D.

- Picasa, the desktop photo organizer described in Chapter 19.

- Google Desktop, the file organization and search utility also described in Chapter 18.

- Google Toolbar, an add-on for Internet Explorer that lets you search from any location on the Web and blocks popup windows.

- Google Photos Screensaver, a screen saver for your computer that lets you display slideshows or your own photos on your monitor when it's idle.

- Mozilla Firefox, the popular freeware browser that's the leading alternative to Microsoft Internet Explorer. Firefox comes with its own version of Google Toolbar pre-installed.

- Adobe Reader, the free reader for PDF files.

- Norton Security Scan, a free utility that scans for viruses and other harmful programs.

- Spyware Doctor Starter Edition, an anti-spyware utility that detects and re-moves keyboard logging programs (programs that can track a user's keyboard entries in order to steal passwords and other sensitive information), Trojan horses, and other spyware programs that you can download without your knowledge and that slow down your surfing as well as threaten your privacy.

In addition to these programs, which give you the basics needed for surfing the Web, you can also choose to download a group of optional add-ons. These are programs that enhance your surfing experience by providing you with multimedia content:

- *Google Talk*—This is Google's IM and chat application, which is described in Chapter 10.

- *RealPlayer*—This popular audio and video player is provided by RealNetworks.

- *Google Video Player*—Even though RealPlayer or Microsoft's own Windows Media Player will play Google Video content, you might want to use this "official" video player to view video clips in case you are a committed Google user and just in case the other two players can't play a file.

- *GalleryPlayer HD Images*—This is a viewing tool for high-quality drawings and photos.

- *Skype*—This software is specially intended to enable Voice Over Internet Protocol (VoIP) conversations—conversations that use your computer as a sort of telephone so you can talk to anyone around the world essentially for free. (Google Talk lets you do the same thing, however.)

You won't notice any Microsoft programs in either the core or optional list. Google Pack is, in fact, Google's attempt to take on Microsoft and make inroads in the browser, audio player, and other software areas.

 Note: You don't need to download all of the optional software programs as a group; you aren't required to download all of the core Pack programs at the same time either. If you want to pick and choose programs individually, you are presented with an Add or Remove Software link during the download process. You can also find out more about each application or download them by going to the respective manufacturers' Web sites, where they are readily available: do a search on Google (where else?) to find them.

When you download Google Pack by clicking the blue button at the top of the Google Pack home page, you use a utility called Google Updater to manage the download; it lets you uninstall any program you don't want to keep or update software when new versions are available; a Google Updater icon appears in your system tray that displays notifications about updates to the Google Pack programs you already have.

Keeping Track with Google Notebook

As you surf pages or work with Docs & Spreadsheets or other Google applications, you'll inevitably want to take notes to record thoughts that occur to you. You can send quick notes to a coworker using Google Talk, or you can e-mail notes to someone else or to yourself using Gmail. But Google Notebook is in fact the perfect note-taking application for working with Google's own business applications or simply for remembering Web sites, making notes about content, or recording thoughts you might comment on later in your blog.

You probably already take notes while you're online by typing in a Microsoft Word or other window. One nice thing about Google Notebook is that it comes with a utility that lets you publish notebook contents to your Google Apps site so members of your workgroup can read and respond. Other colleagues can add their own notes to yours if you give them the ability to collaborate with you.

Google Notebook comes with an optional plug-in application (also called an extension) that makes it more functional if you take notes within a Web browser window. The plug-in lets you use a "mini" version of the Notebook so you don't have to switch between the browser window and the Notebook window. It even records the source of the Web page data you copy, so you can always refer to your Web page links and return to a page later on if necessary.

To get started using Google Notebook, go to http://www.google.com/notebook. Sign in with your Google Account information. The next page prompts you to download the extension for the Web browser you are currently using: if you sign in with Firefox you'll be prompted to download the software for Firefox, and if you use Internet Explorer, you can download the extension for that browser. Click Agree and Download. When a Software Installation dialog box appears, click Install Now. A dialog box will then appear prompting you to quit and restart your browser automatically.

After your browser restarts, you view not your usual startup page, but the original download page. Click the link at the bottom Continue to your notebooks. The blank notebook page shown in Figure 20-1 appears.

If you want to find out more about Google Notebook at any time when using the program, click the Notebook Overview link at the bottom of My Notebook, or whatever you have named the current notebook. You'll find basic instructions on how to use the application. If you're in a hurry and just want to start taking notes, however, you can simply start taking notes by typing or pasting them into the blank box labeled Type here or add section at the bottom of the Notebook window. As you work, a red box will appear on the right side of the window to let you know your changes are instantly being saved. The interface, in fact, is remarkably similar to that of Google Docs, which saves your work almost constantly so you don't have to manually save it. You can use the buttons above the text box to format text in bold, italic, or a color, or to change the font or type size. The Link button allows you to format highlighted text as a hyperlink (see Figure 20-2).

Figure 20-1. A new file called My Notebook is automatically created when you first open the program.

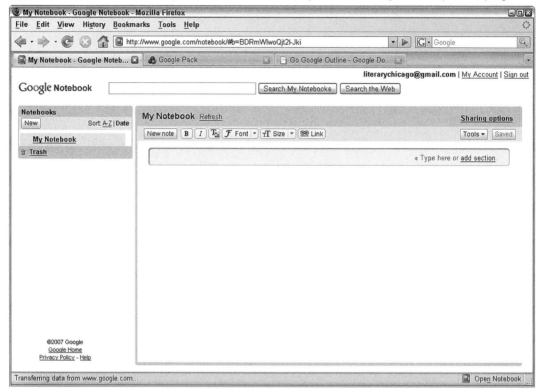

When you're done typing, click New Note to add a new, separate note in your default My Notebook notebook. You don't have to stick with My Notebook, however. To keep your notes organized, you can create custom notebooks at any time and give each one a distinct name. To create a new notebook, click New under Notebooks. A new blank screen will appear with the cursor positioned in a box that lets you enter a title for the notebook. Type the title and click OK. The notebook will be added to the Notebooks column on the left side of the screen. You can create notebooks for both personal and office use, as shown in Figure 20-3.

The browser plug-in version of Notebook provides you with a Notebook icon and an Open Notebook link in the status bar of your browser. Click the link shown in Figure 20-4 to open the Notebook whenever you're surfing the Web.

Expanding Your Reach with Google Mobile

Google Mobile is a service for workers who are on the go and who are able to send and receive information from their cell phone, Blackberry, or other palm device.

Figure 20-2. You can format text or add hyperlinks to your notes.

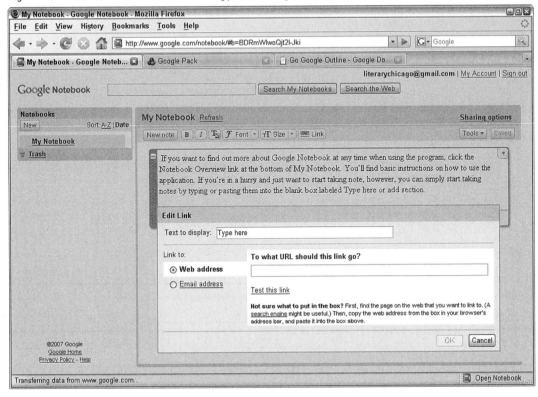

Figure 20-3. You can crate multiple notebooks to organize different types of content.

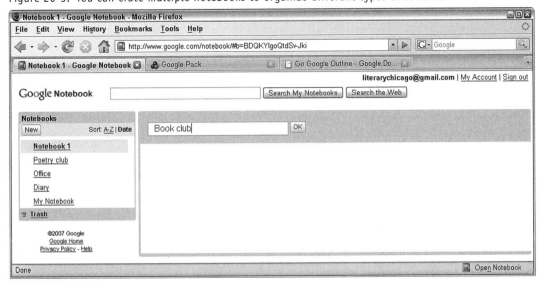

Figure 20-4. The plug-in lets you open the notebook application from your browser's status bar.

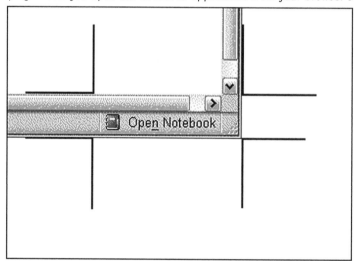

Google Mobile actually is a suite of services, each of which is available in a "small screen" version: Google Search, Google Maps, Gmail, Google News, and Google SMS, the text messaging service.

It's easy to use the service: go to http://www.google.com/mobile. Enter your mobile phone number in the box provided and click the Send me the link button. In a few seconds, your cell phone will let you know a message has been received. You are instructed to click a link embedded in the message. If you don't see a link (I didn't), you have to connect to the Internet to start up your device's browser and then go to http://mobile.google.com. You'll see a screen full of links that will lead you to each of the Google services mentioned in the preceding paragraph; click any one of the links to start using it on your phone.

Joining Business Communities with Google Groups

If you have been encountering difficulties finding buyers and sellers for the products or services in your chosen field, you're sure to find new markets by joining an online discussion group. Some discussion groups are specially designed for B2B transactions. They are vertical communities that bring together businesses in a particular field. By joining—or possibly even starting—an online community, you can:

- increase sales leads
- find new markets

- make valuable business contacts
- mine valuable data about supply and demand in your field.

The same Internet that brings together buyers and sellers of virtually every imaginable product on sites like eBay and online e-commerce stores can provide gathering places for far-flung businesses that need to trade in offbeat, hard-to-find items.

 Tip: You might be able to trade your goods or services through a group you join online. Bartering, like streamlining administrative procedures, is a way to improve your company's bottom line that doesn't involve the usual cash transaction. Get used to thinking about forms of payment other than money, such as equipment or services that will help cut expenses in the long run.

It's Time to Get Going!

By now, you're probably more than ready to Go Google. I suggest you start by signing up for a Google Account. Once you have that, you can sign up for Google Apps, or start using Gmail on an individual basis. Gmail will give you access to Docs & Spreadsheets, Calendar, Talk, and many of the other tools described in this book. Google, in my opinion, is the real deal: its emphasis on free and easy-to-use software puts it way ahead of Microsoft, and guarantees that it will be in the business applications field for years to come. Start working online and sharing with your colleagues and you'll find that you're working faster and more conveniently than you ever could before. I wish you good luck, and happy Googling!

Other Online Tools for Your Office

Despite the many services offered by Google, it never hurts to explore other options for online office tools. Some of these services are analogous to those of Google, while some are not. For a small business, one of the major draws to Google products is their price, which is, for the most part, nothing. While certain services, such as Ad-Words, or the Premier Edition of Google Apps, do come with a price tag, it remains relatively low compared to comparable competing services.

It is important to keep in mind, however, that other companies offer services free of charge, as well, and that there is no way to predict which tools will be most perfectly tailored to fit your particular business's needs without first testing some of them out. Try to think about what types of services you are offering, and what tools or products you will need to implement them. If you simply need an online workspace plus email, for example, then Google Apps is probably sufficient. If, on the other hand, you'll be doing, say, aggressive marketing or business forecasting, then something like Salesforce.com, which costs more, but also provides more robust sale-tracking, might be a better fit. Here are some links to and brief descriptions of competing services or simply other providers of online office tools so you can go and have a look yourself.

Competing Search Engines

According to Nielsen NetRatings, as of June 2006, 49.2 percent of all search engine searches were made through Google. While this is an impressive and dominating figure, it's always worth checking other search engines if a Google search doesn't give you exactly what you're looking for.

Yahoo! (http://www.search.yahoo.com)

Yahoo!, which was launched in 1994, is one of the oldest search engines on the web, and continues to be one of the most popular, accounting for a reported 23.8% of all web searches. Originally powered by Google itself, Yahoo! has used several search engines throughout the years, eventually combining the attributes of each to create its own proprietary engine. Because of its partnership with AT&T, Yahoo! features are automatically integrated directly into the web services of many Internet users. Like Google's search page, Yahoo! offers you the possibility of searching in Web, Images, Video, etc., and has a link to its advertisement embedding service (Ad Programs). Unlike the Google 'Classic Home' search page, Yahoo!'s search page also includes a listing of links to the top daily news stories directly.

MSN/Live Search (http://www.live.com)

Windows Live Search, Microsoft's successor to MSN Search, was launched in its final release form on September 11, 2006. MSN accounted for 9.6% of all web searches in June 2006 (technically before Microsoft's search engine was released in its current form). Like Google, Live.com's basic page presentation is relatively Spartan, and can be personalized according to which features you choose to incorporate. Also similar to Google's Personalized Search, Live.com allows searches to be saved and updated automatically. Unique to Live.com is the ability to view additional search results on the same page, instead of having to scroll through several pages.

Ask.com (http://www.ask.com)

Formerly known as AskJeeves.com, this search engine was founded in 1996, and distinguished itself as a "natural language" search, allowing the user to enter a naturally phrased question, to which an answer would be produced. While now accounting for only 2.6% of all web searches, Ask.com retains its prominent position in the web community due both to its ownership of many web destinations (Excite, MyWay.com, iWon.com, etc.) and to its former mascot, Jeeves. Ask.com now supports keyword searches, as well, and relies on the "ExpertRank" algorithm to list search results in order of authoritativeness. Because Ask.com was slower to index many newer web pages, its user traffic fell behind Google, Yahoo!, and MSN.

Other Search Engines and Metasearch Engines

All other search engines combined account for only 8.5 percent of total web searches. It can be useful, however, to be aware of "metasearch engines," which amalgamate the searches of other sites. Here are a few metasearch sites that I have found useful:

Dogpile (http://www.dogpile.com)

Essentially, this site displays search results from Google, Yahoo!, MSN, Ask.com, and others simultaneously.

Refdesk (http://www.refdesk.com)

This site claims to be "the single best source for facts," and displays not only a Google search, a Yahoo! search, and an MSN search, but also a Dogpile search. It also has links to news, dictionaries, weather, and more.

Surfwax (http://www.surwax.com)

This site is notable because it provides a mix of U.S. Government tools, educational, news, and other sources.

Competing Online Office Space

Not surprisingly, companies offering competing search engines also tend to offer competing online office tools. Therefore, along with Google's search engine, both Yahoo! and Microsoft offer online office tools comparable to those of Google. This barely scratches the surface of what is available, however. Here are some of the better products out there:

Office.com (http://www.office.com)

Office.com provides the Virtual Office application, which consists of 15 services, including email, calendar, address book, etc. It can also send updates to a PDA or pocket PC. The amount of web storage, attachment size, number of users, etc., varies depending on the package you choose:

- Virtual Office Free: free
- Virtual Office Light: $5.95/3 mo.
- Virtual Office Regular: $10.95/3 mo.
- Virtual Office Advanced: $19.95/3 mo.
- Virtual Office Hyper: $34.95/3 mo.

Microsoft Office Live (http://office.microsoft.com)

Microsoft Office Live provides a variety of office suite services, including a domain name, business email accounts, data transfer, and web storage. The amount of storage, business application workspace size, number of features, etc., once again varies based on the package you choose:

- Office Live Basics: free
- Office Live Essentials: $19.95/mo.
- Office Live Premium: $39.95/mo.

Salesforce.com (http://www.salesforce.com)

Salesforce.com provides CRM (Customer Relationship Management) services. Their applications allow you to create an online workspace from which you can track sale evolution, use analytics to conduct business forecasting, maintain a record of prospective clients, general marketing, and other sales-intensive activities. Various packages are available, with prices depending on multiple factors, including number of users and which tools you wish to activate. Some examples:

- Basic Edition starts at: $695/yr. (5 users)
- Team Edition: $1995/yr. (10 users)

Yahoo! Small Business (http://www.smallbusiness.yahoo.com/)

Yahoo! Small Business also provides services such as web hosting, domain names, business email, etc., but they are listed separately, and must be subscribed to separately on its website, and you will have to pay even for the most basic version of any service. Here is a list of the prices at the most starter level of Yahoo! Small Business applications:

- *Web Hosting*—starting at $11.95/mo., $25 setup fee
  Ecommerce—starting at $39.95/mo., $50 setup fee
- *Domain Name*—starting at $9.95/yr.
- *Business Email*—starting at $34.95/yr.
- *Marketing Services*—Customizable deposit amount and maximum payment amount per ad click
- *Internet Service*—starting at $15.95/mo. (first year/dial-up)

Other Business Tools

Score (http://www.score.org/)

Score is a site that you may find helpful as a consultation resource. Score provides you with the ability to search business-related topics on the site, and has links, articles, and tutorials about such topics as cash-flow management, creating a PowerPoint presentation, basic accounting, and may other helpful subjects. Best of all, Score's services are offered free of charge as it subsists on donations and is a Resource Partner with the U.S. Small Business Administration. Score's Consultation Services are available to you for free.

APPENDIX ⓑ

More Google Tools

In addition to AdSense, Google Apps, and other more "business oriented" products, Google offers a variety of other services that do everything from helping you to shop more efficiently online (Google Checkout), to letting you manage your photographs (Picasa). While many of the items presented in the following list may be more useful to you for recreational purposes, you might just find that they have applications in the workplace as well.

All of the utilities listed in this appendix are free (with the exception of Google Checkout). Many of Google's services are still in the beta or "rough draft" stage when they are released to the public. But that doesn't mean they're not already powerful tools. Remember that you can always contact Google and let them know if you've encountered a bug in the beta version of a software program. Go to http://www.google.com/intl/en/options/ for a full listing of Google's other product offerings.

Google Earth (http://earth.google.com/)

Google Earth is a downloadable software package that incorporates the Google search engine with satellite imagery, maps, terrain, and 3D buildings to create a three-dimensional globe that can be navigated in real time. While the basic version is free, you can upgrade to more powerful versions:

- Google Earth: free
- Google Earth Plus: $20
- Google Earth Pro: $400

YouTube (http://youtube.com)

YouTube is a well-known online video repository where anyone has the ability to upload their own videos or watch videos uploaded by other users. Videos on YouTube can range anywhere from episodes of a syndicated television show, to political video blogs, to indie films, and everything in between. YouTube was started independently in 2005 and purchased by Google within a year of its launch after becoming far and away the most popular online video Web site. Although Google has struck deals with many media provider corporations allowing YouTube to exist in its current form, it is currently being sued by Viacom for copyright infringement.

Google Video (http://video.google.com)

Google had already built Google Video, its own online video Web site, before acquiring YouTube. Despite the two sites' inherent similarities, Google has chosen not to dismantle its original proprietary version. Google Video has an interface reminiscent of Google Search, and now cross-references topic searches with YouTube.

Google Maps (http://maps.google.com)

Google Maps is a mapping program that allows you to navigate a map of the world (the United States is still the most comprehensively mapped country to date) using a "drag and drop" system that is both intuitive and efficient. It employs satellite imagery to allow you the choice of either viewing the terrain of interest, looking at an actual map, or viewing a hybrid of both. In addition to providing directions to and from a location, businesses can easily be searched in a chosen vicinity, with links to the establishment's Web site built directly into the results.

Google Groups (http://groups.google.com/)

Google Groups is an online discussion group forum as well as a service for creating and accessing mailing lists. You can use Google Groups to find or create discussion forums organized around a particular topic, such as health, automobile repair, setting up your home audio, and thousands of other topics. You can then read and participate by posting messages to the ongoing conversations.

Google News (http://news.google.com/)

Google News is an automated news aggregator the goal of which is to avoid human bias in the choice of news stories displayed. It is currently being provided in 12 different languages, and is divided into searchable categories for easy navigation. The Google News page can also be personalized through services such as Google Alerts, which sends you messages to your email account concerning news topics of choice.

Google Book Search (http://books.google.com/)

Google Book Search is an ambitious project that allows you to search, within the formidable number of books that Google has thus far scanned into its databases, much as you would through an Internet search engine. Books can be accessed in one of three ways: Full View, which allows you to download the entire text as a PDF document; Limited View, which permits you only to see portions of the book at any given time; and Snippet View, which displays only portions of the text containing your query. The differences between these result types are largely due to issues of ownership and copyright, and Google continues to weather fierce opposition to this project from certain parties. Google Books provides links to publishers and other information about the book you are searching, which is particularly helpful when only the Snippet View is available.

Picasa (http://picasa.google.com/)

Picasa is a downloadable software package that organizes digital photographs into albums. You can use Picasa to quickly and easily rename photos, organize them into folders, rate them, and even put a password lock on selected albums. Picasa has other features, as well, such as photo editing, creation of slide shows, and uploading photos to the Internet.

Google Checkout (http://checkout.google.com/)

Google Checkout is Google's online payment processing service. It can make buying online simpler by allowing you to go through Google Checkout to make purchases at participating websites, rather than through a proprietary payment method for each site. Google Checkout also offers fraud protection and purchase tracking. eBay, which owns PayPal, another online payment service, apparently sees Google as a competitor, and has banned the use of Google Checkout on eBay.

Note: While merchants will eventually be charged 2.0 percent plus $0.20 per transaction, Google is providing processing free of charge through December 31, 2007.

Google-Related Web Sites and Resources

This book presents only one perspective on a limited set of Google's online services. There is much more to Google, and if you really want a fuller perspective on this influential company, it pays to look at some of the many Web sites that collect information and voice opinions on Google. Some of the best-known sites are listed below.

Google Watch (http://www.google-watch.org/)

Google Watch is unabashedly critical of Google and its policies. At this site, you will find such topics as *Google Hires Spooks*, *Google's Toolbar is Spyware*, and *Google's Cache Copy is Illegal*. Google Watch perpetuates discussions regarding issues of privacy and data mining inherent to Google's operating procedures, which some consider invasive. In addition, the folks at Google Watch are of the opinion that Google is in the process of building a monopoly whose existence will prove harmful to the consumer and to civil liberties in general.

Google-Watch-Watch (http://www.google-watch-watch.org/)

As an interesting counterpoint to Google Watch, Google-Watch-Watch seeks to refute the claims made by the former. Ultimately accusing the Google Watch's webmaster of bitterness at having his website snubbed by Google's PageRank system, he addresses the issues raised by Google Watch from a more Google-friendly and sanguine perspective.

PageRank (http://www.google.com/technology)

To gain a little insight into the actual technology behind Google's search engine technology, I prefer the description offered by Google itself. Essentially, PageRank treats links between pages as "votes." On top of this, pages are weighted in proportion to their "importance," so votes from "important" pages will be listed higher in the result rankings.

Hilltop Algorithm (http://pagerank.suchmaschinen-doktor.de/hilltop.html)

The Hilltop algorithm is another of the powerful tools used by Google's search engine to determine search results. It ranks documents by using "expert pages," which are pages about a topic having links to multiple non-affiliated pages on that same topic. The website listed here is not the only description of Google's Hilltop algorithm, but I find its explanation to be clear, concise, and informative.

Matt Cutts' Blog (http://www.mattcutts.com/blog)

Matt Cutts is the current head of Google's Web-spam team. In his blog, "Gadgets, Google, and SEO" (Search Engine Optimization), he shares his perspective on a variety of issues, with categories such as *music* and *food,* but also *productivity* and *how to.* In addition to sharing advice on things to do and eat when in Silicon Valley or his excitement about Neil Gaiman's son coming to work at Google, he offers substantive information about new products or unique insights from someone working in the industry. Recent topics of interest include an entry about improvements made to YouTube's search capabilities, or a discussion of different ways in which Google lets you access your data online.

Search Engine Watch (http://searchenginewatch.com)

This website has everything from blogs to search engine resources, to web search tips. You can also sign up for the monthly search engine report for free. There is quite a bit of fascinating information regarding not only Google, but other search engines as well, including statistical monitoring and comparisons.

Alexa (http://www.alexa.com)

Alexa is a web traffic monitoring site. It allows you to quickly and easily view daily rankings of website traffic, which can be categorized by country, language, or subject. While it can only monitor web traffic from users who have willingly installed its toolbar, causing some to question the reliability of its data, the results certainly seem more or less in line with other Web traffic reporting, such as Nielsen-Net Ratings.

Alexaholic (http://www.alexaholic.com/)

Alexaholic is essentially a free, independently-created online data visualization service that uses Alexa's results to create customized charts and comparisons of web traffic on a website or websites of your choice. Instantly generate a graph comparing Yahoo!, Google, and MSN traffic for that day, for example.

Index